Articulate Necrographies

Articulate Necrographies

Comparative Perspectives on the Voices and Silences of the Dead

Edited by
Anastasios Panagiotopoulos
and Diana Espírito Santo

berghahn
NEW YORK · OXFORD
www.berghahnbooks.com

First published in 2019 by
Berghahn Books
www.berghahnbooks.com

© 2019, 2025 Anastasios Panagiotopoulos and Diana Espírito Santo
First paperback edition published in 2025

All rights reserved. Except for the quotation of short passages
for the purposes of criticism and review, no part of this book
may be reproduced in any form or by any means, electronic or
mechanical, including photocopying, recording, or any information
storage and retrieval system now known or to be invented,
without written permission of the publisher.

Library of Congress Cataloging-in-Publication Data
A C.I.P. cataloging record is available from the Library of Congress
Library of Congress Cataloging in Publication Control Number: 2019014084

British Library Cataloguing in Publication Data
A catalogue record for this book is available from the British Library

ISBN 978-1-78920-304-2 hardback
ISBN 978-1-80539-745-8 paperback
ISBN 978-1-80539-925-4 epub
ISBN 978-1-78920-305-9 web pdf

https://doi.org/10.3167/9781789203042

And what the dead had no speech for, when living,
They can tell you, being dead: the communication
Of the dead is tongued with fire beyond the language of the living.
—T.S. Eliot, *Four Quartets* (1943)

Contents

Introduction 1
Anastasios Panagiotopoulos and Diana Espírito Santo

Part I. Necrographic Frameworks

Chapter 1
Voices and Silences of the Dead in Western Modernity 17
Tony Walter

Chapter 2
Coping with Massive Urban Death: The Mutual Constitution of
Mourning and Recovery in World War II's Bombing War 40
Antonius C.G.M. Robben

Chapter 3
Biographies and Necrographies in Exchange: From the Self to the
Other 63
Anastasios Panagiotopoulos

Part II. Necrographic Observations

Chapter 4
The Making of Spirit Bodies and Death Perspectives in Afro-Cuban
Religion 85
Diana Espírito Santo

Chapter 5
Sensory Necrography: The Flow of Signs and Sensations in the
Corpse 106
Beth Conklin

Chapter 6
Unanchored Deaths: Grieving the Unplaceable in Samburu 125
Bilinda Straight

Chapter 7
The Sociality of Death: Life Potentialities and the Vietnamese Dead 141
Marina Marouda

Chapter 8
"Enlightened" Spirits: Modern Exchanges between the Living and
the Dead under Spiritism 165
Raquel Romberg

Chapter 9
Channeling the Flow: Dealing with Death in an African-Based
Religion 186
Gabriel Banaggia

Chapter 10
Of Shadows and Fears: Nepalese Ghost Stories from Classical Texts
and Folklore to Social Media 205
Davide Torri

Chapter 11
Death Isn't What It Used to Be: Animist and Baptist Ontologies in
Tribal India 227
Piers Vitebsky

Afterword
The Necrographic Imagination 244
Magnus Course

Index 251

Introduction

Anastasios Panagiotopoulos and Diana Espírito Santo

> (A)ny comparative study of morbidity must concede the existence of two breeds of gloomy men: those who think about death all the time and those who never think about it.
> —William F. May, "The Sacral Power of Death in Contemporary Experience"

Death seems to be an object of study that has never actually become trendy (how could it?), nor has it ever gone completely out of fashion—perhaps so that scholars may avoid joining either breed of gloomy people, to paraphrase May. In this broad sense, it can be said that death is situated in a perpetually liminal state (see Palmer 2012). This claim may sound paradoxical, considering the weighty stasis and unambiguous nothingness that the image, actual or imagined, of a dead body might intuitively arouse. But such is death. Excessively static and excessively moving; overtly universal and utterly local or individual; it claims everything and nothing with great certainty and mystery, all at once. Death's link to metaphor has also been noted (see Barley 1995: 151–78; Danforth 1982: 71–115) and, indeed, the claim that "death is the mother of beauty" (Turner 2000) sounds especially powerful; but equally powerful is that it is the mother of ugliness: "Death is the ultimate source of both the tragedy and the beauty of a human life. Moreover, death's tragedy is the source of life's beauty and vice versa" (May 2013: 113). In other words then, death is the mother (father, son, and daughter) of paradox: "This is one aspect of the basic human predicament, that we are simultaneously worms and gods" (Maslow 1963 cited in Becker 2011: 51), something which amounts to "the paradoxical nature of death evidenced as the locus of the supreme veiling and unveiling of being" (Demske 1970: 165). Or, to echo Zygmunt Bauman: "Death reveals that truth and absurdity are one" (1992: 15). All these may, or may not, be interesting philosophical and even existential considerations, but too much deliberation might lead to never-ending playful invention and proliferation of opposites that subsequently come to "die" by being merged once they are thrown into death's hungry pit, to continue with the metaphors.

This collective publication is only indirectly dedicated to death in general, precisely because the excessive and paradoxical nature of the phenomenon also invites the need to draw some lines, no matter how heuristic and negotiable these may be. Our lines mark off the dead themselves, analytically separating them from an overtly abstract preoccupation with death; the focus of examination thus becomes their bodies, their objects and materials, their voices and their trajectories or, as we propose in this volume, their "necrographies," as these are related to or entangled with (see Straight 2006) the trajectories and biographies of the living (for an ethnographically-driven elaboration of "necrographies," see Panagiotopoulos 2017).

We, the editors, have been intrinsically inspired by social phenomena that in one or way or another relate to the theme of death. It is perhaps no coincidence that we have both conducted ethnographic work in Cuba for over ten years, wherein the dead are particularly "contaminating" of the living. Indeed, as much was suggested by an elderly woman once while one of us was purchasing flowers from her stall: "This country is full of *muertos*!" she exclaimed, referring to the dead. "We are all contaminated!" she continued, angrily, fatalistically. Whatever she had meant by this, or however we could classify her state of mind at the time, the image of a contaminating army of ghosts—an immanent, saturating sea of the dead, as Todd Ochoa puts it (2010)—endured in our minds as a powerful trope for the universe we both encountered. We begin this Introduction with some observations grounded in our mutual work in Cuba, then, which open up a series of critical questions.

Cuba, as all places, is a place contaminated by its past. Indeed, this is one of Stephan Palmié's main premises in his alternative history of the Caribbean, in which he argues that "no less than religion, history is, ultimately, an assemblage of collective representations positing realities that are—logically—beyond empirical proof," where "their consequences, of course, are hardly beyond direct experience" (2002: 4). The specter of the dead, he seems to suggest, is omnipresent in the relationships articulated among the living, where the dead are just as real as the documented past. In the case of Cuba, the spirit of the *indígena* or slave, the independence martyr, the communist, the colonized, the colonizer, the visionary and the oppressed: theirs are voices intrinsic to a historical imagination that registers and rewrites itself in the moving present, where their presence is infectious and inevitable. Making sense of the dead is very often to make sense of the living, commonsense tells us, but in Cuba—as in other places in the world—these two realms, kept apart in so many other societies so as to avoid contagion, meet in mutual acknowledgment, confrontation, and very often conflict, in order to make sense of each other and themselves.

One way to understand the weight of the dead in Cuba is through the country's political history and contemporaneity. Cubans are no strangers to the shadow cast by dead political martyrs, independence leaders, charismatic Revolutionaries. The country's public sphere is testament to the endurance of the regime's claim to history through them: el Che looms large on the side of a ministry in Havana's Revolution square; plaster and stone busts of independence war hero and poet José Martí sit diligently in every school and official building; pervasive state-sponsored wall graffiti pay homage to the socialist vision of the omnipresent dead, proclaiming its ever-relevance; and Fidel Castro's recent death is likely to follow a similar path (see Panagiotopoulos and Espírito Santo 2017). The dead are resurrected through the Revolution by its very definition, which implies a forward-moving, unfinished process, that builds on the words and concepts of wise, dead visionaries, whose voices are carried through triumphantly. It is no coincidence that the "magical pathos of politics," in Ken Routon's terms (2010), bleeds effortlessly into post-Soviet Cuban life more generally. On the one hand, Revolutionary officialdom has long been suspected by the populace of seeking recourse to hidden sources of sustenance and power from the world of the spirits and deities. On the other, political magic has infused spiritual altars, discourses, and cosmoses: the likes of Che Guevara and other independence war and "revolutionary" heroes materialize in spiritual centers across the country, appearing alternately in dreams and premonitions, as well as bodies, or as communist spirit-inspired messages and discourse.

But however much Afro-Cuban religiosity expresses a political consciousness, or indeed, a consciousness of history—be it by lovingly attending to the spirit of Martí on a spiritual altar, or by the celebration, as Routon argues, of "a bewildering entanglement of bodies, racial geographies, cosmological domains, and historical fields" (2010: 113)—in spirit-mediumship rites and ceremonies, practitioners are no simple, stereotypic "depositories" of Cuban history. Rather, the dead, co-exist with the living; they are not past but present in their "pastness"; their biographies, or necrographies, are inherent to the constitution of the living and their possibilities, and they are ever-changing and mobile. The dead do not necessarily *say something* about people; they are constitutive of the living, in and through bodies, destinies, and forms of communion and oracular vision and counsel.

This leads us to one of the central points of this volume. The dead, in many of the ethnographic contexts explored here, are not abstract entities in need of commemoration, remembrance, or resurrection, but are *potentials of and for something*, presences to be harnessed, transformed, absorbed, and developed through matter as well as living, pulsating paths. This characteristic of the dead means that death is not the opposite of life, but a peculiar variety of it—perhaps its exaggeration—defying, arguably, anthropological renditions of death as a transition (Hertz 1960), or even of life and death as a continuum (Toren 1999; Cátedra 1992) where there may be life in death as much as death in life. This is not to say that the spirits of the dead in some of these contexts do not undergo transitions of important sorts. Very often the point is not to undo relations or attachments in order to pursue "good deaths" but to re-do them in ways that vitalize or activate death's gifts to life. Indeed, being "dead" can offer up privileged perspectives, from both a more transcendent point of view (spiritual geographies) and more immanent frames of mutuality, co-constitution, and relating. Contrary to Durkheim, the dead here neither replicate the social order nor provide an antithesis to it. While the dead often provide a platform of generative and creative social critique, they do so through their insertion into, not removal from, the vicissitudes of life. More importantly, the dead invariably manifest as registers of the sensuous, emotive body, or conscious, perceptive awareness, as well as through the advent of life blockages, misfortunes, or their opposites.

The clear phenomenological geography implied in religious accounts of the dead is a far cry from the notion that death—and its subsequent rites—undoes "complex social ties which once held the living person together" (Course 2007: 77), disintegrating sociality along with materiality; or that death and the dead imply a passage or journey, linear or otherwise, away from life. As Magnus Course has observed, the anthropology of mortuary practices has a long history based on this assumption (which, needless to say, works well in many societies, such as the Melanesian ones), beginning perhaps with Robert Hertz. Hertz's primary observation (1960) was that in many societies, death is not seen as destruction but transition, one invariably accompanied by the decomposition of physical matter itself. And yet, as Course's own ethnography of the Chilean Mapuche shows, death—and its processes—may actually serve to "complete" or "synthesize" the person, rather than break her down. In the Cuban case, dying affords a myriad of possibilities often implicit in a living state but deterred by other factors, such as the inconvenience of a material body. This may also imply that we reconsider death as a merely "biological" process, however extended or symbolic. In Afro-Cuban religion, for example, the dead are kept happy with food and thrive on the earthly love of their family. This consumption is not thought of metaphorically but substantially, through the "spirit" of certain foods, for example.

Dualist notions of spirit and matter have a complicated life both in Cuba and in many of the societies discussed in this edited book. In Cuba, practitioners of Afro-Cuban religion hold both dualist and non-dualist understandings of soul and body, perhaps in a processual sense, of one leading to the other, and back. In some of the contexts explored here, things can be both alive and dead, where "dead" is neither synonymous with lifeless nor inertness. A new language for these forms of "aliveness," or conversely, "deadness," should perhaps be invented, such as that suggested by Ochoa (2010), for dealing with materiality. Any such language should take unto itself an ontology in which material, even biological, processes are implicated in the continued potency and "life" of the dead. It must also take into account that a person herself may be produced via their contiguity with and encompassment of the dead; and that what counts as "death" must be defined through notions other than the biological, notions that give birth to new ontological configurations and possibilities, some with more articulacy than others. As Italian film director Pasolini once said, "death lies *not* in not being able to communicate, but in no longer being understood" (cited in Meyers and Baxtrom 2006: 153, *our emphasis*).

The theme of death has been relatively underdeveloped, perhaps mostly at a theoretical level of analysis. While numerous excellent ethnographic accounts on and of death have been written over the years, there are considerably fewer efforts to produce a synthesizing approach that offers bold theoretical claims. Thus, Fabian's (1973) complaint that the theme of death, especially from an anthropological perspective, is characterized by "parochialization" and "folklorization," which sounds as current as ever. In this publication our interest stems from from a need to preserve the particularism and empirical rigor typical of anthropology, and at the same time venture an effort to present something broader in perspective and reach. We believe that our general approach critically synthesises the existent academic tradition while attempting to go beyond it. The hope is that this can be initially evinced from the Introduction and, then, from each individual contribution.

What are the "voices" and "silences" of the dead, and how can we muster a "comparative" analysis of death and the dead through them?

Death, like many other social phenomena, has been trapped between certain structural oppositions. In anthropological studies of death there are some that have been more prominent. One of these is that of death and the dead being perceived as having a "voice" or, on the contrary, pertaining to the realm of "silence" (see Agamben 1991; Burke 1952). Most ethnographic accounts study the process of death and mourning as ritual (rather than as a meaningful event for those that are its participants), where death is invariably defined by its formality and routine. Anthropologists have tended to ignore the relationship between the public and the private and to treat death ritual as if it stored a "microcosm of its encompassing cultural macrocosm" (Rosaldo 1989: 15), as *speaking* of the society's cultural repertoire, as well as reproducing it. The focus has invariably been laid upon practices of mourning, memorialization, and social reconfiguration among the living. Death, in the end, is a process that takes time because it is simultaneously a process of social beginning. Indeed, this "voice" supposedly contrasts to that in the West where, as Ariès notes, death ceremonies have become discrete and void of emotion (1991). The dead do not "speak" in "modern" Western societies, although a person's social death may succeed their biological one, and more complex forms of life destabilize taken-for-granted notions of life, death, and the person (Kaufman and Morgan 2005: 330). Despite more recent ethnographies and approaches to death, beginning with Kübler-Ross's call for a more humane and personalized attention to dying (1969), there has typically been a chain of oppositions articulated in the literature, whereby death-as-voice, presence, creation, and social reproduction appears in an invariably "non-Western," "religious" (or "magical"), "rural," "traditional" context, whereas death-as-silence, absence, and social destruction figures in a "Western," "secular," "rational," "urban," and "modern" one. Like many other anthropologists, we believe in the need to go beyond these distinctions.

Reviewing the anthropological literature related to death, one may identify certain structural oppositions that repeatedly make their appearance: continuity and change, remembering and forgetting, embodiment and disembodiment, materialization and dematerialization (or spiritualization), order and disorder, identification and differentiation, social cohesion and social conflict, among others (for a comprehensive list of the relevant literature, see also Chapter 3, Panagiotopoulos). Very broadly put and following a more general paradigm shift in the social and humanistic sciences in the last decades, current studies on death have begun to favor the second term of each of the aforementioned oppositions (with notable exceptions of the embodiment/disembodiment and materialization/dematerialization pairs, where it is the first term that tends to be favored). This has had, in our belief, a double-edged effect. On the positive side, it has opened up death from a previous entrapment in rigid, "Durkheimian" (see Straight 2006: 101) categories, such as remembering, social cohesion, and order. Scholarship of late modernity has discarded the social function of death in exchange for an attention to its subtleties and the manner in which it fundamentally disrupts anthropological givens about what life is. On the other hand, this opening up can go too far, so much that, as many other post-modern efforts, it might come full circle and start chasing its own tail. "Open-ness" has become a cult; all is "becoming," "multiple," and "hybrid," an interminable "process" in "practice." It is not so much that *we have never been modern*, but, to paraphrase Latour, *they too* have always been modern. The danger is to take all this for granted to the extent that the very process is being stripped of its meaning.

Here, we mention two dimensions, one more general and the other more pertinent to the study of death. First, we identify a predominant understanding of oppositions within a framework of conventional dialectics. Simply put, this framework tends to view the relationship between the opposing terms in purely antithetical terms. For instance, order wins over disorder, or vice versa. In Hegelian terms, the relation between master and slave can only be maintained or dissolved (but not transformed within this same framework). This is a deeply metaphysical (Christian perhaps) prism in which historicity is acknowledged (only) to the extent that there is a linear movement towards a preordained *telos*. Where in all of this scheme is there space for simultaneity, for a comparative theory (and practice) of both order and disorder, to use just the previous pair as an example?

The second dimension has to do with death itself more particularly. Venturing a perhaps aphoristic claim, we could argue that death as an object of study has been locked into an overarching opposition: that between "acceptance" and "denial" (for an extensive discussion and references, see Chapter 3, Panagiotopoulos). In this framework the reality of death as the end of existence is either accepted or denied, whether consciously or not. Therefore, the "denial" stance is actually and in final analysis a derivation of the "acceptance" one. Very closely linked to this opposition is a homologous one of silence and voicing. Where there is "acceptance" there tends to be silence, and where there is denial, death and the dead are given a voice. Furthermore, the former is deemed "scientific" and the latter as "religious" or even "magical."

Our basic concern in this volume, apart from an ongoing interest in the ethnographic particularities of phenomena related to death, is how we can go beyond the aforementioned analytical molds. Is giving a voice to death and the dead always and necessarily a "religious" stance or one that denies dogmatically death's finality? Do all these binary terms or oppositions always stand at the expense of, or in a hierarchical relation to, the other antithetical terms, or can they coexist in a fully creative relation? Is "acceptance" and "denial" always a preoccupation in issues concerning death? What exactly is given voice and what is silenced? Beyond rigid binaries but also beyond the infinite regressions of a permanent fluidity, what new avenues do death and the dead forge? How do we simultaneously identify with and differentiate ourselves from death *and* from others who adopt different stances and perspectives?

Articulate and Inarticulate Necrographies

Death as the "other" and the deaths of others are related but not necessarily completely merged or diametrically opposed to the self and life. Beyond these conventional dialectics, perhaps death shows us its own *die-lectics*, or perspectives of life trajectories (biographies), as compared to partially identified with and partially differentiated from death trajectories and perspectives, what we call *necrographies*. What kinds of articulations and inarticulations (inarticulacies or silences, cf. Vitebsky 2008) does death create and how are they attributed to death by the living? Is the concept of "necrography" a useful one when thinking of the mutual constitution of the living and the dead? Can we usefully employ the idea of "necrographies" to understand how the dead interact with the biographies of the living, creating their own? What is the evidence that death gives to the living and how are the dead's voices heard and their silences interpreted?

As is fully elaborated by Panagiotopoulos in his contribution to this volume, there is a dynamic and non-linear relation to be accounted for, both ethnographically and analytically: first, between the living (and their biographies) and the dead (their past biographies as ex-living and their present transforming state, their "necrographies"); second, between the just-mentioned voices (or articulacy) and silence (or inarticulacy) of the dead. The dynamic character of such relations necessitates a novel vocabulary and perspective in order to highlight the simultaneous and partial identification and partial differentiation between the two apparently opposing terms. Just like the living and the dead, biographies and necrographies enter into a dialogue wherein they encounter points of identity and alterity, as do the voicing and silencing pair. For such conceptualization, we propose the analytical lucidity of the term "exchange," as this has been developed by Jean Baudrillard (see Chapter 3, Panagiotopoulos). A vivid kind of exchange is found lacking, then, there is only room for representation or symbolic reflection.

If there is an absence of exchange, then the "dialogues" are essentially "representational," that is, whatever "voices" and perspectives seem to be emanating from the dead are essentially the perspectives *of* the living *about* the dead, whether explicitly acknowledged or not; they are not perspectives exchanged equally between the living and the dead. Representational dialogues are in essence monologues (see Bakhtin 2008): the living *represent* the dead because the latter are not there to *present* themselves (for death's link to representation see Goodwin and Bronfen 1993; Holland 2000: 28; for a similar critique of such a link as offered here, see Tsintjilonis 2007: 173–77).

Although the notion of exchange strongly implies that the dead are vociferous, and representation that the dead are silent, things are not so simple. Even though there might indeed be strong correlations in the aforementioned pairs (see Agamben 1991; Bauman 1992; Burke 1952; Kübler-Ross 1969; Seremetakis 1991; Vitebsky 1993, 2008), it can be argued that exchange might also involve, even if more subtly, a certain kind of silence (for very suggestive explorations, see Conklin 2001; Ochoa 2010; Taylor 1993; Williams 2003), just as much as representation contains a certain kind of voice, whether indirectly, or even metaphorically or ideologically (see, for instance, Harrison 2003; Kalusa and Vaughan 2013; Lomnitz 2008; Merridale 2000; Verdery 1999; Walter 1994). Thus, the most challenging task and question becomes: with what *kinds* of voices and silences are we confronted in conditions of exchange and conditions of representation? How do exchange and representation stand in relation to each other in a broad comparative perspective? In other words, what are the differences and what are the similarities between them? What are the dynamics and tensions of their coexistence, if there are any (see, for instance, Alexiou 2002; Holst-Warshaft 1992)? What are the motives, hopes, desires, or fears behind such stances? Furthermore, one could heuristically ignore exchange and representation and just deal with the voicing and silencing of the dead in a more phenomenological way. All these are possible and equally promising avenues into which, because they suggest an engagement between the living and the dead, one may insert both biographies and "necrographies," rather than merely pondering in general about life and death (for the links between biographies and death, see Course 2007; Desjarlais 2003; Panourgia 1995; Seremetakis 1991; Walter 1996).

Given that a "necrography" can be depicted as the specific trajectory of the after-life of a deceased person, why not simply call it a "biography," albeit one that continues past the threshold of death? The neologism, however, is something significantly more than a metaphor or a play on words; rather, it denotes and highlights, in a true and creative Baudrillardean sense, that while death may indeed be perceived as a different ontological state to life, it is neither radically disconnected from, nor completely identified with it. Difference becomes an integral part of the relation between the two conditions and the term necrography semantically condenses the dynamic continuities and discontinuities with the state that is associated with biography. Necrographies are the present situation, affects and effects of the deceased, whether these are present in the form of representation or (Baudrillardean) exchange. Furthermore, they can discursively or perceptually be related to their own past (their own biographies and legacies) and the biographies of significant living Others. Thus necrographies possess their own biographies and, at the same time, relate to others' biographies. Meanwhile, in the very process of their (dis)articulation, in their voicing and silencing, they are (de)constructed.

The concept of exchange is, thus, not only an ethnographic one, but also a whole angle from which the relations between the living and the dead, biographies and necrographies, and ultimately life and death can be viewed. If anything, when necrographies come to the surface, subtly or explicitly, or when they are silenced, unconsciously or strategically, then a truly dynamic and original process of exchange occurs in identifications and differentiations between them and their own past (their own biographies), just as well as with the biographies of the living. This "optic of death" (Seremetakis 1991: 14), with its accompanying "polyphony of movements and voices" (ibid.: 98), points to the "problematic nature of discrete beginnings and endings" (ibid.: 48; see also Lock 2002; Singer 1994) and proposes the following question: "can theory shift from the familiarization of death to the defamiliarization of social order by death?" (Seremetakis ibid.: 14). Let us conclude with Robert Harrison's answer to why the dead may have such an authority:

> Because the dead possess a nocturnal vision that the living cannot acquire. The light in which we carry on our secular lives blinds us to certain insights. Some truths are glimpsed only in the dark. That is why in moments of extreme need one must turn to those who can see through the gloom. (2003: 158–59)

This "nocturnal vision" afforded by and through the dead, has been also described by Paul Valéry as the "glance of death" or the "panoramic vision of the dying," a kind of glance that goes "well beyond vision" (see Tsintjilonis 2007: 173–74). Each one of us is free to take such propositions more or less literally or metaphorically; yet another possible and fruitful avenue opens up when we put their literal and metaphorical sides into dialogue. Death universally appears as a powerful intuition of radical transformation but with no absolute certainties of exactly in what the transformation will culminate. According to Ingold (2000: 143), the suggestive question becomes the following: "What if death punctuates, but does not terminate life?" (in Tsintjilonis 2007: 175). All the possible perspectives are brought up and entertained through the notion of exchange. Should we need then more reasons to argue for a comparative approach?

A Brief Commentary on the Book's Structure and Contents

Our editorial emphasis on a comparative approach, which, we believe, is a quintessentially anthropological stance, is not one-dimensional and this is reflected in the structure and content of the book. A comparative approach of anthropological interest on a specific subject, death in our case, is conventionally taken to imply a cross-cultural account, with ethnography as the primary methodological tool and material. Although we maintain such foundational premises, we also wish to go beyond such demarcations and explore a wider range of possibilities.

Therefore, the book is divided into two parts. Part I, "Necrographic Frameworks," sets a broader discussion in which a more immediate anthropology of death could (or, better, should be able to) converse with; converse with other disciplines, such as sociology (Chapter 1, Walter), social history (Chapter 1, Walter and Chapter 2, Robben), psychology (Chapter 2, Robben), and philosophy. Panagiotopoulos's contribution takes all these disciplines into account and explicitly attempts to set broad (not just interdisciplinary but also transdisciplinary) frameworks of discussion, without losing a particular interest in the anthropology of death and also in further elaboration of the volume's core concepts and terminology. As such, it could be read as a kind of appendix to the Introduction and, even, be read just after it. It should be noted here, that exactly because the comparative element is among disciplines and broader frameworks of discussion, direct ethnography, although not at all an unknown practice to the contributors of this Part (on the contrary), does not play a monopolizing or explicit role. Nevertheless, we believe, the discussions raised are not only pertinent to the volume's themes but create a field in which ethnography becomes a potential and significant interlocutor.

Part II, "Necrographic Observations," alluding to the tight link with ethnographic (participant) observation, is the most directly anthropological part, given that the contributions are primarily based on first-hand ethnography. Here, the comparative element becomes the vast diversity of geographic and cultural contexts of the chapters, such as, urban Cuba (Chapter 4, Espírito Santo), Amerindian Brazil (Chapter 5, Conklin), tribal Kenya (Chapter 6, Straight), contemporary Việt Nam (Chapter 7, Marouda), Puerto Rico (Chapter 8, Romberg), rural Brazil (Chapter 9, Banaggia), Nepal (Chapter 10, Torri), and India (Chapter 11, Vitebsky). Finally, the very insightful Afterword by Magnus Course offers an encompassing glue, so to speak, to the diversity and richness of the chapters.

Anastasios Panagiotopoulos is a senior postdoctoral researcher at Centro em Rede de Investigação em Antropologia, Universidade Nova de Lisboa, Portugal. His research includes the role of divination in Afro-Cuban religiosity as it relates to issues of personhood, historical imagination, race, and secularism, among others. He has published book chapters, peer-reviewed articles, such as "When biographies cross necrographies: the exchange of affinity in Cuba" (*Ethnos* 2017), and co-edited *Beyond Tradition, Beyond Invention* (Sean Kingston Publishing, 2015).

Diana Espírito Santo has researched spirit possession and mediation, Afro-Cuban espiritismo, and African-inspired Umbanda; she is currently examining ontologies of evidence in parapsychology movements and paranormal investigation in Chile. Her interests include personhood, materiality, divination, witchcraft, and technologies. She has published many articles, written two monographs, and co-edited three volumes, including *The Social Life of Spirits* (University of Chicago Press, 2014) and *Making Spirits* (I.B. Tauris, 2013).

References

Agamben, Giorgrio. 1991. *Language and Death*. Minneapolis and London: University of Minnesota Press.
Alexiou, Margaret. (1974) 2002. *The Ritual Lament in Greek Tradition*. Lanham, MD: Rowman & Littlefield Publishers.
Ariès, Philippe. (1981) 1991. *The Hour of Our Death*. Oxford and New York: Oxford University Press.
Bakhtin, Mikhail M. (1981) 2008. *The Dialogic Imagination: Four Essays by M.M. Bakhtin*. Edited by Michael Holquist and translated by Caryl Emerson and Michael Holquist. Austin: University of Texas Press.
Barley, Nigel. 1995. *Dancing on the Grave: Encounters with Death*. London: Abacus.
Bauman, Zygmunt. 1992. *Mortality, Immortality and Other Life Strategies*. Cambridge: Polity Press.

Becker, Ernest. (1973) 2011. *The Denial of Death*. New York: The Free Press.
Burke, Kenneth. 1952. "Thanatopsis for Critics: A Brief Thesaurus of Deaths and Dyings." *Essays in Criticism* 2: 369–75.
Cátedra, Maria. 1992. *This World, Other Worlds*. Chicago and London: University of Chicago Press.
Conklin, Beth. 2001. *Consuming Grief: Compassionate Cannibalism in an Amazonian Society*. Austin: University of Texas Press.
Course, Magnus. 2007. "Death, Biography, and the Mapuche Person." *Ethnos* 72(1): 77–101.
Danforth, Loring M. 1982. *The Death Rituals of Rural Greece*. Princeton: Princeton University Press.
Demske, James M. 1970. *Being, Man, and Death: A Key to Heidegger*. Lexington: The University Press of Kentucky.
Desjarlais, Robert. 2003. *Sensory Biographies: Lives and Deaths Among Nepal's Yolmo Buddhists*. Berkeley: University of California Press.
Fabian, Johannes. 1973. "How Others Die: Reflections on the Anthropology of Death." In *Death in American Experience*, ed. Arien Mack, 177–201. New York: Schocken Books.
Goodwin, Sarah Webster, and Elisabeth Bronfen, eds. 1993. *Death and Representation*. Baltimore and London: Johns Hopkins University Press.
Harrison, Robert Pogue. 2003. *The Dominion of the Dead*. Chicago and London: University of Chicago Press.
Hertz, Robert. 1960. *Death and the Right Hand*. Edited by Rodney Needham and Claudia Needham. New York: Free Press.
Holland, Sharon Patricia. 2000. *Raising the Dead: Readings of Death and (Black) Subjectivity*. Durham, NC: Duke University Press.
Holst-Warshaft, Gail. 1992. *Dangerous Voices: Women's Laments and Greek Literature*. London: Routledge.
Ingold, Tim. 2000. *The Perception of the Environment: Essays in Livelihood, Dwelling and Skill*. London and New York: Routledge.
Kalusa, Walima T., and Megan Vaughan. 2013. *Death, Belief and Politics in Central African History*. Oxford: Lembani Trust.
Kaufman, Sharon, and Lynn M. Morgan. 2005. "The Anthropology of the Beginnings and Ends of Life." *Annual Review of Anthropology* 34: 317–41.
Kübler-Ross, Elizabeth. 1969. *On Death and Dying*. London: Routledge.
Lock, Margaret. 2002. *Twice Dead: Organ Transplants and the Reinvention of Death*. Berkeley and Los Angeles: University of California Press.
Lomnitz, Claudio. 2008. *Death and the Idea of Mexico*. New York: Zone Books.
Maslow, Abraham. 1963. "The Need to Know and the Fear of Knowing." *Journal of General Psychology* 68: 111–25.
May, Todd. (2009) 2013. *Death*. Durham, NC: Acumen.
May, William F. 1973. "The Sacral Power of Death in Contemporary Experience." In *Death in American Experience*, ed. Arien Mack, 97–122. New York: Schocken Books.
Merridale, Catherine. 2000. *Night of Stone: Death and Memory in Russia*. London: Granta Books.

Meyers, Todd, and Richard Baxstrom. 2006. Review of *Pier Paolo Pasolini and Death*, edited by Bernhart Schwenk and Michael Semff. Ostfildern-Ruit, Germany: Hatje Cantz Verlag, 2006. *Parachute* 124: 153.
Ochoa, Todd Ramon. 2010. *Society of the Dead, Quita Manaquita and Palo Praise in Cuba*. Berkeley: University of California Press.
Palmer, Stephen. 2012. "Dead but not Departed yet: The Exploration of Liminal Space in Jim Crace's *Being Dead* (1999)." *Mortality: Promoting the Interdisciplinary Study of Death and Dying* 17(1): 51–63.
Palmié, Stephan. 2002. *Wizards & Scientists: Explorations in Afro-Cuban Modernity & Tradition*. Durham, NC and London: Duke University Press.
Panagiotopoulos, Anastasios. 2017. "When Biographies Cross Necrographies: The Exchange of Affinity in Cuba." *Ethnos* 82(5): 946–70.
Panagiotopoulos, Anastasios, and Diana Espírito Santo. 2017. "Afro-Cuban Religion's New Man." *Cuba Counterpoints: Public Scholarship about a Changing Cuba*. Retrieved 17th July, 2018, from https://cubacounterpoints.com/archives/5280.
Panourgia, Eleni Neni K. 1995. *Fragments of Death, Fables of Identity: An Athenian Anthropography*. Madison: University of Wisconsin Press.
Rosaldo, Renato. 1989. *Culture and Truth: The Remaking of Social Analysis*. Boston: Beacon Press.
Routon, Kenneth. 2010. *Hidden Powers of the State in the Cuban Imagination*. Gainesville: University Press of Florida.
Seremetakis, C. Nadia. 1991. *The Last Word: Women, Death and Divination in Inner Mani*. Chicago and London: University of Chicago Press.
Singer, Peter. 1994. *Rethinking Life and Death: The Collapse of Our Traditional Ethics*. New York: St. Martin's.
Straight, Bilinda S. 2006. "Becoming Dead: The Entangled Agencies of the Dearly Departed." *Anthropology and Humanism* 31: 101–10.
Taylor, Anne Christine. 1993. "Remembering to Forget: Identity, Mourning and Memory Among the Jivaro." *Man* 28(4): 653–78.
Toren, Christina. 1999. *Mind, Materiality and History: Explorations in Fijian Ethnography*. London: Routledge.
Tsintjilonis, Dimitri. 2007. "The Death-Bearing Senses in Tana Toraja." *Ethnos* 72: 173–94.
Turner, Mark. (1987) 2000. *Death is the Mother of Beauty*. Christchurch, New Zealand: Cybereditions.
Verdery, Katherine. 1999. *The Political Lives of Dead Bodies: Reburial and Postsocialist Change*. New York: Columbia University Press.
Vitebsky, Piers. 1993. *Dialogues with the Dead: The Discussion of Mortality Among the Sora of Eastern India*. Cambridge: Cambridge University Press.
_____. 2008. "Loving and Forgetting: Moments of Inarticulacy in Tribal India." *Journal of the Royal Anthropological Institute (N.S.)* 14: 243–61.
Walter, Tony. 1994. *The Revival of Death*. London: Routledge.
_____. 1996. "A New Model of Grief: Bereavement and Biography." *Mortality: Promoting the Interdisciplinary Study of Death and Dying* 1: 7–25.
Williams, Patrick. (1993) 2003. *Gypsy World: The Silence of the Living and the Voices of the Dead*. Chicago and London: University of Chicago Press.

Part I

Necrographic Frameworks

Chapter 1

Voices and Silences of the Dead in Western Modernity

Tony Walter

Anthropologists have observed a belief in many hunter-gatherer and agricultural societies not only that the dead are aware of the activities of the living but also that the more agentful dead have power to shape the course of events, at least for a time—though the ways such power is manifested are diverse (Straight 2006). A range of scholars have contrasted this with modern Western societies, by which I mean primarily Europe, North America, and Australia/New Zealand, the focus of this chapter. Here, it has been claimed, the dead are absent, their voices silenced. As Baudrillard puts it:

> There is an irreversible evolution from savage societies to our own: little by little, the dead cease to exist. They are thrown out of the group's symbolic circulation. They are no longer beings with a full role to play, worthy partners in exchange, and we make this obvious by exiling them further and further away from the group of the living. (1993: 126)

Historians, sociologists and other scholars have offered religious (Geary 1994), demographic (Blauner 1966), and economic (Berger 2008) reasons for this profound change. In Latin America and East Asia, however, exchange with the dead continues in modern (R. J. Smith 1974; Suzuki 1998) and modernizing (Ochoa 2010; Endres and Lauser 2011; Espírito Santo and Blanes 2013) societies.

Following these diverse scholars, it seems that there is something about Western modernity that silences the dead. But if Western modernity bans the dead as conscious, active agents, are there other ways that the dead affect modern societies? If so, are such effects created by the dead or by those who survive them? Or to put it in Panagiotopoulos's terms (Chapter 3), do contemporary Western dialogues with the dead entail not exchange but simply representations by the living *about* the dead?

The dead's "absence" or "presence" in society, along with their more nuanced "absent presence" are terms used by some sociologists (Mellor 1993) and cultural geographers, and as a sociologist I find these terms illuminating as they suggest structural location. Following Vitebsky (2008), the current, largely anthropological, collection prefers the metaphor of sound—the silences and voices of the dead—and this metaphor usefully hints at the dead's agency or lack of agency. Historian Ariès (1981) uses a metaphor of sight: are the dead visible or invisible? This chapter employs all these metaphors.

Increasingly, scholars are arguing that the dead are not entirely absent from Western modernity, their voices not entirely silenced (Hallam, Hockey, and Howarth 1999; Howarth 2000). They point to ambiguities, to an increasing social presence and even agency of the dead within Western modernity. As long ago as 1860, Burckhardt (1960) argued that the Renaissance's celebration of the individual made death a very individual problem, which Ariès (1981) later called the problem of "my death," inspiring ever greater efforts at this-worldly immortality. If individualism prompts the once living to preserve identity beyond death (Kamerman 2003; Shneidman 1995; Unruh 1983), contemporary capitalism makes money out of resurrecting them. While in Marx's analysis, commodification and objectification turn something living into something dead, contemporary American capitalism now turns the dead into social and economic actors as long as they can continue to generate income: the commodified dead, including halls of fame, exhibited plastinated bodies, deceased musicians and celebrities who earn more in death than in life, etc. In commercializing (Kearl 2010; Jones and Jensen 2005) and politicizing (Kearl and Rinaldi 1983) its dead, contemporary North America and no doubt other Western societies seem impelled to connect with them through memorialization, aboriginal rights politics, the heritage industry, nostalgia, genealogy, the music industry, etc. Yet alongside the commercially preserved posthumous identities of some pop culture celebrities, there is arguably a loss of significant historical memory, especially among Americans—more of whom know about Elvis than about the Great Depression (Kearl 2001).

This chapter aims to identify the main social forces causing the dead to be both absent *and* present within modern Western societies, their voices both heard and silenced. Apart from suggestive hints from Kearl, this has not been attempted before—the authors cited in the previous paragraph focus on just one or at most two factors. Though there is a clear historical trend in the West away from the agency of the dead as personal and intentional, my analysis highlights ambiguity and contradiction—the very same social force can render the dead both present and absent. Along with Panagiotopoulos (Chapter 3), my question is "with what kinds of voices and silences are we confronted in conditions of exchange and in conditions of representation?" How do the biographies (or necrographies) of the dead intersect with the biographies of the living? I am concerned potentially with the social presence of the dead, from those who have just died (who may be visible in, for example, mass mourning) to those who died in pre-history (whose voice may be reconstructed through aboriginal rights claims). It should then be possible to mount a more nuanced argument showing how the dead are present in different ways in different kinds of societies and why, and to indicate the circumstances in which presence entails agentful action by the dead as well as by the living.

My approach is necessarily suggestive and broad—both in lumping together somewhat disparate presences and absences, and in ignoring the many variations within "modern western society." In this, the author (a sociologist prone to generalization) craves the indulgence of anthropological readers who value the kind of ethnographic detail that is necessarily absent from this distinctly "macro" chapter. Psychologist readers may also be frustrated, for I do not consider the considerable literature on private experiences—as when a bereaved person senses the deceased's presence (Rees 1971) or constructs a continuing bond with the deceased (Klass, Silverman, and Nickman 1996). Nor do I analyze here the work of occupations (archeology, pathology, mediumship, journalism) that "read" the dead and perform a story about them in public rites such as museum exhibitions, inquests, séances, and obituaries (Walter 2005). And, though they receive some mention, I do not focus on vernacular practices or beliefs, such as spiritualism (Walliss 2001) or reincarnation (Walter and Waterhouse 1999), which are below the radar of Western modernity's dominant culture and institutions.

I first analyze some social forces that tend to remove the dead from modern Western societies: property, kinship, demography, and religion; and then I analyze some social forces that construct the dead as part of modern society, such as the nation state and ecology. Rapid social change both cuts people off from their forebears and motivates their rediscovery. I do not claim the chapter exhaustively lists all the relevant forces; I simply offer them as suggestions for further analysis. I finish with some concluding reflections on the nature of contemporary contracts with the dead and on the kinds of agency they entail.

Silence: The Absent Dead

Labor

Unlike hunter-gatherers, especially immediate return hunter-gatherers (Woodburn 1982), subsistence farmers know that the harvest this year depends on the previous year producing good seed and a surplus to subsist on till the next growing season, which leads to a general understanding that subsistence relies on previous years and previous generations. This respect for previous generations tends to produce origin myths and a cyclical view of time (Eliade 1971), along with ancestor veneration, specifically a use of ancestors to lay claim to land (Meillassoux 1972; Whitley 2002).

In industrial societies, by contrast, the contribution of the labor of forebears to one's current prosperity or lack of prosperity is more complex and subject to power and to ideological interpretation very different from that found in agricultural societies. In capitalist societies, social class is the major determinant of how prosperity is or is not transferred from one generation to another, not only through property but also through educational advantage and social and cultural capital (Miller, Rosenfeld, and McNamee 2003). How this is experienced by subsequent generations depends on class position and on ideology.

Many working-class people are conscious of class barriers and how their life chances are limited by those of their parents and grandparents. To a greater or lesser degree, they understand that capital has stolen not only their own, but also their forebears' labor, which can shape a shared identity of oppression across the generations (Gordon 1997). They may have what Horkheimer and Adorno term "the correct relationship with the dead," namely "unity with them because we, like them, are the victims of the same condition and the same disappointed hope" (1973: 215). However, insofar as they internalize a meritocratic ideology that an individual's economic position depends solely on his or her abilities, they will not share this sense of intergenerational oppression (McNamee and Miller 2004).

What about the middle classes, now the demographically and politically dominant class in advanced industrial societies? Standing observes that

> Every moderately affluent person in every society owes their good fortune largely to the labour, work, energy and inventiveness of their forebears and the forebears of their lower-income fellow citizens. Today's wealth ... is largely a reflection not of our labour but of that of generations before us. (2009: 300)

Contrast this reality with the ideology, common in liberal Western economies, that "I deserve every cent I have earned" and hence that "taxation is theft." This ideology of "the self-made man" is particularly strong in the US, whose citizens "perceive their biographies to be generally independent of history and the deeds of their ancestors" (Kearl 2001: 12). The labors of the dead undergird everyday affluent life, but their contribution is not seen. Paradoxically, the richer we become and the more the dead's labor is embedded in our prosperity, the less it may be seen.

Farmers and the old rich, however, often share neither the middle class "possessive individualist" understanding of property and self, nor the cutting off from ancestry that this implies. They may instead continue with an understanding of land and other capital as handed down from forebears, to be held in trust for future generations of the family. Even today, actively nurturing and investing in family land can generate a sense of connection to the past. Thus,

> In French winemaking, the notion of *terroir* conveys more than the land or its productive characteristics. It suggests a way of communicating between past, present and future generations, and between them, the earth and the activity of winemaking, as well as a call to those privileged to be attached to it to produce not just fine wine but to reproduce the traditions and the ecology that go with it. (Standing 2009: 20)

Indeed, *terroir* is now used as a strategy to market wines to middle-class customers who themselves are detached from land, place, and ancestry; at least they can drink wine that is rooted in qualities they themselves lack (Demossier 2011). Thus the labor of the dead as well as of the living is commodified. We have already noted other ways in which capitalism commodifies the dead (Kearl 2010). If capitalist ideology typically hides the labor of the dead, this does not undermine capitalism's potential to create opportunities to commodify and re-sell their labor, whether through deceased celebrity earnings or fine wine. The labor of the dead is both hidden by modern property relations and can itself be appropriated by the living as property.

Inheritance

Moving from labor to the property that labor produces, inheritance law and practices in Western Europe and North America tend to undermine property's potential to carry the dead's stories. Distribution of the remaining parent's assets among all the children is required by law in some European countries, and also becomes the legally required position in the UK and the US should the deceased die intestate (Miller et al.

2003). One detailed sociological study of inheritance in the UK showed that, even though not legally required, the remaining parent generally wills the house to all her children, who are then likely to sell it (Finch and Mason 2000). In Britain, the family home is typically created by the couple, so when the surviving spouse dies the home becomes again a house—property to be sold and the proceeds divided. Children who grew up in the home will retain their memories of it, but—once sold—it cannot continue to hold memories beyond their generation.

Apart from the house, specific objects may be willed to or chosen by specific individuals who will remember the deceased through those objects, so these memories become private rather than shared among all family members. Thus, "I remember my granddad by wearing his tie," rather than "That field was planted by our grandfather" (Finch and Mason 2000; Hallam and Hockey 2000). French research shows a similar internalizing of family memories, lasting no more than from one generation to the next (Déchaux 2002). Executors may do their best to keep the memory of the dead alive by ensuring that objects go to people who will cherish them for the memories and stories embodied in them (Christian 2009), but these will likely be lost when the heir in turn dies. Objects that no heirs want are sold, finding their way into junk shops, antique shops, garage sales, car boot sales, and e-bay, in the process losing the stories of the deceased.

There is a paradox here. The will is an instrument that makes the deceased a legal agent; it enables the dead literally to become a social and economic actor. Yet if, as is often the case after an elderly death in the West, the will divides property, then—after the relatively brief postmortem period in which the will is enacted—the family property becomes either private memories or alienable junk, confirming the deceased's social as well as physical death (Mulkay and Ernst 1991). This characterizes owner-occupied homes, a majority of the housing stock in many Western societies; by contrast, small family businesses, not least farms, are more likely to be inherited by just one child.

There is one way, however, in which the contemporary rich can control society after their death, and that is through setting up philanthropic trusts (Kiger 2007). They can thus initiate and control the living-dead relationship, imposing conditions on how their funds are to be used. The dead philanthropist acts on the living, as much as the other way around. His agency, however, is vulnerable to the decisions of subsequent curators and trustees who have to interpret the philanthropist's wishes in the light of new social, economic or political circumstances that the predeceased may not have envisaged or adequately planned for (Emsworth 2010).

Kinship

Closely related to property is kinship. In agricultural societies, the most common kinship structure is unilineal, with ancestry—and typically also land rights—traced through just one parent, either the father (patrilineal) or the mother (matrilineal). In unilineal societies it thus becomes possible to trace ancestors back several generations, and through them to identify as extended family maybe a hundred or so contemporaries with whom one has reciprocal obligations and rights.

However, as far back as historical records go (the thirteenth century), there is no evidence in England of a unilineal peasantry (Macfarlane 1978). The English (and hence many Americans) have long constructed family membership in terms of bilateral kinship, tracing ancestry through both parents. As any modern Briton or American who has researched their family tree has discovered, the number of people who are thus counted as kin soon gets enormous. Non-genealogists typically know little about forebears before their grandparents—bilateral kinship produces a shallow sense of time (Finch and Mason 2000; Verdery 1999). Bilateral "family" is constructed by each individual somewhat differently, and there is relatively little sense of the new spouse joining a family that exists independent of themselves (Finch and Mason 2000). Bilateral kinship typically offers considerable choice in how individuals construct "family," who they count as forebears, and to whom they will their property (Déchaux 1997, 2002; Macfarlane 1978; Strathern 1992). Necrographies become increasingly personal to the individual and vulnerable to the passing of just one or two generations. Aristocratic families differ, of course, with ancestry traced unilaterally through the male line; indeed, it is by documenting ancestry that claims to nobility are made (Halbwachs [1992]).

Aristocracy aside, contemporary Western (and especially Anglo) societies thus have two mentalities, both forms of individualism. One, based in bilateral kinship and a meritocratic understanding of prosperity, cuts me off from the march of generations through time and erases the dead, apart from those personally chosen. The other mentality is one of chosen kin relationships, love matches, affection for children, and chosen friendships (Allan 1996) that create personal attachments that, on death, can lead to intense grief (Lofland 1985; Parkes and Prigerson 1996). Thus contemporary Western grief culture has two incompatible components—a modernism that would leave the dead behind as soon as possible, in tension with a romanticism comprising love attachments that seek to continue a bond with the dead (Stroebe et al. 1992). Philippe Ariès (1981) describes this as a conflict between "hidden" death and "thy" death. Society continues as though the dead never existed, but for some individual mourners, their whole world has fallen apart.

Demography

In an influential article, Robert Blauner (1966) argued that the dead are important in societies in which many people die in the full flow of life. The greater their social, political and economic involvement, the bigger the gap left by their death, and hence their continuing presence, whether as ghost or ancestor. By contrast, members of modern societies tend to die in old age, after they have retired from both child-rearing and work; with major roles relinquished, they can depart this earth leaving but a ripple. To make its own way in life, the next generation requires not property so much as human, social, and cultural capital, and this they already have long before their elderly parents die—so even if the dead exert agency through willing property, this has rather little effect on the inheritors' life chances. Even when an adult dies before retirement, causing a huge personal loss for family and friends, their role in the bureaucratically organized workplace can readily be filled. The consequence of all this is a society oriented to the young and to the future, rather than to the old and to the past.

Though many old people are now recognized to be more engaged (not least as grandparents) than disengagement theorists such as Blauner envisaged, he was correct that the central social institutions of child socialization and paid labor do not depend on those most likely to die, namely the elderly. Continued engagement by old people in chosen, often family, roles means that their death may be deeply felt by a few intimates, but does not significantly disrupt groups beyond the family, or even the family itself. More problematic for Blauner's thesis is that belief in ghosts is buoyant in some contemporary Western societies (Davies et al. 1991), while in the equally long-lived Far East, respect for the elderly and for ancestors is evolving, not collapsing (Endres and Lauser 2011; Kawano 2010; Suzuki 1998). Such findings raise the possibility of religion as an influence on whether the dead continue in social exchange with the living.

Religion

In tribal societies, ancestors are family ancestors. World religions, unlike indigenous religions, are not confined to small communities based on kin, so need not support kin-based ancestry (Steadman et al. 1996) and indeed may oppose it—as in biblical injunctions against using mediums to call up the family dead or Protestant Christianity's prohibitions on praying for the dead. Venerating the family dead is a potential threat to worshiping the one true God, so monotheistic world religions (Judaism, Christianity, Islam) tend either to ban communication with the dead (as Vitebsky [2008] shows for twenty-first century Sora who become Baptists) or incorporate it. World religions, whether monotheistic or not, typically set up their own ancestral founders—whether Abraham, Jesus, Mohammed, or the Buddha—who continue to have considerable social presence and agency today, even for those who do not believe. Claims to descent from Abraham profoundly shape contemporary Middle Eastern politics, while Jesus's and Mohammed's biography, specifically their birthday, "are officially commemorated as national holidays (Christmas, Prophet's Birthday) in 149 and 46 countries, respectively" (Zerubavel 2003: 102). In such religions, the ordinary family dead, however much they are remembered, cease to have agency; this is reserved for founders (such as the resurrected Christ) and saints.

In addition to venerating or worshiping their founder, some world religions (e.g., Catholicism, Christian Orthodoxy, Hinduism) transform their holiest dead into saints who play an ongoing role in the lives of the living, not least in healing. Some religions (such as Catholic and Orthodox Christianity) allow prayers for the dead conducted through channels approved by the religious hierarchy and proscribe unauthorized channels such as spiritualist mediums. Thus world religions attempt to regulate relationships with the dead. Protestant Christianity, however, goes further, by banning (in theory at any rate) any attempts to call up or pray for the dead, causing considerable disruption to popular practices in the seventeenth century (Duffy 1992; Gittings 1984; Koslofsky 2002). In so far as Western modernity is influenced by Protestant Christianity which bans exchange with the dead, and by secularism which considers exchange impossible, there is a very real sense in which the dead are excluded from modern Western societies.

But Catholic regulation and Protestant proscription of living–dead exchange are by no means totally effective. In Asia, sub-Saharan Africa and the Caribbean, syncretism between Christianity and ancestor veneration is common. In nineteenth-century America, sentimental forms of Protestantism expressed continuing bonds between the living and the dead (Kete 2000). In England, bereaved Christians often quietly attend Spiritualist meetings in order to ascertain that their loved one is okay (Walliss 2001). Other vernacular discourses about the living and the dead currently popular within the West ascribe agency to the dead, for example imagining deceased loved ones not as souls, imprisoned in heaven, but as angels able to travel back and forth to earth to perform their work of guiding and caring for the living (Walter 2016). And the gothic and romantic movements (in which the dead play ongoing roles for the living) arguably began in reaction to the seventeenth-century Protestant ban on praying for the dead (Draper 1967), continuing to this day in popular culture through gothic novels, cinema, and goth subculture, all of which thrive in historically Protestant, more than in Catholic, countries (Goody and Poppi 1994).

One religious belief in which the dead continue as agents among the living is reincarnation. In popular, rather than elite, belief this typically entails recognizing a new baby or young child as the reincarnation of a recently deceased relative, who may need to be related to as though he were this older person (Empson 2007) — here biographies and identities of the living and the dead are intimately intertwined. But reincarnation is not taught by Judaism, Christianity, or Islam, even if entertained by some adherents of these religions (Walter and Waterhouse 1999); thus Western religious history tends to exclude the dead as agents in the society of the living.

Absence: Conclusion

Capitalist property relationships, individualism, and the ideology of meritocracy, inheritance, geographic mobility, bilateral kinship structures, longevity, and religious beliefs tend to erase the dead from modern Western institutions and from Western consciousness. Memories of the family dead, and interactions with them, tend to be private and individualized, in sequestered spaces such as cemeteries (Francis, Kellaher, and Neophytou 2005) and spiritualist séances (Walliss 2001). While largely absent from collective consciousness, the dead nevertheless still shape modern Western lives: the high material standard of living, not to mention political developments such as democracy, depend profoundly on the labor and sacrifices of previous generations. We stand on the shoulders of those who came before us.

Voices: The Present Dead

In this section, I outline some social forces that in modern Western societies tend to bring forth the dead, particularly the non-family dead such as national heroes. Advanced communication technologies also amplify the presence of the late modern dead, both the intimately mourned and celebrities (Walter 2015). One could also add commodification (Kearl 2010) that allows the dead to be resurrected, for profit, but this has been discussed earlier as the counterpart of a capitalism that otherwise tends to hide the dead and their labor.

Rapid Social Change

> Among democratic peoples, new families continually rise from nothing while others fall, and nobody's position is quite stable. The woof of time is ever being broken and the track of past generations lost. Those who have gone before are easily forgotten, and no one gives a thought to those who will follow. All a man's interests are limited to those near himself. . . .
> —Alexis de Tocqueville, *Democracy in America*

Social mobility today may not be quite as chaotic as Tocqueville considered it to have been in early nineteenth-century America, but his observation that it results in the individual's alienation from community, both present and past, is perceptive. I have already discussed this in relation to house moving. Moreover, when values change, the once-valued dead are forgotten (Bauman 1992). And yet the rapid social change and the acceleration of time (Rifkin 1987), which is arguably endemic to modernity, has contradictory effects for the social life of the dead, for it can end up resurrecting as well as forgetting them. Change does indeed break the woof of time, but all kinds of cultural, family, and political repairs may be attempted, with more or less success.

Migrants to a new country who are encouraged to leave behind their natal language and traditions (Horkheimer and Adorno 1973) may make great efforts to retain and pass on their cultural heritage to their children, including stories of forebears and how they lived. Marris (1974) argues that both individuals and communities need to retain something of their past if they are to feel secure enough to face change, a tendency noted also by Karl Marx ([1852] 1978) and more recently Paul Connerton (1989). Outside of the West, the dead may be mobilized to help the living adjust locally to an increasingly global economy—as with the tomb groups of the Merina of Madagascar (Bloch 1971), ancestral stories in Zimbabwe (Walter 2015), or consulting the spirits in Southeast Asia (Endres and Lauser 2011).

Modern Western societies typically frame time as linear rather than, for example, tree-shaped (with numerous "dead-end" branches) or cyclical. Thus, the dominant historical narratives are those of progress and decline (Zerubavel 2003); when progress feels no longer like progress, then decline narratives emerge, not least in the form of nostalgia for a world that is lost (Lowenthal 1985; Seabrook 2007). Progress narratives focus on the young and on future generations, decline narratives on the old and past generations. Progress and decline narratives can coexist, as in the heritage industry where leisured members of affluent post-industrial societies pay to remember "The Way We Were" (the name of an industrial heritage museum in Wigan, UK). At heritage sites, the dead come alive again, mostly in stories and pictures but sometimes also in the form of live actors. The contemporary "memory boom" is rooted in twentieth-century war and in the Holocaust (Winter 2006), but it spills over into many other kinds of touristic, media, and intellectual activity (Assmann and Conrad 2010).

If the heritage industry and the memory/memorial boom bring (some of) the humble dead (the factory worker, the Holocaust victim) into contemporary public spaces, genealogy resurrects the family dead for the individual seeking ancestors. Genealogy requires (preferably digitized) archives, along with leisure and education, but is often thought to be motivated by "the multiple discontinuities brought about by migration, war and divorce and separation" (Morgan 1996: 114). It thrives in immigrant societies such as the US and Australia (Meethan 2004), providing a resource for late-modern individuals detached from place and community to create their own identity (Giddens 1991). Genealogists may be surprised by the ancestors they meet, such that "the dead remain social agents with the capability to influence behavior in the present" (Kramer 2011: 392). In more settled England, newly discovered ancestors can provide a tangible sense of kinship for genealogists with few living kin; at the same time, genealogists posthumously restore kinship to the many dead who were excluded from family due to illegitimacy and other forms of shame now recognized as injustices. Thus genealogy can create an exchange in which the dead and the living create kinship for each other (Cannell 2011). Yet for every family member obsessed with genealogy, there are others whom it bores (Kramer 2011), illustrating the paradoxical consequences of social change: some individuals see no problem not knowing their ancestors, others become obsessed with seeking them.

Rapid social change does not mean that the dead are no longer present, simply that *which* dead are present, when, and to whom, can be much more variable, contested and unpredictable than in stable societies.

The Nation State

A group's founders are often central to constructing group identity, from world religions to academic disciplines to business organizations (Rowlinson et al. 2010). In the US, halls of fame (Kearl 2010) are used to construct identity for local communities, interest groups, and industries. But it is the nation state, more than any other collectivity, that in secular modern times has co-opted founders, heroes, and martyrs for its own uses—and with greater consequences for the living (Kearl and Rinaldi 1983). A modern nation cannot exist without its dead.

The national dead are visible on postage stamps and banknotes and commemorated in public holidays, memorial days, and one-off anniversaries (Zerubavel 1996). Their mode of death can be particularly significant. Marvin and Ingle (1999) follow Warner (1959) in analyzing the symbolism of ordinary soldiers who have died for their country, arguing that American patriotism is a civil religion of blood sacrifice which kills its children to keep the group together. Challenging Benedict Anderson (1991), they argue that "Nationalism is a community of blood and not text. . . . Ceremonies of nationalism are about death and not literature" (Marvin and Ingle 1999: 26–27). Other scholars have written about the role of heroic martyrs in nation-building in medieval France, nineteenth-century US, twentieth-century Latin America, and the Soviet Union (DeSoucey et al. 2008; Tumarkin 2011). Others have shown how stories of heroes, martyrs, and victims socialize French children into a national identity (Pellegrini 2008), while pilgrimage to Auschwitz transforms Israeli youth into citizens willing to defend their country (Feldman 2008). British commemoration of its dead in the recent Afghan war identify them as unique personalities, reflecting how "The British . . . no longer live so much in a nation-state but in a community of personalities, united through a shared domestic sphere" (King 2010).

To construct the nation, the dead may need to be present not just in schoolbooks, pilgrimages, and rituals, but also corporeally. "To mark new successor nation-states means to mark territories as 'ours' by discovering 'our sons' in mass graves and giving them proper burial in 'our soil,' thus consecrating the respective space as 'ours'" (Verdery 1999: 98). By gathering some, and excluding others, for reburial, new solidarities are affirmed. To maintain the nation, the dead may need physically to be present, on national soil, as in some Canadian First Nation campaigns to have their prehistoric dead returned from Western museums (Krmpotich 2011) and in the American imperative to bring its military dead back home. America's national myth of a haven for emigrants from poor benighted countries would not be well served by its military dead resting where they fell, overseas in some poor benighted country; they must be brought home to lie in America's sacred soil (Walter 1993). By contrast, until the 1984 Falklands War, Britain's twentieth-century military dead typically lay not at home but around the world in over two thousand Imperial (now Commonwealth) War Cemeteries, symbolizing the spread of Empire.

The nation is therefore constructed not only by including the dead, but also by excluding. America's national myth as a haven for the world's oppressed and a global crusader for freedom is served both by its many Holocaust museums, *and* by its contrasting paucity of slavery museums. Memorials erected by repentant perpetrator countries such as Germany memorialize victims not perpetrators (Young 2008). In the Soviet Union, it was the other way around: "Death spawned a monstrous hierarchy in the Soviet Union. At its top was Lenin—embalmed at the mausoleum—and at its bottom were countless unmarked, unknown, and frequently desecrated mass graves of the millions of the enemies of the people" (Tumarkin 2011: 891).

Thus power can remember certain deceased citizens and forget others; this is central to legitimizing the state and to forming ideal citizens. Kearl and Rinaldi (1983) and A. D. Smith (1986) argue that the nation provides symbolic immortality for its citizens, but contemporary states—even contemporary democracies—provide immortality to but a few, not entirely unlike ancient Egypt where only pharaohs and their entourage gained immortality.

There are, though, those whom the nation state struggles either to include or exclude for its own purposes (Schudson 1989). These are the unquiet dead, those who have died in vain—on the wrong side in civil war, in de-legitimated wars for meaningless causes, in police custody, or in the care of social workers. The unquiet dead haunt society; officialdom and history books try to hide them, but they are always available to be resurrected as martyrs by reputational entrepreneurs (DeSoucey et al. 2008); meeting the excluded ancestors is at the heart of counter-hegemonic history (Gordon 1997) and identity politics (Doss 2010; Misztal 2004). Like the Israeli state, marginalized subnational groups are not just traumatized by painful memories of suffering and exclusion, but actively cultivate painful memory in order to legitimize themselves (Misztal 2004). Holst-Warhaft (2000) has argued that grief has throughout history formed a powerful motive for action to right wrongs, manifested for example in the witness of the mothers of the "disappeared" of Argentina. As Domanska (2006) puts it, Argentina's missing dead are present in their absence, possessing "the power of absence." For Holst-Warhaft, however, it is grief, rather than the dead themselves, that has agency.

One way or another, when ghosts come to haunt the body politic, the state has to exorcise them. The US had to incorporate first the Civil War (Schwartz and Schuman 2000) and then Vietnam (Wagner-Pacifici and Schwartz 1991) into its collective memory. It remains haunted by 9/11. Here exorcism has entailed not just rebuilding and memorializing Ground Zero, not just contentious military ventures in the Middle East, but also an ongoing attempt to incorporate 9/11 into a revised narrative of America and of the West.

But today's memory boom may be related less to nationalist agendas than "to today's identity politics: to diverse social and political groupings claiming voice and vying for representation in the public sphere" (Doss 2010: 48). Misztal has argued that from the late eighteenth century, states monopolized memory, banishing memories of trauma and wrongdoing, but now there is "a public space for counter-memories structured around trauma. . . . The decline in the role of national and religious memories as stable sources of identity reopens the space for search for both authentic and useable pasts" (Misztal 2004: 68, 77). With synchronous media and internet reporting of events around the world, these counter-memories can become more global than national (Assmann and Conrad 2010). The next section illustrates this.

Ecology

Environmental movements generate awareness of both how our world's altered physical environment is the product of the actions of past generations, and how our own actions will affect our children's world. This entails a global sense of both the living and the dead and their effect on succeeding generations—the globe itself becomes the medium through which past, present, and future generations influence each other. The planet is portrayed similarly to how peasants and aristocrats see their land, that is, as the product of their forebears' labor, to be held in trust for their descendants. Nature takes time to nurture, whether it is planting trees or reducing humans' carbon footprint, so the consequences are not felt for a generation or two. Ecology thus revives an agrarian understanding of stewardship and of actions being felt for generations. Of course, many kinds of human activity are felt for generations, but the ecology movement seems to be influencing public opinion about the relation between the living and the dead more than other contemporary social movements. This may possibly be because ecology has made headway in redefining community as global, in turn redefining whom we consider both forebears and descendants.

Conclusion

This chapter has argued that the dead are both present and absent within contemporary Western societies, sketching some factors that either silence the dead or give them a voice. In contemporary Western societies, property relationships, kinship structures, demography, and religion tend to silence the dead; while philanthropy, nationalism, heritage, genealogy, commodification, and ecology tend to render them visible. Rapid social change is more complex in its effects, both killing the dead and offering a pressing reason to reanimate them.

Contemporary social formations not analyzed in this chapter, such as medicine and democracy, also have ambiguous effects. Medicine's focus on keeping the body healthy for this life rather than preparing the soul for the next, and democracy's granting of authority to living voters rather than to inherited monarchical power, downplay the importance of the dead. Yet medicine insists that all deaths have a medical cause; democratic states require the cause of each death to be medically, and if need be, judicially accounted for (by means of death certification, inquests, etc.), so no death can go unnoticed. At least until these procedures are complete, the dead have a formal, official presence. This is very different from undemocratic societies in which the dead can immediately disappear or be "disappeared" (Holst-Warhaft 2000).

In many traditional and eastern societies, the contract between the living and the dead is mutual (Endres and Lauser 2011; R. J. Smith 1974). As a Singaporean student emailed me, "the living offer prayers and offerings to the ancestors in exchange for the ancestor's blessings and protection." In Western eyes, such a contract reflects feudal relations, and sits uneasily with Western notions of democratic, secular modernity. So what kinds of contract between the living and the dead remain or are evolving in the modern West? In some arenas, such as the nation state, religion, and environmentalism, there seems to be a contract. The living need the nation state as a form of symbolic immortality while the nation state needs the sacrifice of its soldiers. Religious founders need followers; believers need a founder. For environmentalists, the planet needs a new contract between the present and future generations. In other arenas, the "contract" seems one-sided and confused. The labor of past generations is both needed by capitalism and, through capitalist ideology, forgotten. Heritage resurrects and commodifies a few of the historic dead, while condemning the rest to social death.

Without a clear mythology or ideology that provides space for the ancestors among the living, their presence can be hard for modern Westerners to detect. For Marx, ideology brings the past both in and out of view, and this chapter has indicated some ideologies that hide from the living the very real presence of the dead within their society. Most modern democratic nations depend on historic violence that must be kept veiled if the nation is to retain legitimacy. The well-off inherit social, cultural, and economic capital from their forebears, yet the ideology of meritocracy blinds them to this, seducing them to believe they have earned every cent of their wage, ignoring the labor of previous generations.

Other ideologies, such as socialism and environmentalism, highlight how actions affect subsequent generations, challenging the current generation to change the accumulated actions of the past and to acknowledge a social contract between the living and the dead.

Parties to a contract have agency, but can the dead have personal, intentional agency? Some scholars argue that they cannot (Schutz and Luckman 1974), but that their material remains can become powerful symbolic objects, capable of being used by claims-makers to considerable effect (Jenkins 2010; Verdery 1999); other scholars consider that the corpse can exert agency in the sense of affecting the living (Harper 2010; Young and Light 2013). Whatever powers the corpse may or may not have or be given, this chapter has argued that in certain circumstances and through certain institutions, the dead can indeed exert agency through, for example, wills, philanthropic trusts, genealogical surprises, and—at least for believers—their religious founder and specific beliefs such as reincarnation. And just as inanimate objects can be causal agents, so the effects of human actions can outlive the agent, as historians clearly acknowledge— not least Marx who famously wrote, "Men make their own history, but they do not make it just as they please; they . . . make it . . . under circumstances directly found, given and transmitted from the past. The tradition of all the dead generations weighs like a nightmare on the brains of the living" (Marx [1852] 1978: 595). Ecology seems to teach the same. Thus there can be more to the dead's social presence than the (highly potent) agency of the living in collectively remembering them, (re)constructing their history, and sooner or later forgetting them; in certain circumstances, even today, it seems that the dead too can exert agency on the living.

Distinguishing two meanings of "agency" may be helpful here. In liberal Western societies people believe that they govern themselves, that they have "the capacity to act independently and pursue their interests" (Endres and Lauser 2011: 10). The dead are no longer believed to exert to agency in this sense. But premortem actions do continue postmortem and exert agency in another sense of the word, namely causation; their actions continue to have effects, in the way that objects and animals exert agency. Objects, animals, and the dead all impact living humans, who must orient their own actions accordingly—as actor network theory suggests (Law 2009).

Max Weber's vision of rationality disenchanting the world portrays rationality and modernity as the effort to "kill" the personal agency in all non-human, non-living beings. In this, Western modernity has largely succeeded—but has not succeeded in killing their effects. The premortem actions of the dead continue postmortem to shape the lives of survivors, in ways as complex as society itself. The more complex the society, the more complex the effects.

The West, especially those parts of the West influenced by Protestant Christianity, has radically excluded the possibility of exchange between the living and the dead, leaving "memory" as the only, and decidedly one-sided, way in which the living can relate to the dead. Hence much of this chapter has concerned collective memory, and the reduction, in some circumstances, of collective memory of the dead to private memory. But in many parts of the world, ancestor veneration allows two-way exchange in which the living perform rites for the dead, who in turn will bless, or at any rate not harm, the living. As several chapters in this book demonstrate, such societies may modernize in ways that allows space for the dead to have active, personal agency. The most obvious highly industrialized country in which such practices are normative is Japan, but "spirited modernities" are also emerging in many other modernizing parts of the world (Endres and Lauser 2011; Espírito Santo and Blanes 2013).

Tony Walter is a sociologist and Emeritus Professor in the Centre for Death & Society, University of Bath. After early writings on religion, landscape, and basic income, he has for the past thirty years researched and taught about death and society. His fifteen books include *Pilgrimage in Popular Culture* (Macmillan, 1993), *The Revival of Death* (Routledge, 1994), *The Eclipse of Eternity: A Sociology of the Afterlife* (Macmillan, 1996), *On Bereavement: The Culture of Grief* (Open University Press, 1999), and most recently *Social Death* (Routledge, 2016), *What Death Means Now* (Policy Press, 2017) and *Death in the Modern World* (Sage, 2020).

References

Allan, Graham. 1996. *Kinship and Friendship in Modern Britain*. Oxford: Oxford University Press.
Anderson, Benedict. 1991. *Imagined Communities: Reflections on the Origin and Spread of Nationalism*. London: Verso.
Ariès, Philippe. 1981. *The Hour of Our Death*. London: Allen Lane.
Assmann, Aleida, and Sebastian Conrad, eds. 2010. *Memory in a Global Age: Discourses, Practices and Trajectories*. Basingstoke: Palgrave Macmillan.
Baudrillard, Jean. 1993. *Symbolic Exchange and Death*. London: Sage.
Bauman, Zygmunt. 1992. *Mortality, Immortality and Other Life Strategies*. Cambridge: Polity.
Berger, John. 2008. "Twelve Theses on the Economy of the Dead." *Left Curve* 31.

Blauner, Robert. 1966. "Death and Social Structure." *Psychiatry* 29: 378–94.
Bloch, Maurice. 1971. *Placing the Dead: Tombs, Ancestral Villages and Kinship Organization in Madagascar*. London and New York: Seminar Press.
Burckhardt, Jacob. (1860) 1960. *The Civilization of the Renaissance*. New York: Mentor.
Cannell, Fenella. 2011. "English Ancestors: The Moral Possibilities of Popular Genealogy." *Journal of the Royal Anthropological Institute* 17(3): 462–80.
Christian, William. 2009. "The Presence of the Absent: Transcendence in an American Midwest Household." *Studia Ethnologica Hungarica* 12: 223–40.
Connerton, Paul. 1989. *How Societies Remember*. Cambridge: Cambridge University Press.
Davies, Douglas, Charles Watkins, and Michael Winter. 1991. *Church and Religion in Rural England*. Edinburgh: T&T Clark.
Déchaux, Jean-Hugues. 1997. *Le Souvenir Des Morts: Essai Sur Le Lien De Filiation*. Paris: Presses Universitaires de France.
———. 2002. "Paradoxes of Affiliation in the Contemporary Family." *Current Sociology* 50(2): 229–42.
Demossier, Marion. 2011. "Beyond Terroir: Territorial Construction, Hegemonic Discourses and French Wine Culture." *Journal of the Royal Anthropological Institute* 17(4): 685–705.
DeSoucey, Michaela, Jo-Ellen Pozner, Corey Fields, Kerry Dobransky, and Gary Alan Fine. 2008. "Memory and Sacrifice: An Embodied Theory of Martyrdom." *Cultural Sociology* 2(1): 99–121.
Domanska, Ewa. 2006. "The Material Presence of the Past." *History & Theory* 45: 337–48.
Doss, Erika. 2010. *Memorial Mania: Public Feeling in America*. Chicago: Chicago University Press.
Draper, John W. 1967. *The Funeral Elegy and the Rise of English Romanticism*. London: Frank Cass.
Duffy, Eamon. 1992. *The Stripping of the Altars: Traditional Religion in England, 1400–1580*. New Haven and London: Yale University Press.
Eliade, Mircea. 1971. *The Myth of the Eternal Return: Cosmos and History*. Princeton: Princeton University Press.
Empson, Rebecca. 2007. "Enlivened Memories: Recalling Absence and Loss in Mongolia." In *Ghosts of Memory*, ed. Janet Carsten, 58–82. Oxford: Blackwell.
Emsworth. 2010. "Nobody to Blame but Albert C. Barnes for the Barnes Foundation's Moving." Retrieved 16 February 2019 from http://emsworth.wordpress.com/2010/03/24/the-barnes-foundations-moving-blame-albert-c-barnes/.
Endres, Kirsten W., and Andrea Lauser, eds. 2011. *Engaging the Spirit World: Popular Beliefs and Practices in Modern Southeast Asia*. Oxford and New York: Berghahn Books.
Espírito Santo, Diana, and Ruy Blanes. 2013. *The Social Life of Spirits*. Chicago: University of Chicago Press.
Feldman, Jackie. 2008. *Above the Death Pits, Beneath the Flag: Youth Voyages to Poland and the Performance of Israeli National Identity*. Oxford and New York: Berghahn Books.

Finch, Janet, and Jennifer Mason. 2000. *Passing on: Kinship and Inheritance in England*. London: Routledge.
Francis, Doris, Leonie Kellaher, and Georgina Neophytou. 2005. *The Secret Cemetery*. Oxford: Berg.
Geary, Patrick J. 1994. *Living with the Dead in the Middle Ages*. Ithaca, NY: Cornell University Press.
Giddens, Anthony. 1991. *Modernity and Self-Identity*. Cambridge: Polity.
Gittings, Clare. 1984. *Death, Burial and the Individual in Early Modern England*. London: Croom Helm.
Goody, Jack, and Cesare Poppi. 1994. "Flowers and Bones: Approaches to the Dead in Anglo and Italian Cemeteries." *Comparative Studies in Society & History* 36: 146–75.
Gordon, Avery F. 1997. *Ghostly Matters: Haunting and the Sociological Imagination*. Minneapolis: University of Minnesota Press.
Halbwachs, Maurice. 1992. *On Collective Memory*. Chicago: University of Chicago Press.
Hallam, Elizabeth, and Jenny Hockey. 2000. *Death, Memory and Material Culture*. Oxford: Berg.
Hallam, Elizabeth, Jenny Hockey, and Glennys Howarth. 1999. *Beyond the Body: Death and Social Identity*. London: Routledge.
Harper, Sheila. 2010. "The Social Agency of Dead Bodies." *Mortality* 15(4): 308–22.
Holst-Warhaft, Gail. 2000. *The Cue for Passion: Grief and its Political Uses*. Cambridge, MA: Harvard University Press.
Horkheimer, Max, and Theodor W. Adorno. 1973. *Dialectic of Enlightenment*. London: Allen Lane.
Howarth, Glennys. 2000. "Dismantling the Boundaries Between Life and Death." *Mortality* 5(2): 127–38.
Jenkins, Tiffany. 2010. *Contesting Human Remains in Museum Collections: The Crisis of Cultural Authority*. London: Routledge.
Jones, Steve, and Joli Jensen, eds. 2005. *Afterlife as Afterimage: Understanding Posthumous Fame*. New York: Peter Lang.
Kamerman, Jack B. 2003. "The Postself in Social Context." In *Handbook of Death and Dying*, ed. Clifton B. Bryant, vol. 1, 302–6. Thousand Oaks, CA: Sage.
Kawano, Satsuki. 2010. *Nature's Embrace: Japan's Aging Urbanites and New Death Rites*. Honolulu: University of Hawaii Press.
Kearl, Michael C. 2001. "An Investigation into Collective Historical Knowledge and Implications of its Ignorance." *Texas Journal of Ideas, History and Culture* 23: 4–13.
_____. 2010. "The Proliferation of Postselves in American Civic and Popular Cultures." *Mortality* 15(1): 47–63.
Kearl, Michael C., and Anoel Rinaldi. 1983. "The Political Uses of the Dead as Symbols in Contemporary Civil Religions." *Social Forces* 61: 693–708.
Kete, Marie Louise. 2000. *Sentimental Collaborations: Mourning and Middle-Class Identity in Nineteenth-Century America*. Durham, NC: Duke University Press.
Kiger, Joseph C. 2007. *Philanthropists and Foundation Globalization*. Edison, NJ: Transaction.

King, Anthony. 2010. "The Afghan War and 'Postmodern' Memory: Commemoration and the Dead of Helmand." *British Journal of Sociology* 61: 1–25.

Klass, Dennis, Phyllis R. Silverman, and Steven L. Nickman, eds. 1996. *Continuing Bonds: New Understandings of Grief*. Bristol, PA: Taylor and Francis.

Koslofsky, Craig M. 2002. "From Presence to Remembrance: The Transformation of Memory in the German Reformation." In *The Work of Memory*, ed. Alon Confino and Peter Fritzche, 25–38. Urbana: University of Illinois Press.

Kramer, Anne-Marie. 2011. "Kinship, Affinity and Connectedness: Exploring the Role of Genealogy in Personal Lives." *Sociology* 45(3): 379–95.

Krmpotich, Cara. 2011. "Repatriation and the Generation of Material Culture." *Mortality* 16(2): 145–60.

Law, John. 2009. "Actor Network Theory and Material Semiotics." In *The New Blackwell Companion to Social Theory*, ed. Bryan S. Turner, 141–58. Oxford: Blackwell.

Lofland, Lyn H. 1985. "The Social Shaping of Emotion: The Case of Grief." *Symbolic Interaction* 8: 171–90.

Lowenthal, David. 1985. *The Past is a Foreign Country*. Cambridge: Cambridge University Press.

Macfarlane, Alan. 1978. *The Origins of English Individualism*. Oxford: Blackwell.

Marris, Peter. 1974. *Loss and Change*. London: Routledge.

Marvin, Carolyn, and David W. Ingle. 1999. *Blood Sacrifice and the Nation: Totem Rituals and the American Flag*. Cambridge: Cambridge University Press.

Marx, Karl. (1852) 1978. "The Eighteenth Brumaire of Louis Bonaparte." In *The Marx-Engels Reader*, ed. Robert C. Tucker, 594–617. New York: Norton.

McNamee, Stephen J., and Robert K. Miller. 2004. "The Meritocracy Myth." *Sociation Today* 2(1). Retrieved 18 March 2019 from http://www.ncsociology.org/sociationtoday/v21/merit.htm.

Meethan, Kevin. 2004. "To Stand in the Shoes of my Ancestors: Tourism and Genealogy." In *Tourism Diasporas and Space*, ed. Tim Coles and Dallen J. Timothy, 139–50. London Routledge.

Meillassoux, Claude. 1972. "From Reproduction to Production: A Marxist Approach to Economic Anthropology." *Economy and Society* 1(1): 93–105.

Mellor, Phillip A. 1993. "Death in High Modernity." In *The Sociology of Death: Theory, Culture and Practice*, ed. David Clark, 11–30. London: Blackwell.

Miller, Richard K., J. P. Rosenfeld, and Stephen J. McNamee. 2003. "The Disposition of Property: Transfers Between the Dead and the Living." In *Handbook of Death and Dying*, ed. Clifton B. Bryant, 917–925. Thousand Oaks: Sage.

Misztal, Barbara A. 2004. "The Sacralization of Memory." *European Journal of Cultural Studies* 7(1): 67–84.

Morgan, David H. J. 1996. *Family Connections: An Introduction to Family Studies*. Cambridge: Polity.

Mulkay, Michael, and John Ernst. 1991. "The Changing Profile of Social Death." *Archives Européennes de Sociologie* 32: 172–96.

Ochoa, Todd Ramón. 2010. *Society of the Dead: Quita Manaquita and Palo Praise in Cuba*. Berkeley: University of California Press.

Parkes, Collin Murray, and Holly G. Prigerson. 1996. *Bereavement: Studies of Grief in Adult Life*. London: Routledge.
Pellegrini, Ann. 2008. "'What Do Children Learn at School?' Necropedagogy and the Future of the Dead Child." *Social Text* 26(4): 97–105.
Rees, W. Dewi. 1971. "The Hallucinations of Widowhood." *British Medical Journal* (2 Oct): 37–41.
Rifkin, Jeremy. 1987. *Time Wars*. New York: Henry Holt.
Rowlinson, Michael, Charles Booth, Peter Clark, Agnes Delahaye, and Stephen Procter. 2010. "Social Remembering and Organizational Memory." *Organization Studies* 31(1): 69–87.
Schudson, Michael. 1989. "The Present in the Past Versus the Past in the Present." *Communication* 11: 105–13.
Schutz, Alfred, and Thomas Luckman. 1974. *The Structures of the Life-World*. London: Heinemann.
Schwartz, Barry, and Howard Schuman. 2000. "History, Commemoration, and Belief: Abraham Lincoln in American Memory, 1945–2001." *American Sociological Review* 70(2): 183–203.
Seabrook, Jeremy. 2007. "The Living Dead of Capitalism." *Race & Class* 49(3): 19–32.
Shneidman, Edwin S. 1995. "The Postself." In *Death: Current Perspectives*, ed. J. B. Williamson and Edwin S. Shneidman, 454-460. Mountain View, CA: Mayfield.
Smith, Anthony D. 1986. *The Ethnic Origins of Nations*. Oxford: Blackwell.
Smith, Robert John. 1974. *Ancestor Worship in Contemporary Japan*. Stanford, CA: Stanford University Press.
Standing, Guy. 2009. *Work After Globalization: Building Occupational Citizenship*. Cheltenham: Edward Elgar.
Steadman, Lyle B., Craig T. Palmer, and Christopher F. Tilley. 1996. "The Universality of Ancestor Worship." *Ethnology* 35(1):63–76.
Straight, Bilinda. 2006. "Becoming Dead: The Entangled Agencies of the Dearly Departed." *Anthropology & Humanism* 31: 101–10.
Strathern, Marilyn. 1992. *After Nature: English Kinship in the Late Twentieth Century*. Cambridge: Cambridge University Press.
Stroebe, Margaret, Mary M. Gergen, Kenneth J. Gergen, and Wolfgang Stroebe. 1992. "Broken Hearts or Broken Bonds: Love and Death in Historical Perspective." *American Psychologist* 47: 1205–12.
Suzuki, Hikaru. 1998. "Japanese Death Rituals in Transit: From Household Ancestors to Beloved Antecendents." *Journal of Contemporary Religion* 13(2): 171–88.
Tumarkin, Maria. 2011. "Productive Death: The Necropedagogy of a Young Soviet Hero." *South Atlantic Quarterly* 110(4): 885–900.
Unruh, David R. 1983. "Death and Personal History: Strategies of Identity Preservation." *Social Problems* 30(3): 340–51.
Verdery, Katherine. 1999. *The Political Lives of Dead Bodies: Reburial and Postsocialist Change*. New York: Columbia University Press.
Vitebsky, Piers. 2008. "Loving and Forgetting: Moments of Inarticulacy in Tribal India." *Journal of the Royal Anthropological Institute (N.S.)* 14: 243–61.

Wagner-Pacifici, Robin, and Barry Schwartz. 1991. "The Vietnam Veterans Memorial: Commemorating a Difficult Past." *American Journal of Sociology* 97: 376–420.
Walliss, John. 2001. "Continuing Bonds: Relationships between the Living and the Dead within Contemporary Spiritualism." *Mortality* 6(1): 127–45.
Walter, Tony. 1993. "Dust not Ashes: The American Preference for Burial." *Landscape* 32(1): 42–48.
_____. 2005. "Mediator Deathwork." *Death Studies* 29(5): 383–412.
_____. 2015. "Communication Media and the Dead: From the Stone Age to Facebook." *Mortality* 20(3): 215–32.
_____. 2016. "The Dead who Become Angels: Bereavement and Vernacular Religion." *Omega* 73(1): 3–28.
Walter, Tony, and Helen Waterhouse. 1999. "A Very Private Belief: Reincarnation in Contemporary England." *Sociology of Religion* 60(2): 187–97.
Warner, W. Lloyd. 1959. *The Living and the Dead: A Study of the Symbolic Life of Americans*. New Haven: Yale University Press.
Whitley, James. 2002. "Too Many Ancestors." *Antiquity* 76(291): 119–26.
Winter, Jay. 2006. *Remembering War: The Great War between Memory and History in the 20th Century*. New Haven: Yale University Press.
Woodburn, James. 1982. "Egalitarian Societies." *Man* 17(3): 431–451.
Young, Craig, and Duncan Light. 2013. "Corpses, Dead Body Politics and Agency in Human Geography: Following the Corpse of Dr Petru Groza." *Transactions of the Institute of British Geographers* 38: 135–48.
Young, James E. 2008. "The Texture of Memory: Holocaust Memorials in History." In *Cultural Memory Studies*, ed. Astrid Erll and Ansgar Nünning, 357–66. Berlin: de Gruyter.
Zerubavel, Eviatar. 1996. "Social Memories: Steps to a Sociology of the Past." *Qualitative Sociology* 19(3): 283–99.
Zerubavel, Eviatar. 2003. *Time Maps: Collective Memory and the Social Shape of the Past*. Chicago: Chicago University Press.

Chapter 2

Coping with Massive Urban Death

The Mutual Constitution of Mourning and Recovery in World War II's Bombing War

Antonius C.G.M. Robben

After surviving the Battle of Stalingrad, where an estimated 250,000 German and supporting troops had died, and after languishing three years in a prisoner-of-war camp in Siberia, Corporal Beckmann returned to Germany where more hardships were awaiting him. His wife was living with another man, and his parents had committed suicide out of desperation over Nazi Germany's defeat. Weighed down by guilt for having lost eleven soldiers during a reconnaissance mission in the woods of Gorodok, Beckmann visited his former commanding officer and pleaded to relieve him of the responsibility for the failed mission, but he was ridiculed and sent off. Desperate for work, Beckmann stopped by a theater to offer his services as a performer, but the director turned him down. And even the river Elbe refused him when he tried to commit suicide by washing his half-drowned body ashore. Beckmann felt abandoned by the world and by a dejected God who bemoaned that no one believed in him anymore. God proclaimed Death the world's new deity: "They believe in you. They love you. They fear you. You can't be deposed. You can't be denied" (Borchert 1996: 80). Death had grown fat, remarked God. "Why, yes," Death responded, "I've put on a bit of weight this century. Business has been good. One war after another. Like flies! Like flies the dead hang on the walls of the century. Like flies they lie stiff and dried up on the windowsill of the times" (Borchert 1996: 80).

The play *The Man Outside* (*Draußen vor der Tür*), written in 1946 by Wolfgang Borchert, became an overnight success upon its radio debut in February 1947 because the plight of the fictional Corporal Beckmann resonated with the misfortunes of Germany's demobilized soldiers, and the anguish of families awaiting the return of around three million troops penned up in Soviet prisoner-of-war camps. Dread and despair dominate the play as one door after another was shut into Beckmann's face. The exception is the Other. The Other is Beckmann's alter ego, the one who explains that life is worth living, that there is always an open door somewhere. When Beckmann asked after yet another disillusion why he should continue living, the Other responded: "For yourself! For life. Your road is waiting. And every so often there are lamps. Are you such a coward that you're afraid of the darkness between them? Do you want only lamps? Come, Beckmann, on to the next one" (Borchert 1996: 114).

The Man Outside is an allegory of death and survival in postwar Germany, this chapter's subject matter, and serves as a starting point for rethinking the dominant anthropological approach to mourning. The anthropology of death has been focusing primarily on the study of the care, dying, death, human remains, and incarnated spirit of the deceased; the grief and liminality of the mourners; and the cross-cultural variations of funerary rituals, ancestor worship, and commemoration (e.g., Green 2008; Palgi and Abramovitch 1984; Robben 2004; Rosenblatt, Walsh, and Jackson 1976; Seale 1998). Borchert's play could easily be interpreted as Beckmann's descent from mental and physical deterioration to suicide, were it not that his alter ego represents a contrapuntal life force that mitigates his many adversities. The anthropology of death has understudied this interrelation of life and death, with some exceptions (Franklin and Lock 2003; Kaufman and Morgan 2005; Lock 2002; Robben 2014).

This chapter intends to demonstrate that the way people cope with death influences the way they cope with life, and vice versa. Rather than treating mourning and recovery as separate processes that develop in different time frames, this chapter addresses the constitutive oscillation between mourning and recovery, and critiques anthropology's overbearing concept of liminality. An examination of war widows in postwar Germany who mourned their dead husbands, and coped with food shortages, destroyed housing, and poor health, demonstrates how coming to grips with past losses and facing everyday challenges influence one another. Many German civilians and troops died on native soil during the final years of World War II. People perished in collapsed cellars and air raid shelters as cities crumbled under the weight of intensive bombardments. Others were killed during the ground offensive by the Allied forces approaching from East and West. Numerous corpses could never be recovered as they were crushed by falling debris or reduced to ashes in fire storms. Citizens and homes were as much united in death as in the postwar efforts to rebuild city and society. After conceptualizing the oscillatory process of mourning and recovery, this chapter elaborates its mediation through varying circumstances of massive death, changing burial rituals, and differentiating practices of social reproduction, and then concludes with the theoretical implications for the anthropology of death.

The Oscillatory Process of Mourning and Recovery

The sadness and suffering upon the passing away of a loved one are so overpowering, and the expressions of grief often so visible and all-absorbing, that these emotions have dominated the scholarly attention to death. Furthermore, throughout the world mortuary rituals have clear beginnings and endings, and the dead body seems to absorb the bereaved entirely because the inobservance of even the smallest funerary prescripts is believed to harm the living and trouble the dead. Mourning has therefore been understood by several founding fathers of the social sciences as a finite process, and one that singularly focuses on the acceptance of painful losses. Durkheim noted the social and spiritual punishment for improperly conducted mourning. Whenever an indigenous Australian aboriginal failed to ritually lacerate himself at his father-in-law's funeral then his wife would be given to someone else, and if he did not mourn the deceased correctly then "the soul of the deceased dogs his steps and kills him" (Durkheim 1995: 401). Durkheim explained this strict social control as a mechanism to strengthen the injured group by sharing the loss in an effervescent ritual necessary to restore people's social and mental health. Malinowski recognized this need for communal and personal stability in the belief of immortality: "Religion saves man from a surrender to death and destruction, and in doing this it merely makes use of the observations of dreams, shadows, and visions. The real nucleus of animism lies in the deepest emotional fact of human nature, the desire for life" (1954: 51). The way bereaved Trobrianders blackened their bodies with soot, and widows were secluded in their huts during an extensive mourning period, demonstrated to Malinowski (1929) the extraordinary significance of separating the dead from the living for the survival of society. Van Gennep (1960) substantiated the validity of this understanding through a cross-cultural analysis of funerals as rituals that occur in liminal time to isolate communal mourning from the flow of everyday life. Finally, Freud understood individual mourning as a natural reaction to loss; a loss that needed to be accepted to prevent worse from happening. "Reality-testing has shown that the loved object no longer exists, and it proceeds to demand that all libido shall be withdrawn from its attachments to that object" (Freud 1955: 244). Freud regarded grief as a bounded emotional process that began with the announcement of death and ended with its acceptance. Melancholia and chronic mourning were the detrimental consequences of attachments that had not been properly severed. In sum, these three founding fathers considered grief and mourning as different manifestations of bereavement; communal mourning took place during liminal time, outside the everyday of regular time; and grief ended when the attachment to the deceased had been cut.

Durkheim, Malinowski, and Freud were of course not blind to the ambiguities of grief and mourning. Durkheim emphasized the discrepancies between emotion, display, and action. "But generally there is no relationship between the feelings felt and the actions done by those who take part in the rite: If, at the very moment when the mourners seem most overcome by the pain, someone turns to them to talk about some secular interest, their faces and tone often change instantly, taking on a cheerful air, and they speak with all the gaiety in the world" (Durkheim 1995: 400). Malinowski pointed at the conflicting emotions of wanting to hold on to but also to let go of the deceased: "There is a desire to maintain the tie and the parallel tendency to break the bond" (1954: 50). Freud theorized this ambiguous conduct in psycho-dynamic terms. "[P]eople never willingly abandon a libidinal position, not even, indeed, when a substitute is already beckoning to them. This opposition can be so intense that a turning away from reality takes place and a clinging to the object through the medium of a hallucinatory wishful psychosis" (Freud 1955: 244). Nevertheless, these three scholars directed the scientific study of mourning narrowly to the coping with loss rather than examining the entire social and behavioral spectrum of bereavement. Somehow, they regarded the everyday lives of the bereaved as inconsequential for and unaffected by the circumscribed mourning process, as is clear from Malinowski's selective description of mortuary rituals on the Trobriand Islands.

Malinowski described the taboos and seclusion of a Trobriand widow inside her house as follows: "She must not leave the place; she may only speak in whispers; she must not touch food or drink with her own hands, but wait till they are put into her mouth; she remains closed up in the dark, without fresh air or light. . . ." (Malinowski 1929: 158). His ethnography of Trobriand mourning is entirely focused on the cultural prescriptions imposed on widows portrayed as passive subjects, and fails to examine how this treatment influenced the ways in which widows coped with their bereavement. In all fairness to Malinowski, he was a product of his times and not sensitive to questions of gender, but even his functional analysis ignores the non-funerary demands placed on the bereaved because they are not conceptualized in an interactional relation to mourning.

Malinowski's influence on the anthropology of death could still be noticed fifty years later in Annette Weiner's ethnography of the Trobrianders. Despite her feminist perspective, Weiner focuses on the contributions of Trobriand women to processes of regeneration and immortality through their ritual exchanges. Surprisingly, the widow's and widower's lives are reduced to a few sentences about how the relation with the deceased spouse is severed by cutting off the mourning neck band during a mortuary distribution of natural fiber skirts. "The spouse may then wash the black from her or his body and wear bright clothing again. A new marriage can now be contracted. A spouse's mourning usually lasts for two years" (Weiner 1983: 81). We get no idea of what happens during the two years of mourning, how the daily lives of the bereaved spouses are affected, and how these circumstances influence the prolonged mourning period.

The narrow understanding of mourning as the coping with loss has been particularly dominant in psychotherapy because of Freud's influential grief work hypothesis. Freud observed that the bereaved have little interest in the outside world, and are absorbed by the mental effort to overcome the loss: "time is needed for the command of reality-testing to be carried out in detail, and that when this work has been accomplished the ego will have succeeded in freeing its libido from the lost object" (1955: 252). This notion of working through grief was further developed by psychologists such as Lindemann (1944) and Bowlby (1998), and counseling was shaped around the central idea that the affectional bond between the bereaved and deceased had to be broken. A productive life could only begin after a successful severance (Stroebe and Schut 1999: 197–99).

This theorization of bereavement shifted when constructivist psychologists demonstrated that grief work might unravel but also refashion the emotional attachment to the dead through narration, active remembrance, and periodic rituals (Klass, Silverman, and Nickman 1996; Neimeyer 2001). Of course, they did not suggest that pathological clinging to the dead does not exist or that some bereaved do not require treatment, but the therapeutic and moral judgment about people with enduring bonds to the dead changed significantly. Similar conceptual developments have taken place in sociology and anthropology. Tony Walter (1996, 1999) observed that people may cultivate durable relations with the dead through conversations with others, and Obeyesekere (2002) demonstrated the cross-cultural existence of cyclical models of life and death. Anthropologists also noticed that the bereaved may incorporate the dead in the flow of life through narration, inner conversations, memorialization, and cemetery visits (Francis, Kellaher, and Neophytou 2005; Green 2008; Hallam and Hockey 2001). Aside from complicated grief, the bereavement process may lead to the cutting of affective ties within an understanding of life as inevitably ending in death or entail an enduring bond that appeals to a cyclical notion of life and death (Kaufman and Morgan 2005: 320).

The second contribution of constructivist psychology has been that counseling is no longer occupied exclusively with affectional disengagement but also with activities and emotions involved in rebuilding a life without the deceased (Worden 2009: 46–54). The conceptualization of bereavement is broadened from a decontextualized intrapsychic process of grief work to a comprehensive dual process of mourning and restoration that encapsulates the bereaved's lifeworld. In particular, the Dual Process Model of Coping with Bereavement (DPM) emphasizes the oscillation between attention to the bond with the deceased (loss orientation) and a complementary attention to a life without the deceased (restoration orientation). Loss orientation includes an array of emotions, from profound sadness and despair to remembrance and happiness, and activities such as handling the deceased's clothing and arranging the funeral. Restoration orientation is directed at the adjustment to what has been also called secondary losses, namely loneliness, a declining income, and assuming a new identity as a widow or orphan. Anxiety and fear, but also pride and a sense of achievement, may accompany these challenges. Furthermore, the oscillation between attention to primary and secondary losses is a regulatory mechanism encapsulated in an everyday life occupied with unrelated, distractive activities (Stroebe and Schut 1999, 2001, 2010).

Psychology's dual process model can provide an important corrective to the one-sided attention to loss orientation in the anthropology of death that originated in the works of Durkheim, Freud, and Malinowski. This new perspective requires a translation of the oscillatory process of loss and restoration orientation from the psychic to the sociocultural level, and an incorporation of the growing scholarship that regards death not as separate from but intertwined with life (Kaufman and Morgan 2005; Robben 2014). Two steps are necessary. First, the terms loss and restoration orientation need to be replaced by sociocultural mourning and recovery orientation to avoid a confusion between the psychological and anthropological approach, and to emphasize the empirical shift from grief as an intrapsychic process to mourning as a sociocultural process that oscillates with life processes. Second, the two mutually constitutive processes exist in a societal context whose multilayered complexity leads to a differentiation of sociocultural mourning and recovery into personal, social, and collective mourning and recovery.

Personal mourning applies to sociocultural manifestations of individual bereavement. Unlike grief, which is an intrapsychic process investigated by psychology, personal mourning includes cultural externalizations of bereavement, such as cemetery visits, displaying mementoes, and exchanging memories about the deceased. Social mourning concerns people with affective bonds to the deceased and the bereaved, such as members of parishes, neighborhoods, ethnic groups, professional organizations, political parties, and so forth. Common expressions of social mourning are historical accounts, exhumations, burials, and commemorations. Collective mourning involves the coping with human losses by a heterogeneous bereaved population that is defined by living in a city, region, or country. The common denominator is not attachment or affection but coexistence and therefore includes people who are strangers to the deceased, indifferent, or maybe even responsible for their death. For example, perpetrators are also participants in the collective mourning, simply for being residents of a city or country. They have to face the harm inflicted on society and may try to influence processes of national mourning and recovery for self-serving reasons. Moreover, national governments may try to orchestrate expressions of collective mourning and influence when, where, and whether to mourn the dead.

Like mourning, recovery is manifested on the personal, social, and collective level because the bereaved need to reconstitute their lives without the deceased in multiple domains. Personal recovery includes the adjustment to a new social status as widows, widowers, orphans, or childless parents. Furthermore, the bereaved have to strengthen family ties or conjugal relations and run the household. The emphasis lies on the bereaved person situated in the center of an egocentric network. Social recovery involves the reconstitution of damaged group ties; the start of which is often a funeral or memorial service where participants renew their group relations. Dependent on the circumstances of death and the social life of the bereaved, additional occasions and expressions of recovery may be organized beyond the mortuary rituals. For example, the renewed social coexistence requires particular attention when many community members died through war or natural disaster. Collective recovery is seldom manifested when one person dies, unless it concerns a popular figure or a prominent statesman whose death requires not only public mourning but also efforts to prevent societal upheaval. Likewise, massive death requires collective recovery to rebuild the broken society and work towards postconflict coexistence.

This conceptual approach will be illustrated with an analysis of the oscillatory process of the sociocultural mourning and recovery by German war widows during and after World War II. Their predicament lends itself well to such analysis because the intertwinement of life and death is starkest during times of war. I will make an anthropological analysis of data derived from historical studies, restrict the analysis to confirmed dead civilians in Germany, and focus on the mourning and recovery of German women. First, the causes of death and the collection of human remains will be described. The competition between relatives and Nazi authorities over the funerals demonstrates how personal and collective mourning can be in conflict. Next, the everyday challenges of the survivors will be analyzed, and how personal and social recovery influenced mourning. A comparison of how Jewish and non-Jewish women dealt with the hardships of pregnancy and procreation demonstrates the mutual consequences of mourning and recovery. I will conclude with a critique of liminality as a conceptual approach to mourning and emphasize the continuities between mortuary rituals and everyday life.

Collecting, Burying, and Reburying the Dead

German troops and civilians were killed mostly abroad during the greater part of World War II, especially during massive battles and major extermination campaigns in the East. Many fallen soldiers were buried locally, while assassinated Jewish deportees were cremated or dumped in mass graves. Death was first brought to Germany through British-American aerial attacks, particularly since 1943. The bombings were intended to cripple the German war industry and break the morale of the German people. Bombardments during World War II killed at least 353,000 German citizens, mostly civilians. The final Allied ground assault in 1945 raised the number of dead to unprecedented heights, with an estimated 1.3 million German soldiers who lost their lives between January and April 1945 on the Eastern front (Overy 2013: 477; Bessel 2011: 52).

The Allied bombardments on German cities were denounced by the Nazi regime as terror attacks against women and children. The German people were exhorted to show the same resilience and resolve as the frontline troops. But civil courage was put severely to the test when the dead were strewn in streets and squares, as happened in Kassel on 22 October 1943 when an RAF raid killed 6–8,000 people, razed 60% of the city, and destroyed the tank and locomotive factories (Arnold 2011: 1, 31–33). For days, the charred and dismembered remains of people lay exposed on the sidewalks. Many dead were collected from air raid shelters where they had suffocated from carbon monoxide poisoning. Others had been completely incinerated by petrol and phosphorus bombs. Throughout Germany, scenes could be found similar to the following from a Dresden air raid shelter: "About thirty to forty people, mostly elderly, women, and children were dead, sitting on the benches against the wall. Only a few had fallen to the ground" (Friedrich 2006: 377). Inmates from prisons and concentration camps were faced with far more gruesome discoveries as they were ordered to climb into cellars and retrieve the deformed bodies. A policeman, searching for his loved ones in the rubble, reported: "I have found many wedding rings, but not the one of my wife. I have held in my hand children's vertebrae and skulls . . . But I have found no trace of my family" (Arnold 2011: 53).

The air war casualties were a matter of state when the death toll was still low. They were appropriated in funerary rituals that did not evolve around the dead themselves or the personal mourning of the bereaved relatives but focused on sacrifice, resilience, and rebirth in the Third Reich. The elaborately staged funeral ceremonies were held at city halls and public squares. Early in the war, the ceremonies were centered on coffins covered with swastika flags to emphasize the collective identity of the dead, but such open display of the dead was avoided as their number increased. Memorials were used in their place. Private citizens were encouraged to attend these commemorations at which the bereaved were prominent yet passive recipients of the eulogies by local party leaders, and the faith in Adolf Hitler and Germany's final victory was professed. The principal orator was accompanied by delegations from the Nazi party, the state, and the German army to represent the national mourning (Arnold 2011: 76–82). Sociocultural mourning was thus compartmentalized in separate funerary rituals according to the type of mourning at stake. Personal mourning was expressed at private burials, social mourning was important at memorial services for the missing dead and at mass burials, while collective mourning was central in funeral ceremonies to advance state interests.

Personal mourning might be woven through the collectivization of loss, as happened in Hamburg where relatives placed small crosses and altars with letters and photos at the edge of an official mass grave containing thirty thousand dead that were portrayed by the state as a community of shared fate. Also in Hamburg, memorials were erected for neighborhoods erased after the British-American Operation Gomorrah killed an estimated 37,000 people in July 1943 and destroyed 61% of all housing (Overy 2013: 335). The Nazi authorities attempted to turn the dead into eternal collective heroes, and the state-controlled press emphasized how quickly the city residents had adjusted to the massive losses as they visited a mass grave in Ohlsdorf near Hamburg: "Cheerful voices of boys are sounding somewhere. Life, life goes on. It must go on so that someday also the army of silent sleepers can be said to have been victorious—despite everything" (Thiessen 2007: 69–70). The army of the future and the army of the dead were supposed to unite in a final victory won at great sacrifice. The Nazi regime gave meaning to the massive deaths by linking them explicitly to Germany's hailed millennial Third Reich, and thus hoped to motivate a new generation to fight for its future. The massive losses were presented as enhancing the fighting spirit of the German people rather than lowering morale.

In the face of death and ruination throughout Germany, the Nazi authorities tried to sway the coping with these losses from national mourning to national recovery through a redemptive discourse about the return to normality. Life would go on, as it had always been in a city that had been struck repeatedly by disaster. Hamburg's history was represented as an endless cycle of destruction and reconstruction that included the medieval plagues, the Napoleonic invasion, the Great Fire of 1842, and the cholera epidemic of 1892. Reconstruction became a metaphor for healing the city and its inhabitants. For example, a commemoration on 9 November 1943 of Hitler's failed putsch in 1923, began with mourning Hamburg's dead, and then transformed into a demonstration of combativeness and comradery with a defiantly sung "Our Dead": "This way the people found itself / and for a few seconds / the heart of the strongest grows weak.—But now raise the standards, / Germany shall wait no longer, / stand firm, you holy Reich!" (Thiessen 2007: 64). The destruction–reconstruction cycle was compared to a cycle of death and rebirth. Time for mourning was fitting, but the flags, hanging half-mast in respect of the dead, were soon raised high to salute the holy fatherland. The regional party leader Kaufmann imagined Hamburg's rebirth through the mobilization of its citizens in a total war that would lead to a final victory and would give meaning to the sacrifices of soldiers at the front and civilians in Hamburg (Thiessen 2007: 52–55, 64–66).

Where Durkheim and Malinowski regarded funerals as rituals with largely unchanging structural qualities, the burial of the war dead, if they were buried at all, changed rapidly under the mounting assault on Nazi Germany. The sacredness of an extinguished life dissolved as the dead multiplied, and mortuary rituals could no longer be held. Hitler had prohibited mass burials, but cemeteries could not handle the rising number of dead. In October 1943 the city of Frankfurt am Main assigned the dead to three forms of individual burial, according to the number of dead after a particular bombardment. A toll of two thousand entitled the dead to standard coffins. Anywhere between two thousand and six thousand dead were placed in half coffins covered with paper, and higher casualty numbers were buried in large paper bags. If the dead were foreign laborers and concentration camp inmates, then they were thrown in mass graves (Friedrich 2006: 380).

Many dead could not be identified after being disfigured by incendiary bombs and demolished air raid shelters. Flame throwers were used to incinerate the dead stuck under the debris. Cities with massive casualties resorted to open-air cremations, as happened in Dresden after heavy bombardments in February 1945: "They were cremated at the Old Market, where iron girders were built into huge grates on which roughly five hundred bodies each could be stacked into a funeral pyre, drenched with gasoline, and burned" (Friedrich 2006: 378). A technique developed in Germany's extermination camps was now used for the casualties of air raids in total disregard of the symbolic and ritual needs of the dead and the bereaved.

The public cremation of the dead exposed the waning strength of the Nazi state and altered the oscillations of sociocultural mourning and recovery. The Allies continued to be blamed for the bombings but people began to fault the German military for failing to protect them. The Nazi funeral ceremonies were increasingly replaced by mortuary services organized by local pastors who could also offer spiritual care and help restore the damaged community of believers. The bereaved began to demand openly from the authorities that their dead be interred in individual or family graves. The Nazi state was losing its grip on the population and had to concede to these requests (Arnold 2011: 89–90, 53).

One remarkable example of the oscillation between mourning and recovery was the postmortem or corpse marriage. Hitler decreed in 1941 that engaged women could marry fiancées who had died at the front, especially when children were expected. The premarital deaths directly affected the social status of these unwed mothers who could now be honored by the state with pensions and legal rights as official war widows. The Nazi authorities even steered the personal mourning of these women by allowing older widows to live as housewives, while obliging young widows to overcome bereavement by working, raising children, and possibly remarrying. Older widows who had lost their husbands in World War I, and were now grieving over their dead sons, were portrayed as exemplary mothers who had sacrificed everything to the Nation and kept the memory of the fallen alive (Heineman 1999: 47–56). The three types of widows were thus accorded other positions in society that affected their coping with bereavement, and differentiated their personal and social recovery.

With the Allied forces entering deeper into Germany and defeat becoming inevitable, large numbers of Germans began to commit suicide. The Germany Security Service reported in early 1945: "Many are getting used to the idea of making an end of it all. Everywhere there is great demand for poison, for a pistol and other means for ending one's life. Suicides due to genuine depression about the catastrophe which certainly is expected are an everyday occurrence" (Bessel 2011: 54). These suicides were generally not provoked by an inconsolable grief over the violent death of loved ones but by despair about the future. Personal, social, and collective recovery was all seen in a negative light. People were fearful about survival under occupation. Could they feed, clothe, and house their children? Would the Allied victors take revenge on the German people? Suicide is not only an individual deed, as Durkheim explained, but also very much a social phenomenon. People could no longer rely on neighborly assistance because of the disintegration of the social fabric. The downfall of Nazi Germany made them the anxious orphans of the Allied rulers, whose revenge was dreaded as the knowledge about Nazi crimes spread across Germany and shortages of food and housing made the future precarious.

The victorious Allies were not allowing self-pity among the defeated German people and forced them to confront the horrors of the recent past. Photo exhibitions displaying emaciated survivors in the Buchenwald concentration camp, and piles of victims of typhoid fever at Bergen-Belsen, were held throughout Germany. Germans in the American Zone were obliged to watch the documentary *Death Mills* (*Die Todesmühlen*), which visualized the human degradation at several liberated concentration camps and showed how civilians from nearby towns were filed past the dead strewn out in open fields and forest groves (Barnouw 2008: 7–9; Olick 2013: 98–99). Having just buried their own dead, they were now forced to rebury dehumanized fellow human beings, such as Jewish deportees, Russian prisoners of war, and foreign forced laborers. An embodied memory was impressed on civilians by obliging them to collect decaying corpses barehanded and exhume mass graves. The Allied authorities were thus attempting to make the German people acknowledge their common humanity with these victims, honoring the defiled dead with decorated individual graves, and reburying them on German cemeteries with the proper religious ceremony. More important for the Allies, these obligatory tasks were to instill a collective responsibility and guilt about the atrocities (Barnouw 2008: 12–22; Bessel 2011: 60). Some individuals may have felt remorse, but this sentiment was collectively overridden by feelings of victimization, both from Nazi warmongering and the Allied invasion. The mother who shielded her son's eyes, and the woman who covered her mouth and nose in sight of the rotting corpses, might have felt horror but not necessarily compassion (Barnouw 2008: 30–33). More than likely, they were reminded of their own dead and missing who had been buried in mass graves along the retreating Eastern front.

The number of urban dead had been so high in 1945 that the cemeteries were overflowing or could not be reached because of the door-to-door fighting. In cities like Berlin and Nuremberg, the dead were buried hastily in parks, squares, and gardens or kept at home until the streets were safe again. Mass burials were also carried out by the victorious Soviet authorities to prevent contagious diseases from spreading. Black (2011: 69) has argued that mass graves represented for Berliners a loss of civilization, which until then had only befallen people who were considered racially inferior, such as Jews, Slavs, Gypsies, and the mentally handicapped. Demanding a "proper burial became a way of dissociating oneself from the past, and of redeeming German cultural traditions from the experience of Nazism" (Black 2011: 86). Emergency graves, as they were called to avoid an association with the mass graves of racial outcasts, were opened during the war and the dead reburied individually. Once defeated, former Nazis were ordered to unearth and properly bury their executed victims. Cemeteries were stripped of Nazi memorials to the dead, and the SS and SA insignia on the graves of soldiers were removed. In fact, distinctions between soldiers and civilians were erased. Both groups were regarded as victims of the Nazi regime and its fatal embrace of total war. Numerous civilians reburied their loved ones in wooden coffins at cemeteries, although others defended improvised graveyards as dignified places of mourning and memory (Black 2011: 74–80; Gregor 2008: 162–4).

Ambiguous Procreation and Widowhood

Both life and death had been degraded during the Nazi regime. Lives were extinguished in extermination camps, on front lines, in the occupied territories, and increasingly also in German cities as the war intensified. This dehumanization debased also the respect for the dead. Postwar reburials became a symbolic means to pick up the cycle of rebirth again; a cycle that reincorporated the dead in a resurging community, despite the suicides, abortions, and premature deaths from malnutrition and poor health. Reburials symbolized a return to proper social relations. The humanization of death entailed a humanization of life, and the recreation of a community. This reconstitutive oscillation of humane mourning and humane recovery through proper burials makes sense on a cultural level but is not necessarily plausible on an individual level. Death, deprivation, and a bleak future were postwar conditions that reinforced one another for many German citizens, and resulted in downward oscillations of mourning and recovery that ended numerous lives.

In 1946, the British publisher Victor Gollancz made a six-week journey through Germany to assess the state of well-being in the British Zone. Shocked by the starvation and deplorable health of the German population, and conscious of the fact "that Belsen and Auschwitz were far worse," he urged the British government to improve food supplies, medical care, and housing (Gollancz 1947: 64). This precarious situation affected bereaved families in the broad sense of survival and procreation. Malnutrition not only lowered female fertility and increased infant mortality, but the anxiety about food also influenced the feelings about having children. "Instead of desiring a child many women are now succumbing to a deep despondency, thus the diagnosis of a new pregnancy often arouses fits of despair. The women are weighed down by the anxiety how to procure the most necessary things for the expected baby. There are no beds, no bedding, no baby-clothes and diapers. . . . Abortions are on the increase" (Gollancz 1947: 44–45). Gollancz added that the main source of income of general practitioners was performing abortions. These abortions were often procured after rape by Allied soldiers, but also caused by demoralization and despair about the future (Grossmann 2007: 61). Instead of reinvigorating German society with a new generation to make up for the millions of dead of warfare and genocide, non-Jewish German women resorted to abortion and suicide as self-inflicted reactions to massive death.

Abortions were also frequent in an embattled Berlin. The defense of Germany's capital was so tenacious because Nazi propaganda had warned about the mass rape of women and children by subhuman Red Army soldiers. The refusal to surrender and the brutal treatment of captured Soviet troops made the ominous threat become a reality for German women and girls (Grossmann 2007: 50–53). The Red Army assault was in fact accompanied by mass rapes. The raping decreased within weeks of the final victory but nevertheless continued until early 1947. According to one conservative estimate, 110,000 women in Berlin were raped multiple times (Grosmann 2007: 49), as was the anonymous author of a diary about the first two months of the Soviet occupation: "One of them grabs my wrists and jerks me along the corridor. Then the other is pulling as well, his hand on my throat so I can no longer scream. I no longer want to scream, for fear of being strangled. They're both tearing away at me, instantly I'm on the floor" (Anonymous 2012: 72). Not only the death of a loved one, but also such harrowing experience, and others that followed, was mourned as a personal loss or even as a loss of self.

Much has been written about the fate of German women during the postwar years, but the relation of rape and bereavement has hardly been studied. We can imagine that the intermingling of the mourning over a deceased husband and the multiple personal violations may have made women decide to terminate pregnancies. The two experiences evoked feelings of victimization and abandonment that ran counter to the cultivated public image of steadfast German rubble women (*Trümmerfrauen*) who cleared the ruins of Germany's bombed-out cities. Recovery from loss was for many women a negative process burdened by malnutrition and poor health. The confrontation with the horrors of the Nazi regime further increased the emotional load of personal ordeals because the same German men who had slaughtered defenseless civilians and committed genocide against Jews and Gypsies were some of the same men who were unable to protect German women because of their incarceration in prisoner-of-war camps.

According to the anonymous diarist from Berlin, the losses suffered from the rapes were "... a collective experience, something foreseen and feared many times in advance, that happened to women right and left, all somehow part of the bargain. And this mass rape is something we are overcoming collectively as well. All the women help the other, by speaking about it, airing their pain and allowing others to air theirs and spit out what they've suffered. Which, of course, doesn't mean that creatures more delicate than this cheeky Berlin girl won't fall apart or suffer for the rest of their lives" (Anonymous 2012: 174). Like rape, bereavement in Germany was a highly personal as well as a collective experience in which personal mourning and recovery translated collectively into low birthrates and high suicide figures. Forgetting the war years of plenty, when Nazi Germany appropriated property and natural resources from occupied countries and forced millions of foreign men to work on German farms and in German factories, seemed understandable as the daily postwar struggles dominated the oscillation of mourning and recovery in adverse ways.

Different oscillations become visible when the predicament of Jewish women in postwar Germany is compared to that of non-Jewish women. Whereas numerous non-Jewish women committed suicide, had abortions, and avoided pregnancies, Jewish women had in 1946 the world's highest birthrate (Grossmann 2007: 184). Within weeks of liberation they married other survivors because of a primary need, "to seek some link on earth. ... This came before food and shelter" (Levin quoted in Grossmann 2007: 185). Newborns could not mend the gap left by six million dead but at least help restore the Jewish community, both as a way to redeem the future and as a procreative revenge for the Holocaust. "Indeed, in some significant ways, the generation of new life was not only a signal of survival and hope but also an acknowledgment of loss" (Grossmann 2007: 200). These collective aspirations were complemented by personal considerations. Jewish women wanted to recover a sense of agency, and offset fears of infertility due to the deprivations suffered in concentration camps. However, there were also women who interrupted their pregnancies. Having survived starvation and the traumatic onslaught of the concentration camps, they worried about their baby's mental health and the fate of raising children in Germany. Some survivors had abortions after being raped by Allied soldiers (Grossmann 2007: 191–6). These divergent experiences reflected the different oscillations between processes of mourning and recovery among Jewish survivors, including the desire to build an independent Jewish state away from Europe.

Fraternizing with Allied troops and foreigners was one way of survival for non-Jewish war widows: "Light, warmth, a cup of hot cocoa, the prospect of being able to spend a couple of carefree hours often brings a young woman into a soldier's apartment...." wrote a contemporary sociologist (Thurnwald quoted in Moeller 1993: 23). Popular memory has it that German women fraternized with British and American soldiers but were raped by Soviet soldiers. Although not denying the generalization, Heineman argues that it revealed people's notions about Eastern and Western Allies, and "reflected a troubling tendency to consider consensual and violent sex two sides of the same coin" (1999: 77). Consensual relations between German women and Soviet men to obtain food and affection were hushed up because of the massive rapes during the siege of Berlin. These relations dwindled in the summer of 1947 as Soviet troops were confined to military barracks because commanders feared the corrupting influence of the bourgeois German women. In the American Zone, however, young Americans without combat experience were rotated into Germany, and they readily struck up friendly relations with German women (Heineman 1999: 96–98).

The immediate postwar years witnessed a preoccupation with marital crisis in Germany brought about by the demographic imbalance of men and women, high divorce rates, and an anxiety about male sexual dysfunction due to wartime license, postwar imprisonment, and malnutrition (Herzog 2003). In Berlin, the male–female ratio was 100:146 in October 1946, and the divorce rate in 1948 was almost 80% above the 1946 level (Moeller 1993: 27–29). The family as a fundamental cornerstone of society remained intact but this ideal clashed with the harsh postwar reality. Where young war widows had been told by the Nazi state that remarrying and having more children were national obligations, postwar widows were less willing to give up their hard-earned independence and marry men who had returned wounded from the front or demoralized from a prisoner-of-war camp (Heineman 1999: 52, 108–11; Moeller 1993: 28–30).

Living life as a single mother was complicated because of the state's conceptualization of widowhood. The different treatment of war widows with children in West Germany and East Germany demonstrates how mourning and recovery were intertwined differently. The Allied authorities suspended the military pensions to widows as a measure to demobilize German society and remove all privileges for the armed forces. This policy was perceived by the German people as a revictimization of women who had endured the wartime bombings, postwar shortages, and the loss of husbands and breadwinners. Within years the official attitude towards widows in East and West began to diverge.

In 1950, the West German government adopted the Law to Aid Victims of War that entitled war widows with small children to pensions in order to allow them to be homemakers, and thereby assure society that the families of soldiers dying in future wars would be supported. Young childless widows received only minimal pensions because they were expected to work. These policies were not without controversy as memories of wartime conduct and peacetime behavior raised doubts about the victimhood of widows. Accusations of adultery, illegitimate children, and concubinage were railed against widows who were drawing pensions unlawfully. A press report estimated that as many as one hundred thousand widows were living with men while receiving pensions. One women's organization turned on them in 1955: "the war widows are the worst practitioners of concubinage; they take women's husbands, above all the husbands' money, move them into their apartments . . . and live as if married. These women don't think about marriage at all, because they certainly don't ever want to lose their 'well-earned pension,' which they acquired through the death of their fallen husbands" (Heineman 2002: 221). In one decade, the image of war widows who had toiled in the debris of German cities, and had been victimized by Allied abuse, were turned into fraudulent women who were morally corrupt (Heineman 2002: 218–24).

East German war widows received a different treatment from the Soviet authorities, who wanted them to join the work force rather than lead domestic lives. Legislation was imposed in 1948 that awarded pensions only to disabled widows or widows with at least two small children. The contrast between East and West was remarkable. The population of

West Germany was three times that of East Germany in 1954, but there were almost 1.2 million official war widows in West Germany, while less than sixty thousand widows received pensions in East Germany (Heineman 2002: 222–24). The fate of living inside or outside the Soviet Zone in 1945, and later the German Democratic Republic, had a significant influence on the ways in which widows coped with their losses and reconstituted their lives and families.

Conclusion

In 1950, Hannah Arendt made a journey to Europe, and noted apathy and melancholy throughout the continent because of the destruction, the Holocaust, and the dissolution of Western civilization's moral structure. In an often-quoted passage, she wrote:

> But nowhere is this nightmare of destruction and horror less felt and less talked about than in Germany itself. A lack of response is evident everywhere, and it is difficult to say whether this signifies a half-conscious refusal to yield to grief or a genuine inability to feel.... And the indifference with which they walk through the rubble has its exact counterpart in the absence of mourning for the dead, or in the apathy with which they react, or rather fail to react, to the fate of the refugees in their midst. This general lack of emotion, at any rate this apparent heartlessness, sometimes covered over with cheap sentimentality, is only the most conspicuous outward symptom of a deep-rooted, stubborn, and at times vicious refusal to face and come to terms with what really happened. (Arendt 1950: 324)

Arendt's observation that Germans did not speak about the urban destruction and mourn their dead has been criticized recently by historians who demonstrated convincingly that there was an extensive local postwar memory culture about Germany's material and human losses (Arnold 2011; Gregor 2008; Moeller 2003; Thiessen 2007). My critique of Arendt's conclusion that the German people refused to face reality takes another approach. Were Arendt observations influenced by her Freudian understanding of the mourning process? Did people refuse to confront the painful reality or were they oriented more towards the recovery pole of bereavement than to mourning?

Like Freud, Arendt opposed mourning to melancholy, which Freud described as "a profoundly painful dejection, cessation of interest in the outside world, loss of the capacity to love, inhibition of all activity, and a lowering of the self-regarding feelings...." (1955: 244). Melancholy leads to a permanent sense of loss. The attachment to the deceased is not unraveled because that person is an inextricable part, in life and death, of the bereaved's self. Death is not the loss of a loved one, but the loss of a part of self. Santner (1990: 3) has remarked, however, that mourning and melancholia are not separate states of bereavement but constitute a continuum. Nevertheless, even this understanding of mourning remains imprisoned in a singular orientation on the dead and ignores that the recovery of a life without the deceased is also part of the bereavement process.

An understanding of the German struggle over massive losses and postwar collapse demonstrates precisely the oscillation between the processes of mourning and recovery. Mourning the dead was intertwined with malnutrition, the difficulties of social reproduction, poor health, and housing shortages. The coping with bereavement by German widows during the postwar decade confirms the mutual constitution of mourning and recovery, and how this oscillation may lead to divergent responses to loss. Differences in age, social position, marital status, and ethnicity, together with personal experiences of loss, affected the possibilities of coming to terms with the past, the choices made, and the reconstruction of lives and homes. Furthermore, these differences do not only exist on the level of personal mourning but also between personal, social, and collective mourning. Arendt's observations about the German people's inability to mourn their losses may refer to official national manifestations of mourning but not to people's private experiences or the local ways of urban populations.

Anthropologists have commonly studied the cultural ways in which people mourn their losses, but have rarely examined their relation to formative life processes following the deaths. The overwhelming emotions at the death of loved ones, as affirmed by the anthropologist's personal experience of bereavement, help to explain this bias to a certain degree while the cultural dominance of mortuary rituals and their anthropological conceptualization in terms of liminality does the rest. The forceful models developed by Hertz and Van Gennep, however, fail to pay attention to the spatial and temporal continuities between mortuary rituals and everyday life or at least to the positioning of sacred time and space in the life world. After all, as Leach has remarked, rituals "*create time* by creating intervals in social life" (1968: 135), and the same argument applies to the creation of space. Liminality only exists by virtue of its interruption of the flow of everyday life, and vice versa. This critique has two implications for the concept of liminality, and the anthropology of death. First, mortuary rituals should not be treated as separate processes that unfold in distinct, self-contained temporal and spatial frames. Rather, mortuary rituals and personal, social and collective mourning are given existence and meaning through their interconnections with everyday social life. The linear sequencing of liminal and everyday phases should be replaced by a more dynamic conceptualization that does justice to the interactive flows of meanings and practices. I am of course not denying the existence of funerals and the accompanying ritual practices, but I want to emphasize their permeability by the processes of everyday social life. Second, rather than treating mourning and recovery as separate sociocultural processes, this chapter has addressed the constitutive oscillation between mourning and recovery because a death does not stand alone in liminal time but affects the ways in which the bereaved continue to lead their lives in the absence of the deceased. Death does not stand apart from life in an exclusionary way because the spiritual lives of the dead and the living constitute one another, and life and death become each other's horizon.

Antonius C.G.M. Robben is Professor of Anthropology at Utrecht University, the Netherlands, and past President of the Netherlands Society of Anthropology. His monographs include *Political Violence and Trauma in Argentina* (University of Pennsylvania Press, 2005), which won the Textor Prize from the American Anthropological Association in 2006, and *Argentina Betrayed: Memory, Mourning, and Accountability* (University of Pennsylvania Press, 2018). His most recent edited volumes are *Necropolitics: Mass Graves and Exhumations in the Age of Human Rights* (with Francisco Ferrándiz, University of Pennsylvania Press, 2015), *Death, Mourning, and Burial: A Cross-Cultural Reader* (2nd ed., Wiley Blackwell, 2017), and *A Companion to the Anthropology of Death* (Wiley Blackwell, 2018).

References

Anonymous. 2012. *A Woman in Berlin*. London: Virago Press.
Arendt, Hannah. 1950. "The Aftermath of Nazi Rule: Report from Germany." *Commentary* 10(October): 324–53. Retrieved 26 May 2015 from https://www.commentarymagazine.com/article/the-aftermath-of-nazi-rulereport-from-germany/.
Arnold, Jörg. 2011. *The Allied Air War and Urban Memory: The Legacy of Strategic Bombing in Germany*. Cambridge: Cambridge University Press.
Barnouw, Dagmar. 2008. *Germany 1945: Views of War and Violence*. Bloomington: Indiana University Press.
Bessel, Richard. 2011. "The Shadow of Death in Germany at the End of the Second World War." In *Between Mass Death and Individual Loss: The Place of the*

Dead in Twentieth-Century Germany, ed. Alon Confino, Paul Betts, and Dirk Schumann, 51–68. New York: Berghahn Books.

Black, Monica A. 2011. "Reburying and Rebuilding: Reflecting on Proper Burial in Berlin after 'Zero Hour.'" In *Between Mass Death and Individual Loss: The Place of the Dead in Twentieth-Century Germany*, ed. Alon Confino, Paul Betts, and Dirk Schumann, 69–90. New York: Berghahn Books.

Borchert, Wolfgang. (1949) 1996. *The Man Outside*. London: Marion Boyars Publishers.

Bowlby, John. (1980) 1998. *Attachment and Loss*. Vol. 3, *Sadness and Depression*. London: Pimlico.

Durkheim, Emile. (1912) 1995. *The Elementary Forms of Religious Life*. New York: The Free Press.

Francis, Doris, Leonie Kellaher, and Georgina Neophytou. 2005. *The Secret Cemetery*. Oxford: Berg.

Franklin, Sarah, and Margaret Lock, eds. 2003. *Remaking Life & Death: Toward an Anthropology of the Biosciences*. Santa Fe: SAR Press.

Freud, Sigmund. (1917) 1955. "Mourning and Melancholia." In *The Standard Edition of the Complete Psychological Works of Sigmund Freud*, vol. 14, translated by James Strachey, 243–58. London: The Hogarth Press.

Friedrich, Jörg. 2006. *The Fire: The Bombing of Germany, 1940–1945*. New York: Columbia University Press.

Gollancz, Victor. 1947. *In Darkest Germany*. London: Victor Gollancz.

Green, James W. 2008. *Beyond the Good Death: The Anthropology of Modern Dying*. Philadelphia: University of Pennsylvania Press.

Gregor, Neil. 2008. *Haunted City: Nuremberg and the Nazi Past*. New Haven: Yale University Press.

Grossmann, Atina. 2007. *Jews, Germans, and Allies: Close Encounters in Occupied Germany*. Princeton: Princeton University Press.

Hallam, Elizabeth, and Jenny Hockey. 2001. *Death, Memory and Material Culture*. Oxford: Berg.

Heineman, Elizabeth D. 1999. *What Difference Does a Husband Make? Women and Marital Status in Nazi and Postwar Germany*. Berkeley: University of California Press.

———. 2002. "Gender, Public Policy, and Memory: Waiting Wives and War Widows in the Postwar Germany." In *The Work of Memory: New Directions in the Study of German Society and Culture*, ed. Alon Confino and Peter Fritzsche, 214–38. Urbana: University of Illinois Press.

Herzog, Dagmar. 2003. "Desperately Seeking Normality: Sex and Marriage in the Wake of the War." In *Life after Death: Approaches to a Cultural and Social History of Europe During the 1940s and 1950s*, ed. Richard Bessel and Dirk Schumann, 161–92. Cambridge: Cambridge University Press.

Kaufman, Sharon R., and Lynn M. Morgan. 2005. "The Anthropology of the Beginnings and Ends of Life." *Annual Review of Anthropology* 34: 317–41.

Klass, Dennis, Phyllis R. Silverman, and Steven L. Nickman, eds. 1996. *Continuing Bonds: New Understandings of Grief*. Washington, DC: Taylor & Francis.

Leach, E. R. 1968. *Rethinking Anthropology*. London: The Athlone Press.

Lindemann, Erich. 1944. "Symptomatology and Management of Acute Grief." *American Journal of Psychiatry* 101(2): 141–48.
Lock, Margaret. 2002. *Twice Dead: Organ Transplants and the Reinvention of Death.* Berkeley: University of California Press.
Malinowski, Bronislaw. 1929. *The Sexual Life of Savages in North-Western Melanesia.* New York: Eugenics Publishing Company.
_____. 1954. *Magic, Science and Religion.* Garden City, NY: Doubleday and Company.
Moeller, Robert G. 1993. *Protecting Motherhood: Women and the Family in the Politics of Postwar West Germany.* Berkeley: University of California Press.
_____. 2003. *War Stories: The Search for a Usable Past in the Federal Republic of Germany.* Berkeley: University of California Press.
Neimeyer, Robert A., ed. 2001. *Meaning Reconstruction and the Experience of Loss.* Washington, DC: American Psychological Association.
Obeyesekere, Gananath. 2002. *Imagining Karma: Ethical Transformation in Amerindian, Buddhist, and Greek Rebirth.* Berkeley: University of California Press.
Olick, Jeffrey K. 2013. *In the House of the Hangman: The Agonies of German Defeat, 1943–1949.* Chicago: University of Chicago Press.
Overy, Richard. 2013. *The Bombing War: Europe 1939–1945.* London: Allen Lane.
Palgi, Phyllis, and Henry Abramovitch. 1984. "Death: A Cross-Cultural Perspective." *Annual Review of Anthropology* 13: 385–417.
Robben, Antonius C.G.M., ed. 2004. *Death, Mourning, and Burial: A Cross-Cultural Reader.* Malden: Wiley Blackwell.
_____. 2014. "Massive Violent Death and Contested National Mourning in Post-Authoritarian Chile and Argentina: A Sociocultural Application of the Dual Process Model." *Death Studies* 38(5): 335–45.
Rosenblatt, Paul C., R. Patricia Walsh, and Douglas A. Jackson. 1976. *Grief and Mourning in Cross-Cultural Perspective.* New Haven: HRAF Press.
Santner, Eric L. 1990. *Stranded Objects: Mourning, Memory, and Film in Postwar Germany.* Ithaca, NY: Cornell University Press.
Seale, Clive. 1998. *Constructing Death: The Sociology of Dying and Bereavement.* Cambridge: Cambridge University Press.
Stroebe, Margaret, and Henk Schut. 1999. "The Dual Process Model of Coping with Bereavement: Rationale and Description." *Death Studies* 23: 197–224.
_____. 2001. "Meaning Making in the Dual Process Model of Coping with Bereavement." In *Meaning Reconstruction and the Experience of Loss*, ed. Robert Neimeyer, 55–73. Washington, DC: American Psychological Association Press.
_____. 2010. "The Dual Process Model of Coping with Bereavement: A Decade on." *Omega* 61: 273–89.
Thiessen, Malte. 2007. *Eingebrannt ins Gedächtnis. Hamburgs Gedenken an Luftkrieg und Kriegsende, 1943 bis 2005.* Hamburg: Dölling und Gaitz Verlag.
Van Gennep, Arnold. (1909) 1960. *The Rites of Passage.* Chicago: University of Chicago Press.
Walter, Tony. 1996. "A New Model of Grief: Bereavement and Biography." *Mortality* 1(1): 7–25.

_____. 1999. *On Bereavement: The Culture of Grief.* Buckingham: Open University Press.
Weiner, Annette B. 1983. *Women of Value, Men of Renown: New Perspectives in Trobriand Exchange.* Austin: University of Texas Press.
Worden, J. William. 2009. *Grief Counseling and Grief Therapy: A Handbook for the Mental Health Practitioner,* 4th ed. New York: Springer.

Chapter 3

Biographies and Necrographies in Exchange

From the Self to the Other

Anastasios Panagiotopoulos

The present chapter is somewhat idiosyncratic, in the sense that it does not deal extensively with the broad ethnographic literature produced over the years concerning death-related phenomena. This is partly because a number of good reviews on the subject have already appeared (see Kan 1992; Kaufman and Morgan 2005; Palgi and Abramovich 1984; Straight 2006; for similar reviews in the field of sociology, see Riley 1983; Walter 2008). More importantly though, in an effort to trace a larger tradition of thought, as well as proposing critical insights which may help take discussion beyond some of that tradition's important limitations, broad outlines of understanding from a variety of fields are more pertinent. Although, from an anthropological perspective, the ethnographic focus on the production of theory is granted a broader comparative perspective is also vital; not just spatial or temporal, but also among various disciplines.

The first section, "Denial and Acceptance: From the Death of the Self to the Death of the Other," examines the long-term philosophical and psychoanalytical framework of "denial and acceptance" (which can retrospectively be called "tradition"), which is perhaps the most dominant within the scholarly study of death, although it acquires more "individualist" or more "collectivist" undertones depending on context and scholar; it is argued here, however, that the denial/acceptance paradigm is geared more towards the individualistic death of the Self (loosely following the terminology of Ariès 1991). The second part of the section presents broad efforts to go beyond the denial/acceptance model, towards what is referred to as the "transition" framework, acknowledging Hertz as its most illustrious and influential representative. Transition, apart from being an analytical viewpoint from which death can be seen productively, also has methodological implications, pointing towards the more anthropological and sociological dimensions of death, as well as the death of the Other. Instead of seeing this effort as a completely distinct tradition, however, I claim that its venture to go beyond denial/acceptance is *partial* and, although very welcome, limitations stemming from the earlier paradigm remain. It should be noted here that it is not so much a matter of chronological sequence that divides these two facets of a single tradition, but rather a matter of where significance is placed.

In the second section, "Beyond Denial and Acceptance: Exchange Versus Representation," a perspective is explored that seems to offer a fruitful avenue which goes beyond both denial/acceptance and transition, one inspired by Jean Baudrillard's understanding of death as "exchange." The dynamic qualities of such a framework offer us an *original* paradigm which can function as a completely alternative model to denial/acceptance or, at least, in a complementary role.

Denial and Acceptance: From the Death of the Self to the Death of the Other

Being-Unto-Death or the Death of the Self: Philosophical and Psychoanalytic Explorations

The title of this sub-section acknowledges a direct intellectual link to a tradition of thought that finds a moment of illuminating condensation in Martin Heidegger. In order to summarize Heidegger's approach to death and life (or "being" as he would have preferred), this account will be based on an extremely useful shortcut provided by James M. Demske in his book *Being, Man, and Death: A Key to Heidegger* (1970).

For brevity's sake, this rich trajectory of the concept of death in Heidegger's thought will be summarized into broad propositions with some significant yet deliberate omissions. Demske's analysis (commencing with Heidegger's seminal work *Being and Time*) intimately links the theme of death with Heidegger's main philosophical preoccupations, namely, the concepts of "being" and "man," and probably the largest part of Demske's analysis is dedicated to these two concepts, precisely because Heidegger did so, too. The most significant omission in the present exposition is that these fundamental concepts are simplified considerably, a choice justified by the wish to do justice to the theme and interests (and thus limitations of space) of this present volume.

The basic understanding of death as an event, according to Heidegger, is that it is the exact opposite, the ontological negation, of "being," i.e., non-being and non-existence. This insight can hardly be said to be Heidegger's intellectual property; on the contrary, one could argue that it is a basic, though not the only (more on that later), human "intuition" concerning death. But death as a phenomenon is much broader than this, precisely because in relation to humanity it is not just an event that occurs but also an event that is the object of human awareness. In other words, it is an anticipated event. Just as humans are conscious of their "being-in-the-world" and creatively reflect upon it, they are equally conscious that this "being" is finite; that in fact at any potential point, from the individual's perspective, this being will cease to be and dissolve into nothingness. This existential and ontological awareness is not merely a brute fact or piece of futuristic knowledge, however, nor is it just a negative event; its reflexive quality shapes the way humans live their lives, because they live them in light of it, in the light of ultimate darkness, one might say. This particularly human "mode of being" (Demske 1970: 25) is what the Heideggerian concept of "being-unto-death" (ibid.: 2) signifies. Thus, "the not-yet of death is not something outstanding, but something 'before-standing'" (ibid.: 24); it is here with us in the present in the form of potentiality and anticipation. Demske reminds us of the folk wisdom that expresses this in its own graphic way: "As soon as a man is born, he is old enough to die" (ibid.: 25).

Death as the end of being, as "finitude" (ibid.: 76) and "shattering" (ibid.: 112), is the object of human awareness and, thus, it gives life a "horizon" (ibid.: 86), and makes of it a "journeying" or "pilgrimage" (ibid.: 141) towards that horizon: an "advancing towards death" (ibid.: 65). This is precisely what confers man with "temporality" (ibid.: 76), in fact, with history: "No history would be possible if men were eternal, immutable, and timeless, for they could not *become* anything; they would simply *be* what they are. Thus history, becoming, transitoriness, and temporality are all interconnected" (ibid.: 111; emphasis in the original). For the moment, the analysis sounds all-encompassing and inevitable, just as death itself appears to be. In other words, death as awareness of finitude appears inscribed in humanity's DNA, in its very nature. Heidegger's answer to this is that we are not dealing with plain certainties but potentials, confronting them with an opposite tendency which he calls "inauthentic being-unto-death" (ibid.: 30).

The inauthenticity of such a tendency lies in the effort of this same humanity to "misunderstand" or "forget" (ibid.: 138) the finitude of death. This means that humans, just as they are capable of being aware of death-as-finitude, are equally capable of denying to themselves such awareness. This (in-)capacity, according to Heidegger, is particularly characteristic of our "modern" age: "Our age is destitute not only because God is dead, but because the mortals can scarcely recognize and cope with their own mortality. The mortals are not yet in possession of their essence. Death withdraws and becomes an enigma. The mystery of pain remains veiled" (Heidegger, cited in Demske 1970: 138). Here, the awareness of death-as-finitude, from a seemingly primordial and eternal truth, becomes an achievement in potential or a "breakthrough" (ibid.: 140). Man, in order to be authentic, needs to "accept" (ibid.: 157) death as such; it is an "act which he actively performs" (ibid.: 159). This involves accepting the ontologically structural (and structuring) premise that we are finite, and that we "go along with" it (ibid.: 157):

> Death is unique and distinctive precisely because it is a border-line phenomenon, which can be only partially incorporated into the analysis ... It remains finally "un-ontological" or "un-intelligible" ... man's self-understanding [is] the realization that he understands himself most fully when he sees that he does *not* understand himself fully. (ibid.: 191; emphasis in the original)

This is a very brief outline of Demske's sophisticated summary of Heidegger.

Another extremely useful and critical shortcut is that of Ernest Becker and his book *The Denial of Death* (2011), which presents an immensely clear systematization of ideas, mainly from the field of psychoanalysis but also philosophy, with respect to the theme of death. The point of critical departure is Freud (see also Bataille 2011; Willerslev 2013), and the two thinkers most prominently showcased are Otto Rank, for his critical post-Freudianism, and Søren Kierkegaard, for his anticipation of such a stance (for original references, see Kierkegaard 2013; Rank 1978; see also Brown 1970). As was the case with Demske's exposition of Heidegger, only broad propositions will be offered here, this time in light of what has been already said. The understanding is that Becker's (Rank's, Kierkegaard's, and others') points are definitely part of the tradition of which Heidegger is an illuminating instance (it must be noted that Kierkegaard's work precedes that of Heidegger). Becker's points organically complement such a tradition by adding depth and critical sophistication to it. What will be sought is what is missing from Becker's book, namely, a positive synthesis with Heidegger (the philosopher and not the citizen), beginning where Becker begins in his preface:

> The main thesis of this book is that ... the idea of death, the fear of it, haunts the human animal like nothing else; it is a mainspring of human activity — activity designed largely to avoid the fatality of death, to overcome it by denying in some way that it is the final destiny for man ... death is indeed a universal in the human condition. (Becker 2011: xvii)

The great affinity these propositions show with the Heideggerian view is evident: the "fear of death" springs from the particularly human awareness that death is the end of existence and it is precisely this awareness that "haunts" man. But, again in accordance with Heidegger, this is not seen in necessarily negative terms because the anticipation of death-as-finitude pushes humans to take advantage of their living conditions and actively participate in them: "it is the mainspring of human activity" (see also Becker 2011: 21). Furthermore, both Heidegger and all the psychoanalytic and philosophical tradition condensed in Becker's approach suggest that all such propositions are "universal." It is at this point that Heidegger's and Becker's approaches appear to diverge but, as will be argued, not to such an extent that two diametrically opposed views on death can be claimed to emerge clearly. On the contrary, their differences are such that they are better seen in a broader framework of synthesis.

Heidegger seems to be opting for a tendency to view the acceptance of death-as-finitude as the positive choice of humanity, which he calls the "authentic being-unto-death." On the other hand, the equally possible choice of humanity to deny death-as-finitude tends to be seen in negative terms, as the source of "inauthentic" living. Initially, Becker's approach seems to be opting for a contrary evaluation of the two opposite tendencies of denial and acceptance. He seems to be viewing denial as a positive tendency. It is more productive, however, to understand the dialectical quality that emerges, more consciously through Becker than with Heidegger, in the relationship between the two tendencies.

In the very beginning of *The Denial of Death* Becker explains that humanity throws itself into the activity of creating symbols, roles, rules, traditions, and so forth, in a "heroic" effort aimed towards "obliviousness" (ibid.: 17) of the otherwise fearful fact of death (ibid.: 1–24); in more psychoanalytic terms, this heroic denial is termed "repression" (ibid.: 20). As mentioned before, however, this repression is used "creatively" (ibid.: 21). Therefore, the consciousness of death-as-finitude undergoes a creative concealment, hiding a "mass of internal scar tissue" (ibid.: 29) which is placed as backdrop to a stage that is built in such a way that its actors will move about on it without ever facing this background directly. Life, accompanied by the prospect of the finality of death, if taken too wholeheartedly, is problematic: "[W]hat bothers people is incongruity, life as it *is*" (ibid.: 34; emphasis in the original). Therefore, the healthy reaction is a *"necessary* and basic dishonesty about oneself and one's whole situation" (ibid.: 55; emphasis in the original), a "confident denial" (ibid.: 63), a "creative illusion" (ibid.: 258). In other words, the "problem" is reality itself, taken literally and in its fullest dimension, as the road to extinction. If for Heidegger the acceptance of such a reality is the "authentic" way, through Becker it seems that denial is the "healthy" stance.

At this point Becker introduces Kierkegaard more systematically, as the predecessor of the post-Freudian psychoanalytic turn with which he is concerned (ibid.: 67–92). It is here that traces of a more dialectical approach than the seemingly definitive favoring of *denial* appear, even if elusively. What Becker terms "denial" Kierkegaard calls "shut-upness" (ibid.: 70), but such negation is a positive one which helps man bypass the anxiety of death. Here we are being offered a more complex image as an alternative to plain and absolute denial. The term that perhaps illustrates this better is that of "half-obscurity" (ibid.: 70), a quality that opens up a more complex avenue wherein *denial* and *acceptance* are not by definition two diametrically opposed stances but can also coexist in, and exactly because of, this "halfness." "Half-obscurity" suggests that there is room for "half-enlightenment," if we could call it that. The "authentic," "healthy" stance is neither absolute denial nor absolute acceptance, but a dialectical and balanced relation between the two, so as to retain an understanding of our finality without its paralyzing us into failing to fully live our lives. This more balanced and, arguably, more dynamic view is further hinted at in certain passages in Becker's text.

For instance, at some point he exclaims: "[M]an wants the impossible: He wants to lose his isolation and keep it at the same time" (ibid.: 155); and shortly after: "[M]an cannot live closed upon himself for himself. He must project the meaning of life outward, the reason for it, even the blame for it" (ibid.: 158). When analyzing Rank's ideas more deeply, Becker mentions an illuminating psychoanalytical term, "partialization" (ibid.: 178), which essentially involves the *partial* "refusal of reality" (ibid.:178), thus implying that it is not *total*. A vital part of such reality is the very fact of realization of death-as-finitude, apart from other aspects which are equally important and ultimately interconnected, such as the partial realization that we are not all-powerful, that we need others just as much as we need to be ourselves (points also raised by Heidegger). The rest of the book becomes much more psychoanalytic in content and terminology.

To recapitulate the most salient features of this stream of scholastic tradition: death as an event is axiomatically taken as finitude, as the absolute cessation of the existence of being, and humanity is in the distinctive position of being aware of such an event and able to shape its being in light of it, a being-unto-death. Because this awareness, which is also understood to be "naturally" daunting, is bound to provoke, if not despair and anxiety, at least mystery and puzzlement, humans have three broad paths to choose from: one is to deny completely such an awareness; the second to accept it completely; and the third is to do both at the same time, but only partially. Even though within this rich tradition there might be some slight tendencies favoring either denial or acceptance as the most "authentic" and "healthy" choice, thus pathologizing the alternative, the overall conclusion to be drawn seems to be that sanity lies in a balanced and partial embracing of both denial and acceptance. However, this conclusion is merely implied and never unequivocally stated; therefore, by highlighting it here, it is hoped that it may be more fully embraced. Meanwhile, discussions relevant to the proposition have been initiated in the studies of grief and mourning since the 1980s and particularly the 1990s (see Klass 2006; Klass, Silverman, and Nickman 1996; Robben 2014; Stroebe and Schut 1999; for similar insights drawn from the anthropological perspective on the ritualization of lament, see De Martino [1958] 2014; Seremetakis 1991). Unarguably, the axiomatic position that death is the end of life, the complete and absolute annihilation of being, leads almost by definition to the premise that, however dialectically related in empirical terms, denial and acceptance are derivative of each other: from the point of view of the person who takes the death-as-finitude stance, acceptance is the primordial element, existentially or ontologically speaking, while denial is a derivative product, a *re-action* to the former.

Ultimately, the axiom of death-as-finitude and as the absolute negation of life builds an insurmountable wall between life and death, obstructing a more dynamic dialogue between them. Certainly, while reflections on the meaning of life in general and the various paths it takes are impossible to condense in any single tradition, let alone by one thinker or book, the weaknesses discussed here also relate to that aspect of life that is explicitly concerned with death. Ultimately, therefore, attitudes, thoughts, emotions, and behaviors concerned with death cannot be fully accounted for within the denial/acceptance frame.

Yet, other interconnected elements may be added to this particular perspective, some of which stem from the essential and utter fear that the first axiom (death-as-finitude) arouses, which has as its perspectival center the Self, the individual. It is the Self that fears death-as-finitude, stemming from the Self projecting its own complete annihilation. Meanwhile, the death of the Other and all the fear, anxiety, or grief that it may provoke, is secondary and ultimately encompassed by the centrality of the fear of the death of the Self. This might explain the predominance of philosophy and psychology in the tradition sketched so far. Both fields share the centrality and universality of the Self, of the self-reflexively thinking and acting subject. In relation to death, the Self universally knows or intuits that death is the end (of itself) and is equally and universally flooded with the fear of this. What individuates the Self is that the *re-actions* towards such universals may differ, leading towards more or less "authentic" and "healthy" behaviors. Complementary to this is that the death of the Self is essentially a matter of anticipation, of projection into the future (no matter how this may affect the present or how close or far this future is). It is not so much an event of the past or the present.

Thus, it is apparent that other interconnected elements may be added to the tradition sketched so far to make it more complete, including the understanding that the death of the Self is complemented by the death of the Other, as well as views of death as actuality and as possessing history. These themes find illustrative examples predominantly in the field of anthropology, but also in sociology (see Bauman 1992; Glaser and Strauss 1965, 1968; Gorer 1965; Seale 1998; Walter 1994, 1999); social history (see Ariès 1991; Kellehear 2007); modern philosophy (see Choron 1963; Derrida 2008; Levinas 2000); and more interdisciplinary approaches (see Van Brussel and Carpentier 2014). The following section explores important differences but also similarities between these lines of understanding, thereby casting light on why we should consider them as part of one larger tradition.

Death as Transition or the Death of the Other: Anthropological Explorations

Robert Hertz's essay "A Contribution to the Study of the Collective Representation of Death" (2009), originally published in French in 1907, commences with the claim that death is not a mere physical fact: "To the organic event is added a complex mass of beliefs, emotions and activities which give it its distinctive character" (Hertz 2004: 27). True to his Durkheimian foundations, Hertz claims that death is the "object of a collective representation" (ibid.: 28). Nowadays this is hardly a revelation, especially within the humanities and social sciences, disciplines which are now well established in the scholarly world. The reason it is mentioned is to point to the fact that the insight both belongs to the intellectual current described above while diverging from it in innovative ways. Although "emotions" are mentioned, the emphasis is now placed not on the individual but on the "collective," and this brings into the frame a host of other dimensions.

Although Hertz's theorization relies heavily on secondary ethnographic data gathered on the Dayak of Borneo, the focus here lies on the more generalizable points he produces as a result. Just after the universalist claim that death is not a merely physical phenomenon, Hertz makes his first cross-cultural comment. Because it is a social phenomenon, accompanied by "a complex mass of beliefs, emotions and activities," he suggests that death may vary depending on the form this "complex mass" acquires: depending, in other words, on the particular social group with which we are confronted. Hertz claims that "we" (let us heuristically not question who this "we" is supposed to include) generally accept "that death occurs in one instant" (ibid.: 28), while societies such as the Dayak approach death as a *transition*—what in a nutshell could be contrasted as death-as-an-instant and death-as-transition. It is interesting that death-as-an-instant implicitly parallels the view of death-as-finitude presented earlier, and clearly differs from the understanding that "death is not a mere destruction but a transition" (ibid.: 48).

Herein lies a typically anthropological perspective that potentially offers a slightly different direction to that provided by philosophy and psychology, without completely estranging itself from them. Hertz, after these short preliminary remarks, goes on to present the ethnographic data which best exemplify this transitional character. The Dayak, when faced with the death of an individual, perform a "double burial" (ibid.: 28). Briefly, the overall process involves a slow and progressive handling of the body of the deceased so as to effect a proper (expected) transition—from living to dead—directly linked to the fate of its soul or spirit, which ideally then enters the land of the ancestors. The first phase of this "double burial," is the "intermediary period" (ibid.: 29–53) wherein, running parallel to the process of the decomposition of the body, lie a host of activities meant to prepare the soul for its ultimate journey. This period is quite unstable because the fate of the deceased has not yet been secured and, indeed, is in its most liminal of situations.

This extremely liminal period is potentially dangerous for the living, especially the relatives, and it is thus characterized by cautious behavior, taboos, propitiatory rituals, offerings, and a large degree of isolation, both of the corpse and the close kin, from the rest of the community. In contrast, the second phase, the "final ceremony" (ibid.: 53–76), normally acquires a more decisively transitional and collective, rather than liminal, character. There are three main objectives of this second and final phase: first, to bury in their final place the physical remains of the person; second, to secure an unproblematic entry of the soul to the world of the dead; and third, to free the living from all the previous obligations of mourning, which were fraught by ambiguity and vulnerability. The end of this "final ceremony" essentially effects an end to the transition; it delivers closure.

To summarize, the first phase is characterized by liminality and the second by the resolution of the previously precarious transition period. In both phases, there is a parallel process occurring on two levels. As far as the deceased is concerned, the state (liminal and then transitional) of the body is parallel with the fate of the soul; however, both the living and the dead undergo a process in which (liminal) uncertainty is succeeded (after transition) by resolution and relief.

Hertz seems to be ascribing wholeheartedly to the "fear of death" tradition when he speaks of a state of confusion and anxiety that permeates both the deceased and the living, especially in the intermediary, liminal period. In fact, what is implied, although not extensively analyzed, is that the purported fear, anxiety, and confusion of the soul of the deceased are essentially reflections of the actual fear, anxiety, and confusion felt by the living in response to the very event of death. Should, for instance, Heidegger have read Hertz (they were contemporaries after all), it is very likely that he would have interpreted the Dayak as an example of humanity's "being-unto-death." Nevertheless, the Hertzian fear is not the fear of the self-reflexive individual that ponders its own death-as-finitude; it is not the death of the Self that acquires a protagonistic role. The Hertzian anxiety rests much more on the death of the Other. This is why he turns his gaze more closely to the actual event of death, rather than the existential and anticipatory reflection of it; his gaze is on the funeral activities, the processes of mourning and the "collective representations" that take place, such as the indigenous views of the body and the soul and the person that accompany such activities.

This change of focus has some important effects. To begin with, fear loses its monopoly as an individual emotion and becomes a collective one. It is not only fear of impending existential destruction but of something that has already occurred: the destruction of the social ties that attached the deceased to the living, and thus it is not fear, but grief. This approach is a considerable enrichment of the existential-ontological tradition, as it throws the denial/acceptance pair into the realm of the collective in a more creative manner: social ties are also severed by death, therefore denial/acceptance may also come into play in terms of this kind of collective destruction. As mentioned earlier, the universalist reach of the pair in existential-ontological terms offers a powerful claim of great transcendence, especially to those who share the implicit understandings of the Self that accompany it. But, at the same time, it tends to leave us without a clear indication of what to do with it apart from repeating it in an almost mechanical way. If all of life's achievements and failures are essentially a manifestation of the tension, no matter how dialectical, between the denial and acceptance of death, then specific achievements and failures—that is, the basis of choice of specific paths adopted in life—are left untheorized. So, however useful the pair may prove, there is definitely more to the phenomenon of death. The Hertzian, anthropological, and sociological view is a productive avenue, although it ultimately also appears to succumb to the pressure of the denial/acceptance model.

It can be claimed that Hertz's formulations are ambiguous, even slightly paradoxical, something which reflects an inherent, equally frustrating but productive anthropological quality more generally. Arguably, this unresolved and thus constantly regenerative paradoxical quality *partially accepts* the denial/acceptance pair and *partially denies* it. It accepts it insofar as it is implied in the form of a transition from temporary denial (exemplified in the "intermediary period") towards acceptance (manifest in the "final ceremony"). Yet, it denies it insofar as it turns its gaze towards the Other: in Hertz's case, the Other being the Dayak, but also death as an event occurring to others (within the Dayak society) and not as something impending for the Self. Therefore, death appears as a relational phenomenon, as something which affects certain ties. The gaze is, therefore, turned towards such ties (for other classical examples, see Battaglia 1990; Baurraud et al. 1994; Bloch and Parry 1996; Damon and Wagner 1989; Goody 1962; Humphreys and King 1981; Metcalf and Huntington 1991; Parry 1994; Robben 2004; Rosenblatt, Walsh, and Jackson 1976).

Hertz's analysis often refers to the state of the deceased in the form of spirit or soul. Despite the underlying message that this is a reflection of the state of the living, Hertz does not dedicate all his discussion to such a reflection, something that the denial/acceptance frame would tend to do. As his framework *denies* to exhaust all discussion to the strict causality of the denial/acceptance pair, this enables him to give detailed ethnographic depth to the state of the deceased, inscribing the state in the very process of transition and in light of the relational approach implied by the severance of social ties involved. On the other hand, if one were to directly argue that death-as-transition presents the "denial" of death in the indigenous idiom (something like an indigenous unconscious), then the discussion would be more likely to fall short of an otherwise rich description of death, social ties, the body, the spirit or soul and personhood, as well as the possible transitions all these may undergo through and because of death. Therefore, without having to wholeheartedly accept, as the Dayak appear to do, that deceased people may continue their journey after death and that the living play their own role in it, *partially accepting* it may lead to the quintessentially anthropological approach of *engaging* with it, rather than hastily explaining it away by subsuming it under the "universal" axiom of death-as-finitude.

The creatively paradoxical stance of anthropology may thus be condensed into a self-perpetuating effort to forge a third kind of perspective which does not fall safely into the categories of either denial or acceptance (of other peoples' views of death): a framework that reflects the emic perspective anthropology has of itself. Such an effort has important outcomes, whether one acknowledges its productive character or argues for its frustrating futility. Death is viewed more comprehensively in its relational dimension (in light of the social ties of which it is a part and which it may originally create or destructively sever) than as an existential-ontological reflection. Therefore, death-as-finitude is much less axiomatically embraced by the analyst, because its creativity and destructiveness provide the greater focus of attention. Death-as-finitude therefore becomes one possible explanatory path among others, taking up a position in a more egalitarian and comparative perspective. These other paths, constantly appearing in anthropological approaches and in comparison with the former (as in Hertz's work), lead to a tendency to ponder death in particular rather than death in general, and deaths in the plural and the deaths of the Others more specifically. Equally, death itself gets personalized and localized to the dead themselves, "biographized" one might say, by being incorporated into their bodies and the objects that relate to them (see, for instance, Hallam and Hockey 2001). The discussion, the gaze of the researcher, is directed towards the dead or the dying (see Earle, Komaromy, and Bartholomew 2009; Richards and Rotter 2013) and their relations with the living, rather than towards the more abstract themes of death and life. As Harrison proposes, from the Heideggerian "being-toward-death" we turn our gaze to "being-toward-the-dead" (2003: 97), even if the contexts are those of professionalization (see Suzuki 2000) or violence and its socio-political ramifications (see De Boeck 2005; Klima 2002; Mbembe 2003; Scheper-Hughes 1992; Whitehead 2002). However, this does not mean that the dead are always highly individuated. Processes of collectivization, commemoration, ancestralization or anonymity, oblivion, silence and undifferentiation may equally be present (see McLean 2013).

Does this all mean that we are left with an extremely local view of death that, due to its multiplicity and fluidity, is unable to lead to broader theoretical claims, doomed to perpetual circularity and relativism or, as Fabian (1973) would have it, "parochialization" and "folklorization?" Not necessarily, although it is *partly necessary* to assume this: even if one is arguing for death's essentially manifold character, then one is, by definition, making a universalist claim. While partial universalism and partial relativism help to check each other's excesses, here a purely universalist claim is being made that is more fully explained in the next section. If a universal claim can be made about Death, keeping the comparative tool wielded by anthropology in mind, it is that it always appears as a definitive change in the course of life. Thus death-as-finitude may be encompassed by something broader which can be termed death-as-change. Change might refer to finality, to complete annihilation, but it may equally signify other kinds of changes, either equally total (death effects a radical change other than finality) or more partial (death effects changes, while preserving certain continuities). The Hertzian transition frame definitely inspires a broader notion of change, although, as argued below, it still suffers from a rigid linearity that could be overcome. Whatever the specific (ethnographic) case, the level of change effected by death is *universally* a significant one, which always involves relational, ontological, emotional, and existential reflections and reactions. Exactly because death effects important transformations on these various levels, it is, collectively, always a significant event. The following section aims to give more substance to such a proposition, while exploring the idea of death not only as change but also as *exchange*.

Beyond Denial and Acceptance: Biographies and Necrographies in Exchange

This section examines ways of going beyond the denial/acceptance perspective by drawing inspiration from Baudrillard's *Symbolic Exchange and Death* (1993), suggesting that perhaps a more useful distinction lies between exchange and representation: first, because it points to the interactions between the dead and the living (rather than the much more abstract and elusive issue of death); and second, because it encompasses the denial/acceptance theme itself. In that respect it proves a more useful analytical and comparative angle from which to view death.

Baudrillard makes the distinction between the view of death as "exchange" (see especially Baudrillard 1993: 131–44), and that which is forged through what he calls "political economy" (ibid.: 144–48). The latter is a negative relation to death, characterized by "exclusion" (ibid.: 126), instituted "prohibition" (ibid.: 130), "melancholy" (ibid.: 135), "discrimination" (ibid.: 144), "irreversibility" (ibid.: 158), "dereliction" (ibid.: 182). Death is an "unthinkable anomaly . . . thrown into a radical utopia" (ibid.: 126), a "social exile" (ibid.: 128), a "hostage" (ibid.: 130), "a disjunctive code," and a "phantasm" (ibid.: 133); it is "extraterritorial" (ibid.: 182) and "pornographic" (echoing Gorer 1955; ibid.: 184). In a similar vein to Hertz, Baudrillard places "our" political economic view of death as one among others, the latter schematically classified under the umbrella category of exchange. With no implied derogatory connotations (on the contrary) and, therefore, no sense of modern anthropological guilt, the "exchange" model clearly belongs to the "savages" or "primitives" (ibid.: 131), just as "our" politically economized death is displaced from its universalist imperialism. This means that death-as-finitude dissolves as an axiom and becomes a specific socio-historical formation.

This approach offers Baudrillard an analytical angle from which the exchange model is independent from, rather than a derivation of "our" axioms. An orthodox adherence to the denial/acceptance framework would tend to interpret different views on death, such as the exchange model, as culturally-specific versions of the universal instinct (or drive, in more psychoanalytic terms) of denial. As argued previously, if denial is ultimately a derivation of the acceptance stance, then in the case of exchange we would have a double derivation, the derivation of a derivation: exchange derives from denial which, in its turn, derives from acceptance. Meanwhile, the more we distance ourselves from the "original" source towards further derivatives, the less *original* descriptive and analytical attention we pay to the latter, precisely because the "original" lies somewhere else and beyond. In contrast, if we break the hierarchical chain of derivations, then each term is seen in its (relative) independence and we are more likely to engage with it fully. As noted earlier, the exchange model distances itself from existential-ontological pondering on death (essentially of the Self) and enters, in a more visceral way, into a reciprocal relation with *the deaths of the Others* and with *the dead*. This kind of distance is not reactive behavior to a universal axiom but, on the contrary, it is an "original" and independent stance. It can stand on its own without having to respond (existential-ontologically) and apologize to the denial/acceptance model.

In Baudrillard's line of thinking exchange is a quintessentially human and social activity; what he calls "symbolic," something that in the present analysis is put aside due its complex and not always unambiguous or unproblematic significations. Reciprocal exchange acknowledges, if not an equal agency, at least a certain amount of subjectivity between the exchanging parties. In those "primitive" and "savage" societies where death is not the complete opposite of life, the dead enter into reciprocal relations with the living similar to those which the living develop among themselves. Therefore, exchange continues after death. This means that the dead have agency and subjectivity while not being identical to the living. Here is where Baudrillard's line of argument acquires considerable sophistication. He adopts as a point of departure the (Hertzian) notion of transition but goes well beyond it by virtue of the concept of exchange. Without dogmatically abandoning transition, he manages to radicalize it:

> When the primitive showers the dead with signs, it is in order to make the transition towards the state of death as quick as possible, beyond the ambiguity between the living and the dead which is precisely what the disintegrating flesh testifies to. It is not a question of making the dead play the role of the living: the primitive concedes the dead their difference, for it is at this cost that they will be able to become partners and exchange their signs . . . [They refuse] to let death signify, take on the force of a sign. (Baudrillard 1993: 181)

Arguably, Baudrillard commences precisely where Hertz leaves off and thus performs a bolder escape act from the ultimate over-determination of the denial/acceptance framework. The way transition is employed by Hertz tends to lay a path, however dynamic and uncertain, which finally leads to a single destination, at least ideally. This is that the dead decisively "leave" this world, physical decomposition followed by the social, finally residing in the land of the ancestors, from which little, if any, interaction occurs between them and the living. In terms of the denial/acceptance model, it seems that the Hertzian transition is just a more prolonged (hence the term *longue durée*) version of our more "instantaneous" behavior, passing from an initial denial of the bodily tissues and social ties that death severs into a progressive acceptance of this *very fact*. Thus Hertz's transition tends to end, if only belatedly, in the "universal" axiom of finitude, shattering, and annihilation (for similar critiques, see Course 2007; Tsintjilonis 2007). It thus appears as ultimately *teleo-logical*, that is, *telos* (end, and more precisely death as end) is its final *logic*.

Exchange continued after death does not abandon the idea of transition, not even as a kind of end, but makes it an end of something and the beginning of something else; rather than just closure we are also offered a novel starting point. As the previous quote suggests, the "primitives" acknowledge that death is a distinct condition, and they actively participate in facilitating such transitions. It is precisely this transitional process of differentiating the once-living from the now-dead that becomes the prerequisite for developing reciprocity between dead and living. Thus, the "savages" do not confuse the dead with the living, and they do not deny in any way the *fact* of death. But this very fact is not an end (in and of itself) but a transformation, a change, on which the continuation of exchange relies. On the other hand, it is "our" radically oppositional understanding of death that creates the notion of "immortality" as the imaginary opposite of our factual axioms, namely, death-as-finitude:

> When the dead are there, lifelike [*vivants*; sic] but different from the living [vivants; sic] whom they partner in multiple exchanges, they have no need to, and neither is it necessary that they should, be immortal, since this fantastic quality shatters all reciprocity. It is only to the extent that they are excluded by the living that they quietly become immortal, and this idealized survival is only the mark of their social exile. (Baudrillard 1993: 127–28)

It is the extreme acceptance of death-as-finitude that leads to its extreme denial. Intentionally paraphrasing Victor Hugo, who pointed to the irony of the transference of dirt to the very hands of the obsessive cleaner, Baudrillard exclaims: "[B]y dint of being washed and sponged, cleaned and scoured, denied and warded off, death rubs off onto every aspect of life" (ibid.: 180). Extreme and oppositional differentiation (read "acceptance") of life and death is part of a "cultural" system that has as its complementary end extreme identification of the two (read "denial"). It is here that Baudrillard becomes highly critical of the imperialist universalism that permeates the denial/acceptance model, which invents the "death drive" so as to encompass the whole of humanity in its fatalistic perspective:

> Political economy is an economy of death, because it economises on death and buries it under its discourse. The death drive falls into the opposite category: it is the discourse of death as *the* insurmountable finality. This discourse is oppositional but complementary, for if political economy is indeed Nirvana (the infinite accumulation and reproduction of dead value), then the death drive denounces its truth, at the same time as subjecting it to absolute derision. It does this, however, in the terms of the system itself, by idealising death as a drive (as an objective finality). As such, the death drive is the current system's most radical negative, but even it simply holds up a mirror to the funeral imaginary of political economy. (Baudrillard 1993:154; emphasis in the original)

To conclude, denial/acceptance, from an all-embracing archetype, becomes a relatively closed and independent system, just as much as exchange becomes another one. This stance strongly implies that the exchanges occurring between the living and the dead are not to be seen as (unconscious) idioms of denial but in their own originality. In other words, such exchanges may not hide anything unconscious (or at least not the kind of unconscious we ascribe to them) but simply be originally and actively, if the apparent paradox may be permitted, *indifferent* to our denials and acceptances. From the particularity of exchange as a specific, "ethnographic," "local," "cultural," "cosmological," "traditional," "non-Western," "enchanting," or what have you, phenomenon, we might gain broader analytical perspectives and insights that may go beyond the "parochial," to use Fabian's terminology once more. This is hardly exhausted in the fact that a cross-cultural or a cross-temporal dimension may be offered. Exchange can also be a broad but dynamic framework in which, the living and the dead, their biographies and necrographies, their voices and their silence, their identity and their alterity, their past, present, and future are put into dialogue and are a relation of reciprocity. Without losing their relative autonomy, they remain unaffected by the other side.

Anastasios Panagiotopoulos is a senior postdoctoral researcher at Centro em Rede de Investigação em Antropologia, Universidade Nova de Lisboa, Portugal. His research includes the role of divination in Afro-Cuban religiosity as it relates to issues of personhood, historical imagination, race, and secularism, among others. He has published book chapters, peer-reviewed articles, such as "When Biographies Cross Necrographies: The Exchange of Affinity in Cuba" (*Ethnos* 2017), and co-edited *Beyond Tradition, Beyond Invention* (Sean Kingston Publishing, 2015).

References

Ariès, Philippe. 1991. *The Hour of Our Death*. Oxford and New York: Oxford University Press.
Bataille, Georges. (1957) 2011. *Death and Sensuality: A Study of Eroticism and the Taboo*. Whitefish, MT: Literary Licensing, LLC.
Battaglia, Debbora. 1990. *On the Bones of the Serpent: Person, Memory, and Mortality in Sabarl Island Society*. Chicago and London: Chicago University Press.
Baudrillard, Jean. (1976) 1993. *Symbolic Exchange and Death*. London: Sage Publications.
Bauman, Zygmunt. 1992. *Mortality, Immortality and Other Life Strategies*. Cambridge: Polity Press.
Baurraud, Cécile, Daniel de Coppet, André Iteanu, and Raymond Jamous. 1994. *Of Relations and the Dead: Four Societies Viewed from the Angle of their Exchanges*. Oxford and Providence, RI: Berg.
Becker, Ernest. (1973) 2011. *The Denial of Death*. New York: The Free Press.
Bloch, Maurice, and Jonathan Parry, eds. (1982) 1996. *Death & the Regeneration of Life*. Cambridge: Cambridge University Press.
Brown, Norman O. (1959) 1970. *Life against Death: The Psychoanalytical Meaning of History*. London: Sphere Books LTD.
Choron, Jacques. 1963. *Death and Western Thought*. New York: Collier Books.
Course, Magnus. 2007. "Death, Biography, and the Mapuche Person." *Ethnos* 72: 77–101.
Damon, Frederick H., and Roy Wagner, eds. 1989. *Death Rituals and Life in the Societies of the Kula Ring*. DeKalb: Northern Illinois University Press.
De Boeck, Filip. 2005. "The Apocalyptic Interlude: Revealing Death in Kinshasa." *African Studies Review* 48(2): 11–32.

De Martino, Ernesto. (1958) 2014. *Morte e Pianto Rituale nel Mondo Antico*. Torino, Italy: Universale Bollati Boringhieri.
Demske, James M. 1970. *Being, Man, and Death: A Key to Heidegger*. Lexington: The University Press of Kentucky.
Derrida, Jaques. (1995) 2008. *The Gift of Death and Literature in Secret*. Chicago and London: The University of Chicago Press.
Earle, Sarah, Carol Komaromy, and Caroline Bartholomew, eds. 2009. *Death and Dying: A Reader*. Milton Keynes: The Open University.
Fabian, Johannes. 1973. "How Others Die: Reflections on the Anthropology of Death." In *Death in American Experience*, ed. Arien Mack, 177–201. New York: Schocken Books.
Glaser, Barney, and Anselm Strauss. 1965. *Awareness of Dying*. Chicago: Aldine.
———. 1968. *Time for Dying*. Chicago: Aldine.
Goody, Jack. 1962. *Death, Property and the Ancestors: A Study of the Mortuary Customs of the Lodagaa of West Africa*. London: Tavistock.
Gorer, Geoffrey. 1955. "The Pornography of Death." *Encounter* 5: 49–52.
———. 1965. *Death, Grief, and Mourning in Contemporary Britain*. London: Cresset.
Hallam, Elizabeth, and Jenny Hockey. 2001. *Death, Memory and Material Culture*. Oxford and New York: Berg.
Harrison, Robert Pogue. 2003. *The Dominion of the Dead*. Chicago and London: University of Chicago Press.
Hertz, Robert. (1960) 2004. *Death and the Right Hand*. London and New York: Routledge.
Humphreys, Sally, and Helen King, eds. 1981. *Mortality and Immortality: The Anthropology and Archaeology of Death*. London: Academic Press.
Kan, Sergei. 1992. "Anthropology of Death in the Late 1980s." *Reviews in Anthropology* 20: 283–300.
Kaufman, Sharon, and Lynn M. Morgan. 2005. "The Anthropology of the Beginnings and Ends of Life." *Annual Review of Anthropology* 34: 317–41.
Kellehear, Allan. 2007. *A Social History of Dying*. Cambridge: Cambridge University Press.
Kierkegaard, Søren. (1849) 2013. *The Sickness unto Death*. Milwaukee, WI: Wiseblood Books.
Klass, Dennis. 2006. "Continuing Conversation about Continuing Bonds." *Death Studies* 30(9): 843–58.
Klass, Dennis, Phyllis R. Silverman, and Steven L. Nickman, eds. 1996. *Continuing Bonds: New Understandings of Grief*. New York and Oxon: Routledge.
Klima, Alan. 2002. *The Funeral Casino: Meditation, Massacre, and the Exchange with the Dead in Thailand*. Princeton: Princeton University Press.
Levinas, Emmanuel. (1993) 2000. *God, Death, and Time*. Stanford: Stanford University Press.
Mbembe, Achille. 2003. "Necropolitics." *Public Culture* 15(1): 11–40.
McLean, Stuart. 2013. "'Seaweeds and Limpets will Grow on Our Grave Stones': On Islands, Time, Death and Inhuman Materialities." In *Taming Time, Timing Death: Social Technologies and Ritual*, ed. Dorthe Refslund Christensen and Rane Willerslev, 17–39. Surrey: Ashgate.

Metcalf, Peter, and Richard Huntington. (1979) 1991. *Celebrations of Death: The Anthropology of Mortuary Ritual*. Cambridge: Cambridge University Press.
Palgi, Phyllis, and Henry Abramovitch. 1984. "Death: A Cross-Cultural Perspective." *Annual Review of Anthropology* 13: 385–417.
Parry, Jonathan P. 1994. *Death in Banaras*. Cambridge and New York: Cambridge University Press.
Rank, Otto. (1936) 1978. *Truth and Reality*. New York and London: W. W. Norton & Company.
Richards, Naomi, and Rebecca Rotter. 2013. "Desperately Seeking Certainty? The Case of Asylum Applicants and People Planning an Assisted Suicide in Switzerland." *Sociological Research Online* 18(4). doi:10.5153/sro.3234.
Riley, John W. Jr. 1983. "Dying and the Meanings of Death: Sociological Inquiries." *Annual Review of Sociology* 9: 191–216.
Robben, Antonius C.G.M. 2014. "Massive Violent Death and Contested National Mourning in Post-Authoritarian Chile and Argentina: A Sociocultural Application of the Dual Process Model." *Death Studies* 38(5): 335–45.
_____, ed. 2004. *Death, Mourning, and Burial: A Cross-Cultural Reader*. Malden, MA and Oxford, UK: Blackwell Publishing.
Rosenblatt, Paul C., R. Patricia Walsh, and Douglas A. Jackson. 1976. *Grief and Mourning in Cross-Cultural Perspective*. New Haven: HRAF Press.
Scheper-Hughes, Nancy. 1992. *Death Without Weeping: The Violence of Everyday Life in Brasil*. Berkeley and Los Angeles: University of California Press.
Seale, Clive. 1998. *Constructing Death: The Sociology of Dying and Bereavement*. Cambridge: Cambridge University Press.
Seremetakis, C. Nadia. 1991. *The Last Word: Women, Death and Divination in Inner Mani*. Chicago and London: University of Chicago Press.
Straight, Bilinda S. 2006. "Becoming Dead: The Entangled Agencies of the Dearly Departed." *Anthropology and Humanism* 31: 101–10.
Stroebe, Margaret, and Henk Schut. 1999. "The Dual Process Model of Coping with Bereavement: Rationale and Description." *Death Studies* 23(3): 197–224.
Suzuki, Hikaru. 2000. *The Price of Death: The Funeral Industry in Contemporary Japan*. Stanford, CA: Stanford University Press.
Tsintjilonis, Dimitri. 2007. "The Death-Bearing Senses in Tana Toraja." *Ethnos* 72: 173–94.
Van Brussel, Leen, and Nico Carpentier, eds. 2014. *The Social Construction of Death: Interdisciplinary Perspectives*. Hampshire and New York: Palgrave Macmillan.
Walter, Tony. 1994. *The Revival of Death*. London: Routledge.
_____. 1999. *On Bereavement: The Culture of Grief*. Buckingham: Open University Press.
_____. 2008. "The Sociology of Death." *Sociology Compass* 2(1): 317–36.
Whitehead, Neil L. 2002. *Dark Shamans: Kanaima and the Poetics of Violent Death*. Durham, NC and London: Duke University Press.
Willerslev, Rane. 2013. "Rebirth and the Death Drive: Rethinking Freud's 'Mourning and Melancholia' through a Siberian Time Perspective." In *Taming Time, Timing Death: Social Technologies and Ritual*, ed. Dorthe Refslund Christensen and Rane Willerslev, 79–98. Surrey: Ashgate.

Part II

Necrographic Observations

Chapter 4

The Making of Spirit Bodies and Death Perspectives in Afro-Cuban Religion

Diana Espírito Santo

Introduction: Substances and the Construction of Animated "Bodies"

Practitioners of the popular religious cosmos in Cuba—the various branches that have become known collectively as "Afro-Cuban religion" (cf. Palmié 2013 for a critique of the term)—are inherent dualists. They believe that matter and mind—body and spirit—are entirely different substances, acting on the world in different ways and belonging to different realms. But neither of these concepts, "spirits" and "bodies," should be seen simplistically—that is, spirit as merely immaterial, on the one hand, and body as merely material, on the other. Both of these instead turn on axes that may alternatively fluidify or crystallize bodies, and that may make some spirits more dense, or material, than others (Espírito Santo 2010a; Wirtz 2009). It is a truism to say that these "transgressions" form uncomfortable right-angles with modernist ideology, not simply secularism, which necessarily divides spheres of distinct logics, but also radical Christian separation of the material and spiritual (cf. Cannell 2006, Miller 2005, C. Taylor 2007). If scientific rationalism has banished concepts of the divine from the realms of nature, entirely governed now by blind quasi-mechanical laws, then it has also reified the Cartesian notion that what is truly distinctive about human beings is their souls (Murphy 2006), read either religiously (given by God) or scientifically (as unique minds and consciousness). Against this Aristotelian dualism, practitioners of the major religions of African inspiration in Cuba, work with a plasticity of elements that, if superficially dualist, belies the constructed—humanly fabricated—nature not simply of "spirits" and "bodies," but also of "spirit bodies."

This chapter will explore the manner in which the dead are "reconstructed," so to speak, so as to have new "bodies": first, in a religious complex of Bantu-Congo inspiration called Palo Monte, and second, in Creole Espiritismo, a practice that melds nineteenth-century spiritualist philosophy with Afro-Cuban religious and material concerns. Palo Monte promises the yearning dead life, through materials that produce agentive pseudo-bodies; though the ritualizing of "materials," the dead are reborn to a state that necessarily recognizes their value *as* dead, separate from a healthy, good existence. Espiritismo provides a corps of techniques to manifest spirits that are not beyond but constitutive of living bodies and destinies. In this case, the dead are produced through "things" (spirit representations) that serve as instruments of cosmogony: the spirits are brought to life in their own image by and through mediums' bodies and environment.

I will argue that these instances cannot be theorized as either death-accepting or death-denying (Becker 2011; see Introduction), but as positing death and the dead as particular *perspectives*, produced in and through the material "bodies" at hand. Thus, the people in this ethnography are constructivists, through and through; but, they are ontological rather than epistemological constructivists, using materials, substances, and their own bodies, literally, to fashion and breathe life into spirit entities. This, in turn, has substantial recursive effects on the maker: in Palo Monte, the initiate gains a new "body," free of illnesses or trials; in Espiritismo, the medium gains "sight" (clairvoyance) from the materialization of her *muertos* and their nearness to her own Person. At stake is a particular cosmology of Self, body, and substance that allows these ontological transactions to take place and to lead to a product or effect.

Re-corporifying the Dead in Palo Monte

About four months into my initial anthropology fieldwork in Havana, where I mostly studied spirit mediums of the Espiritismo tradition, I was invited to an Ifá celebration—Ifá is a prestigious divination cult of West-African inspiration—at the house of a marine biologist, a practitioner of Palo Monte. The celebration was the last day of a *yoryé*, an Ifá initiation, and I had been called by an acquaintance to participate in the only ceremony allowed for women, *aperterbis*—a dancing rite. I spent most of the day speaking with Arturo, a slightly nervous man of about sixty years, the marine biologist, and Palero, whose house it was. At one point Arturo took me down a flight of stairs to a dungy, damp basement. The walls were made of dark earth, and the place smelt intensely of something I could not put my finger on. In the center of the room, was Arturo's *nganga,* or *prenda,* as it is also called. It was a large, dark three-legged metal cauldron, sat atop a couple of train rails that Arturo had decided to bring to his house. Inside the object were all manner of sticks, herbs and plants, stones, minerals, earth taken from "sacred" places (such as the cemetery or the crossroads), insects, sacrificial animal remains, and importantly, the bones (shin, cranium, or other) of a deceased person. Some food offerings had been placed at the foot of the *prenda,* some coffee and some bread from the party.

Arturo explained to me that he had inherited this *prenda* when he was an adolescent, from a religious friend of his mother's. It was apparently "Belgian" and dated back a couple of centuries or more, probably having come from Africa. He seemed quite convinced of this and insisted that he had never used it to provoke harm on anyone (doing *brujería*). After he began to work on the *prenda* he needed a spirit or *muerto* to go "inside" it, or to be "fixed" to it. One day, Arturo and a special friend of his went to an ossuary to find this *muerto.* While the friend kept a watch outside, Arturo scoured the ossuary to find a suitable box of bones. Although the bone warehouse was not so large, he kept getting lost and inexplicably would end up standing beside the same box of bones over and over again. They were "calling" to him, so he took them without investigating who they belonged to or what would happen next. Whereas the normal procedure is to perform a short divination session there and then to ascertain whether the spirit is willing to be taken, Arturo justifies his actions by saying that if the *muerto* was adverse to being used in Palo, something would have happened—a car breaking down, people being caught, an accident, and so forth. In any case, the ceremony that consecrated the spirit and its bones to the *nganga* was initially fraught with troubles, since one of Arturo's own protective spirits—a lawyer—had put a stop to it unless he committed to constructing it alone. He did, and the *nganga spirit,* called a *perro de prenda* (prenda "dog"), or *nfumbe,* was quickly integrated into its functioning. Arturo now says that he talks to this *muerto* as if he were a normal living person in his home. He tells me that the overarching entity of his *nganga* is Sarabanda, the Bantu-Congo god of war, iron, and train tracks, and that his *perro* has proved itself to be tough, like this god.

Prendas can be inherited from family members or religious kin, as well as made, as Arturo's story shows. Generally, they are "born" from the substances of older *prendas* belonging to the initiate's godfather, the *Tata Nganga*. They can also be found. Roberto, a fifty-five-year-old Palero I interviewed in 2013, revealed how he had come to "acquire" his *perro de prenda* and his *nganga*. Fifteen years old in 1968, Roberto was sent to the army in Sancti Spiritus, a province half-way across Cuba. While he was in army, he met a Haitian-descendant, a man everyone around them feared and avoided. Roberto says he was a hermit and lived far from others. One day this man saw him carrying small tortoises and asked Roberto to sell him one. Roberto, who had never feared him, offered him one for nothing in return. After this point the two began to visit each other and became friends. "People used to say that he had a spirit that walked behind him, a light, and that at night, strange noises came from his house." Time passed and Roberto retired from the army and returned to Havana.

About two years later, he had a dream with the "Haitian." He appears to Roberto signaling for him to dig in a place he did not recognize at first. This dream seemed auspicious; but at the same time ominous, since it was unlikely that the Haitian's spirit had visited him in his dream unless he was dead. Again time passed, and about three years later Roberto returns to Sancti Spiritus and indeed, the Haitian's house was gone; neighbors told of his passing. Roberto then finds this piece of land and digs the earth, and there, underneath, he discovers a small *prenda*. The object had the face of the devil, a forlorn image ragged with time and dirt that Roberto reconstructed once he got back. Roberto figures that the Haitian must have sensed he was dying and buried this sacred object. Its face is the devil because while he was alive he practiced "black magic." But the *prenda* also came with its *muerto*—"the one who responds to all the work I now do": Taitica. Taitica is a spirit of an invalid man, who is so crippled that he lets himself be seen as dragging through the floor, with the small *prenda* between his legs. "He was a very black man, almost blue," says Roberto. Taitica does not come in trance, but his old Haitian master, Venancio, does. Roberto says that he's unwilling to incorporate Taitica in possession for fear that the latter may pass on his ailments to his medium. However, because he is also a clairvoyant, Roberto notes that Taitica exhibits a vitality he would not otherwise have were it not for his long-held *prenda* through which myriad operations are possible.

Ngangas are miniature worlds, microcosms where the universe is modeled or simulated by the expert, using natural elements, so that he can subsequently perform his "magical" disassemblies and reassemblies, manipulations of the order of things. Paleros communicate with their *perros* via oracles such as the *chamalongos*, five pieces of round polished coconut shell, or the *vititi mensu,* an object which carries a mirror, or indeed, by mediumship and trance. It is no wonder that Palo is known as the ultimate form of witchcraft or sorcery in the Afro-Cuban religious cosmos. *Dios en el cielo, y Dios en la tierra* (God in the Heavens, and God on earth) goes a typical saying in Palo, suggesting that concerns with immanent deities or rules are of little importance (cf. Figarola 2006). But the *nganga* is not simply a container (of spirits or things); it is also alive, pulsating to life's contingencies—through the Palero—and responding to offerings of blood, honey, and alcohol. If it provides the *perro*'s casing, however, it is far from an inert "body," so to speak.

First of all, this is because each *nganga* "belongs" or is consecrated to a more powerful deity, called a *mpungo*. Mpungos are associated by syncretistic processes in Cuba to *orichas*, the gods of the popular West-African inspired Cuban religion of Santería, and in turn, associated with Catholic saints; so that, for example, a *nganga* sanctified to the *mpungo* Siete Rayos will have its counterpart in the *oricha-*god Changó and in the Catholic Santa Barbara (cf. Bolívar Aróstegui and Diaz de Villegas 1998; Fuentes Guerra and Gomez 1996). But it is not just the *mpungos* that make the *nganga* powerful. Here is how Lydia Cabrera describes the *nganga*:

> It is a spirit, a supernatural force, but it is also a recipient, a clay pot, a metal three-legged cauldron, and in a time now distant it was once a cloth casing or wrapper in which one placed earth from a crossroads and from a cemetery, sticks, herbs, the bones of birds and animals, and other components that would constitute a *nganga* and that were the supports that the spirits and forces over which the mother or father [owner] of the *nganga* exerted their dominion, needed to fulfill their orders. The *nganga* also means the dead. (my translation, 1979: 15–16)

Secondly, the qualities and contents of the *nganga* are of extreme importance to the *perro* who is tied to it, not just because the latter will tend to manifest the characteristics of the deity to which the *nganga* is consecrated, as Artro's example shows, but because it will have at its disposal the *nganga*'s full range of forces to use malleably, even metamorphically. Calleja and Alpizar (2012), for example, argue that the Palero, or *criado-prenda,* can be possessed by animal (serpent, dog, vulture) and tree spirits (royal palm, and so forth) whose essence he has placed inside his *nganga* for accrued powers. But the authors understand that it is ultimately the *perro* spirit who acquires these forces and possesses his master, for instance, by making him crawl on the ground like a snake. The *perro* in this sense gains as many other "spirit bodies" as the Palero has added to his ritual receptacle. This multiplicity is commented on by Walterio Carbonell, one of Cuba's foremost observers of popular African-inspired culture. He says that for Paleros, "The world is governed by a universal substance of spirit, (Nsambi or Zambi) ... This universal spirit has the capacity to materialize, that is, to take on the form of an animal, vegetable, mineral or human being. Everything takes its inspiration from the life-giving breath of Nsambi" (Carbonell quoted in Barnet 2001: 93). It may be interesting to note here that in effect, the *nganga* is also a materialization of a protective spirit's will—for, as many have noted, Palero's must only be initiated if they "have" at least one spirit guide that "knew of those things." This is generally ascertained through Espiritismo, through which concepts of "spirit guide" take shape, as will be explored in the next section.

But even *muertos* are not simply just "spirits" in Palo, meaning incorporeal, nonquantifiable agencies (cf. Espírito Santo 2015a). Eduardo, one of my main *espiritista* and Palo interlocutors and friends, argues that while the *nganga*'s founding *perro* or *nfumbe* is its central agentive piece, there is in effect all manner of assemblages of "bits" and "pieces" that come to look and act like spirits, but are not in the ways typically conceived (cf. Espírito Santo, Kerestetzi, and Panagiotopoulos 2013). Protective objects for the famed *muertos oscuros*—dark, lowly spirit forms sent for the purposes of destroying the victim's life—are often examples of these spirit "fabrications." Indeed, *guardieros, mpakas,* and other ritually-confectioned amulets are composed of partial spirit "bodies," say, the spirit "skin" (or appearance) of a person who once lived, and "filled" or "programmed" with elements from nature, the vitality of blood, and the intentionality of their maker. Eduardo was once firm with me that these were *not* spirits proper—which, for instance, could be pleaded to, or set free—but assemblages that respond to the actual *nganga,* and which can subsequently be "unmade." These complexes (Palmié 2006) are irreducible to the material substances that comprise them, on the one hand, and to the invisible beings or pseudo-bodies that seem to animate them, on the other.

Indigenous understandings of Palo's efficacy lend themselves to popular forms of mythmaking, aggrandizement and even demonization, even within Palo contexts themselves. Notions of the effect of materiality heavily mediate these understandings; and indeed, the notion of "matter" in this and other Afro-Cuban contexts is tied to ideas of morality as well. Both Paleros and other *religiosos* say that Palo magic can save or kill a person in a matter of days. This is largely because the *perro* is literally bound to the *nganga,* part of whose power comes through the spirit's attachment to matter. It is no longer a free-floating entity of "space" manifest through certain bodily sensations or representations, as with most *muertos* worked by other experts, but instead it agrees to live not just *in* but *as* matter, leaving the recipient only to perform errands and carry out its duties. In this contractual arrangement, the *perro*'s work is pliable in as much as it receives material forms of attention, care and incentive, particularly sacrificial animal blood. In this sense, while there are always exceptions, the *perro* becomes less an amoral creature than one whose morality becomes obsolete, along with its individuality.

It is not a coincidence, in this regard, that Paleros speak of valuing certain "types" of spirits over others, namely those whose lives and deaths were characterized by accident, violence and crime. This kind of "primitivity" breeds unreflexivity, which is an invaluable asset for an efficient *perro*. Even Roberto does not have much knowledge of his *prenda*'s Taitica spirit; perhaps because it had "come" with the object in the first place, but also because in general there is little forthcoming information about *perros*—it is unrelated to their "jobs." However, there is a balance that must also be sought between a *perro*'s necessary experience of his own death and an overly long period whereby the spirit can turn into an "enlightened" being (*ndoqui*) with no interest in the *prenda*. Joel James Figarola says as much:

> In general it is preferable that several years have gone by since its physical death, so that the nfumbi has had a certain experience of the life of the dead and has found in it a certain amount of comfort and satisfaction ... on the other hand, it is not convenient that so much time has gone by that its memories of life and the temporal have vanished ... you cannot wait that nfumbis turn into ndoquis ... ndoquis have very different interests to the nfumbis ... (2006: 37–38)

I have been told that Havana's Cementério Colón keeps detailed lists of incoming corpses and their causes of death with officials establishing a black-market for bones destined for Paleros seeking eligible spirits for their new *ngangas*. According to these rumors, the bones of murderers, rapists, and the insane raise the price because an *apego* (attachment) to the material world and its pleasures may be inferred. According to Luis, a middle-aged long-time interlocutor of mine in Havana who has practiced Palo Monte for many years, "you can study religion your entire life; you can have great spirits who assist you; but if you don't have anything 'material' to work them you can get into a lot of trouble." Thus, if the *perro*—now anonymized, separated from its previous life—has gained a new "casing" or "skin," the person too has acquired a new "material" foundation. This foundation has its dangers. Luis says that *ngangas* can go either way—good or bad ("Christian" or "Jewish" as Paleros say), and that the latter "consumes" the Palero eventually.

> You can only work once a year, or when something very grave occurs because you're working with the Devil. If not you get sick. Your legs start to get weak, you lose your memory, you start to talk shit and offend people, to threaten

them. And one day you can throw yourself on the road in front of a car. I know some people like this. They die young. (Luis, pers. comm., 2008)

This may indeed be the shadow side of a Palero's own new "body."

It is well known that being *rayado*—initiated—in Palo Monte, has tangible, health effects. A person is said to be "reconfigured" physiologically once he has received his consecration. Julio, for example, a Palero I interviewed on several occasions in 2008, was *rayado* at the age of thirty because he had been the object of bad sorcery. But immediately he noticed that the spinal problems he had, disappeared. His granddaughter initiated just a few years ago at age five, suffered from intense asthma and lung-related illnesses, and her health has been in a perfect condition since. For Julio, the *nganga* does two things. First, the person is powerfully, physically "nourished" by the vitality of the animal blood fed to the *nganga* and the *perro*—the spirit gives them strength. Second, there is a "rebirth" of the person through her initiation that eliminates some of her "karma," read as disagreeable events or situations that she has to experience in life. These physiological and moral changes may be unsurprising given that for many, the *rayamiento* (or *juramiento*) involves the death of the *nfambi* (neophyte) and his subsequent cosmic birth in the world of the dead. Indeed, Paleros, also known as *nsó-nganga*, are also known in some Cuban provinces as *muerteros*, "those who deal with the dead." Katerina Kerestetzi, in her section of a co-authored article, quotes one of her interlocutors suggesting this proximity:

> Some of the sequences enacted during these early rituals [by which she means initiation]—induce in the neophyte the impression of spatial proximity and ontological affinity with the dead. These impressions lead paleros to make statements such as: "the one who is initiated in Palo Monte dies. He goes to the cemetery, he goes to the world of the dead, and becomes a dead man himself." (Kerestetzi, in Espírito Santo et al. 2013: 200)

The initiation rite is too complex to describe here, but it involves the purification or cleansing of the neophyte, the ritual cutting of several parts of his body with a blade, the mixing of his blood with his godfather's *nganga* and with his own newly born *nganga*—so as to breathe life into it—and the rubbing of sacred (and secret) substances on his incisions (powder, made with human bones among other things). Kerestetzi sees the incisions making the neophyte's body permeable to the "flow of the dead ... allowing the spirit to integrate and occupy the palero's body" (Kerestetzi, in Espirito Santo et al., ibid: 202). A further identification with the dead occurs at the end of the rite whereby the neophyte is made to lie on the ground, with only candles lit around him, covered in a white sheet. He becomes the object of chants, such as "the one who died won't come back, the bone changed, it's alright" (Kerestetzi, in Espírito Santo et al. 2013: 202). At this point the *nsó-nganga* initiate has undergone a "mystical birth" (Calleja & Alpizar 2012: 53) and "signed" a pact both with his own *nganga* that now "lives," and with that of his "house." He or she must now venerate and obey his *taita* or *yaya* (godfather or mother) and respect his ritual "siblings" from this point on.

The concept of a "body" in Palo is clearly multiple; you cannot reduce it to a material substrate for meanings, because often it is not even a material thing at all. For Kerestetzi, the *nganga* becomes the new "material envelope" for the spirit of the deceased person, one that allows the spirit to "believe" he is still alive, somehow (Espirito Santo et al. 2013: 200). But she also contradicts herself further on by citing Bazin (1986: 271) on ritual objects in Mali. The *nganga*'s fabrication, she says, "does not merely represent the 'embodiment of a spirit but, in the opposite direction to death, the carnation of a skeleton'" (Kerestetzi, in Espirito Santo et al. 2013: 201). This suggests that what happens in Palo is less of "giving back" of a *muerto*'s (original, virtual) body and more of furnishing him with an entirely *new form of body*. In effect, Paleros rely on an inherent ambiguity in their *perros*' psyche, so to speak: they must know they're dead, and consequently want life, desperately even, but they must want it in a way that confirms and instantiates their "deadness" as well. It is not exactly a "living body" that they gain, for deadness brings different "physical" properties. No wonder most *religiosos* are so fearful of being harnessed for Paleros' *prendas* after they pass away. The question seems to be here how to redefine "death" itself in this ethnographic context.

A possibility for understanding these differences can be sought, perhaps, in a Palo cosmology of Self. Bolívar, González, and del Río (2007: 154–5) describe how for many Paleros man is divided in two primary parts: an exterior perishable material body and an "internal entity," which is the "essence of man," not seen from the outside (ibid.: 154). This internal essence can be divided in two: the *nsala* and the *mwela*. Nsala is the soul of the person, the principle of life that abandons the person once they die. And it has a "shadow" which also departs after death. The *mwele*, on the other hand, is the breath of life, "the organ through which man lives and breathes" (ibid.: 155). It also separates from the body at death, but, like the *nsala*, it can leave the body during sleep to wander through other lands, and the future. When a man loses his life, his *mwele* goes to the land of the dead. While this explanation is unconfirmed by my research data on Palo Monte, it hypothetically lends scope for a concept of the "soul" that is neither entirely dualistic nor immaterial, in that part of it—the *mwele*, for instance—can be revived or re-animated through substances. Therefore, what kind of dualism or non-dualism is being espoused here? It could be argued that Afro-Cuban religion, in particular Palo Monte, espouses both, sequentially, so to speak. Both spirit and matter potentially survive death, but in order to gain life, must be redefined, or reassembled, into a kind of "re-death" which defies the "dissociational" processes that death ordinarily brings.

Spirit-izing the Human Body: Espiritismo's Technologies of the Self

On one of my last occasions in Havana, in 2013, I participated in a rite called a *misa espiritual*, spiritual mass, performed amongst mediums of Creole forms of Espiritismo, known by some scholars as Espiritismo *cruzado*. Cuban Espiritismo (cf. Espírito Santo 2012, 2015b; Millet 1996) inherits movements and doctrines from nineteenth-century French and Anglo-American spiritualism, especially those of Allan Kardec, Spiritism's French "codifier." Very loosely, in its current form, Creole Espiritismo articulates a view of the soul as an entity superior to the body, that reincarnates many times and "evolves" to "higher" levels of existence. Special people, according to Espiritismo, can communicate with disincarnate spirits through many modes: from dreams, visions, and sensations to bodily trance. It also posits the person as the recipient of the care and protection of a number of spirit guides—*espiritus protectores*, or simply *muertos*—that do not simply "encircle" the person but are intimately tied to her experience of herself. These contrast with other types of *muertos* with whom a person does not necessarily forge long-term ties of embodiment proper, such as deceased family members and religious or ritual ancestors. In the *misa* I attended—dedicated to investigating whether a man could "receive" a minor initiation in Santería—both kinds of spirits made their presence felt, and there were qualitative differences between them, that is, differences felt as shifts in the body's emotional and somatic density. *Misas espirituales* are indeed often used for precisely these purposes: to ascertain the person's suitability for further Afro-Cuban religious rites (Castellanos and Castellanos 1992: 195). In the end, as most *religiosos* maintain, there are strong correlations between an individual's religious destiny, and the spirit elements present in their *cordón espiritual* (group of spirit guides), be they African, indigenous, European, Arab, Gypsy, or any other identity.

The *misa* took place at the third apartment of Eduardo and Olga, a couple I have known since 2006 and who with time have become close friends and religious godparents (Eduardo is mentioned above). I have also known their spirits for a long time. First in line in this *misa* was Lázaro Martinez, an old *muerto* of Olga's who had been a Santero while alive, and who came to sanction and provide guidance for the initiation. Then, Robertico, a "young" *muerto* with whom the couple has only been recently acquainted but who has proven invaluable to their "house" and its functioning. And then came Olga's Native American spirit, the *Indio*, who arrived essentially to rid Olga's body of unwanted currents of energy. While Lázaro's presence was mild and wise—he gave his blessing and told us a (Yoruba-based) story about a princess, or "a ray of light," who was divided between two princes until Orula, the god of divination, decided between them—Robertico's energy was more emotional, scattered, and heavy. Emotions are felt strongly in trance with spirits because there is no physical body to parse or attenuate them. It was no wonder that he tired out Olga's body immensely. Robertico's emotional charge was an evident danger to her *materia*, which is why it was so imperative that the Indio possess Olga straight after to cleanse her thoroughly. He was nostalgic, sad even, particularly when I asked how he felt when he died, and how it was in the "spirit world." This is interesting in that the difference between these two spirits—the first from Olga's *cordón*, and the second from outside it—is also a matter of *biography*. Whereas we knew, from this *misa* and others, all about Robertico's childhood spent barefoot playing baseball on the streets of Havana, being chased by his mother to study, and how since he was a boy he had wanted a motorcycle—perhaps encouraged by his father's work with old cars—on which he eventually died in an accident at the age of twenty-seven in the 1980s, we knew relatively little about Lázaro Martinez, except that he was a knowledgeable "Santero" in Cuba, sometime in the early twentieth century.

Cordón spirits go strangely amiss when it comes to their lives and deaths. As noted elsewhere (Espírito Santo 2014), very few spirit mediums can tell us full *biographical stories* about their protective *muertos*. There may be a few reasons for this, including a sophisticated cosmology of Self that psychologizes these spirits by positing them in a relation of mutual and emergent production with the person. But more interesting for the purposes of this chapter is how they are *produced* in and *as* the body of the medium. There is a sense that, as *cordón* spirits are integrated into a medium's extended Self they lose their own situated biographical Selves, at the same time, parts of their personalities get exacerbated. This occurred with Lázaro Martinez: if the personal specifics of his life were in some way "erased" as he was acknowledged and developed as a protective *muerto*, he now comes in function of his Santería expertise, which he passes on to Olga both in trance and in more silent forms of communion.

While the *cordón* spirits do not disappear entirely from "view," so to speak, the goal in Creole Espiritismo is for the medium's body to manifest them in its totality (body, mind, spirit—in action). This concept could translate into a literal sort of spiritualized chemistry, as some more studious Kardecist espiritista groups that we have observed in Havana would note (Espírito Santo 2010b). For one *"Espiritismo científico"* society with which I did fieldwork in 2005/6, the body is not merely a receptor of spirits but is *constituted* on spirits at many levels of its structure; and because these spirits bring their own energetic patterns from past lives, these patterns get entangled with the medium's own material system, engendering, in this way, a spirit-ized bodily biochemistry, altering her own thoughts and behavior. But, if for this group, the point of mediumship is to "metabolize" and eventually "digest" these protective spirits' traumas and negativities, freeing the person from their effects, then in the more popular Creole Espiritismo, spirits are more organically developed and accepted as natural *parts* of one's Self.

This is evident, among other things, during consultations where the Espiritista medium often "connects" spontaneously with the client's own *muertos*. In one consultation I had, for example, the medium, a well-known lady in her sixties who worked with an unusual oracle—porcelain plates—asked me to say my name, then passed a white, clean plate on my forehead, torso and limbs, and then, placing it upside down, lit a candle underneath. The result was an elaborate burn pattern on the inside of the plate that looked like two dark vortices that she then interpreted. Marta, the medium, explained that she was "catching" my "guardian angel," my most important of *cordón muertos,* or better, the "information" that she could catch from it, which was materializing on the plate. The assumption was that my own energy, accessible to others as easily as through consultation, was somehow permeated with or even equal to that of my spirit guides, who could be "read off." In Espiritismo the divination act is a thoroughly collaborative affair, depending on a cosmology of Self that has the *muertos* as engrained aspects of what Wirtz calls the "perspicient" body (2014: 125). But this is not an arbitrary immanence, since it is via the medium that they pour forth through the enactment of their presence in necessarily material forms. Thus, from constituting and manifesting via what Ochoa (2007) has coined "sense un-certainty," in the form of chills and goose bumps, for instance—early and visceral indicators of a spirit's presence—the developed dead can assume physical and social certainty: they are thought, felt, acted, and seen into existence.

On the one hand, Cuban Espiritistas inherit a superficial, albeit strong dualism from Euro-American Spiritualism. It is not just that they distinguish between "material" or "spiritual" causes of events, illnesses, or misfortune, for theirs is a mission of careful and discerning classification. These are also differing "methodologies," or indeed, discourses, for the development of spirits, with corresponding moral universes (Espírito Santo 2010a; Wirtz 2009, 2014). But on the other hand, in practice, this dualism plays itself out in much subtler ways. Espiritismo also articulates an "Afro-Cuban" understanding of things (including bodies) that are permeable and whose substances are transmissible, somehow forming a chain of vital forces (Morris 1994: 121). Espiritismo, then, also inherits Palo Monte's and Santería's *vitalism*, so to speak; it has both vertical and horizontal axes of cosmogony. The body "receives" spirits, is the site for the identification and strengthening of the world of the dead, but it can also "lose" itself; the person's "matter" can cause her to go insane. She may also leave "parts" of her body—nails, hair, and dust from the skin—that are akin to *her Self* in the sense that they may be used to effect sorcery on *her*. Mind and body are different substances, but body is not purely mechanical, divorced from the world "out there" and *its* mechanics, nor from the deep recesses of the person's own psychic vitality. It is absolutely contiguous with the substantial "matter" of the world itself, changing it and being changed by it. Spirits yearn to partake of this worldly "matter" as well, urging their mediums to furnish them with spaces of "representation," such as spirit dolls and other items, and identity-driven songs. But this "representation" is more of a "re-presentation," in the sense that the object or song performs the spirit's condition as being *of* the world and simultaneously *without* it. Espiritista mediums perform this identification often even in exaggerated forms, for instance, through songs. When Robertico comes through Olga in a *misa espiritual*, for instance, Eduardo sings the following verse, to pay him homage:

Virgen de la Caridad / ilumina a Robertico / para que pueda bajar a la tierra / y pueda darse un traguito
Virgin of Charity / cast your light on Robertico / so that he can come down to this earth / and have himself a little drink

This brief *plegária* is evocative not because it suggests that Robertico will "come down" to have himself a drink, but because Eduardo overperforms the spirit's attachment to "things" in order to enact his respect for its trajectory in his religious house. As Schieffelin has observed, performances do more than represent reality: they "create and make present realities vivid enough to beguile, amuse or terrify" (1998: 194), and in some cases, even heal.

We could ask in what sense the body is something that grows denser, materially, when mediums have "developed" their *muertos*; certainly, they are more protected physically, but that is not all. There is also a sense in which the body is fabricated in relation to the dead and their various characteristics. As it grows stronger in its connections to its *muertos*, the person's own spirit expands and "sees" through these connective "branches." The person becomes less and less vulnerable to intrusion by others, especially through witchcraft. There are parallels that could be made to the manner in which bodies are made in the Amazon, such as among the Mebengokré-Xikrin in the North of Brazil, studied by Clarice Cohn (2011). According to her descriptions, when a child is born it has a body (*í*) and a *karon*, sometimes translated as "soul." The skin of this body needs to be strong so as to contain the *karon*, and as it grows from soft to hard, the child needs less care. The skin is the site where the person's internal aspects—material and immaterial—are expressed (Giannini 1991: 153 in Cohn 2011: 99), similar to what Terence Turner argued for the Kayapó's "social skin" (2012).

Discussion: On the Body

One possible avenue in a discussion on both Palo and Espiritismo understandings of "death-created" bodies, so to speak, is to look at the concept of "substance" as it has been articulated by anthropologists of Amerindian societies, particularly in relation to bodies, and their "unstable and relational character," in the words of Aparecida Vilaça (2005: 445). For instance, according to Cecilia MacCallum, for the Cashinahua of Western Amazonia, "bodies are the accumulated product of human intervention and individual experience, where knowledge and skills extracted from the visible and invisible environment take an embodied material existence" (1999: 443). Here the body, as well as moral personhood, active and constituted on knowledge and skill, must be perpetually achieved. But, according to Vilaça, what is defining in many senses about Amerindian cultures is that they present anthropologists with "structural principles based on a system of relations between bodies" (2005: 446), which Vilaça quotes Seeger, Da Matta and Viveiros de Castro as terming "physio-logics" (1979: 13 in 2005: 447). Substances here, such as blood, semen, and food, are fundamental to the construction of both bodies and moral personhoods. For the Wari' that Vilaça describes, a child's body is made by the circulating substances of mother and father, the very definition of kin. Indeed, kin-making activities are focused on precisely these circulations, which construct and modify bodies (ibid.: 450).

According to Conklin and Morgan, these views do not just reflect radically different orientations to what the body is (1996: 664) to those, say, of American culture, but also how personhood is accrued or attained (ibid.:

667). The point here is that what these authors call "ethnophysiological models of shared substance" (ibid.: 668) embed notions of a person's relationships and social and individual position that are mutable and fluid, with dividends, among other things, for notions of knowledge and knowing. Bodies here are not a "material substrate upon which meaning is encoded" (ibid.: 670), but *are* meaning or meanings themselves, literally, physically. The radical indissociability of substance and symbol is further articulated recently by Cristóbal Bonelli in his analysis of the notion of *mollvün* among Pehuenche communities in Southern Chile (2014). Bonelli shows how *mollvün* does not just refer to the bodily substance of blood but is constitutive of morality and aspects of personhood, as well as kinship and belonging. Further, it is something that can be *extracted,* depleted from the person, through witchcraft for example (2014: 119). *Mollvün* is irreducible either to matter or to meaning—but neither is it a merger or hybrid of the two (ibid.). Rather, *mollvün* is in some sense subjectivity itself: simultaneously capacity to see, perceive, act, and relate, and a transmissible, even edible thing.

These examples demonstrate ethnographic instances where "mind" (meaning) and "matter" (bodies) do not simply blur but become obsolete as concepts; individuation occurs on a level other than the "individual." If we take these substance-based ideas and apply them to boundaries of life-death, can we regain the notion, as Charles Taylor has argued for European populations before the Middle Ages (2007: 66), that death is a further stage in the "career of existence"? Scholarship on spirit mediumship and possession has done little to analytically bridge this gap; most studies assume that the (ready-made, moral) person contacts the (transcendent) "other world" and somehow embodies it through her (ready-made) material body. But people are not constituted a priori. And the body, as Janelle S. Taylor has stated, "is not so much a thing as an –ing" (2005: 745). The body is not one thing, but a process—one cannot think of it "as an object nor a text, nor only as a locus of subjectivity, but rather as a contingent configuration, a surface that is made but never in static or permanent form" (ibid.: 747).

One of the aims of this chapter was to explore the notion that death—through the dead—is not in the "beyond" but in and of things, bodies, objects, and events. Death is itself a "contingent configuration" that takes shape through the perspectives it takes on, bodies included. These are not simple perspectives. In Palo Monte, a new "body" needs to be furnished for the spirit who will slave for the Palero; the spirit of the deceased *becomes* something it was not before—it is both itself and not itself in its new condition. Furthermore, the object in which it labors, a metal recipient called *nganga,* in effect the spirit's own *new* casing, must *also* be fed bodies of animals. In Espiritismo the spirits gain a new body—the medium's—from which to manifest their virtues and traumas, mediated as they are by the espiritista's own perspective and situated Self. This body also changes with time; both spirits and the person animate it. In Cuba there is a (very dualist) sense in which bodies are animated by something which pre-exists them—the "person," the spirit of the dead, and so forth. But this is not a straightforward relation: the animation itself changes the "animated." The body is what creates the perspective—both from the viewpoint of the living, and of the dead.

Scholars of death practices since Robert Hertz (1907) have tended to reify distinctions between "us" and "them" with regards to death beliefs: death-accepting for "modern," technologically-scientific, religiously "repressed" societies, and death-denying for "non-modern" ones, where death is seen as a process, albeit one that does not destroy the "spirit" of the ancestor but re-makes it. This is a fallacious dichotomy of course, tailored to ethnocentric assumptions, among which is that the "native's" personhood is tied to their collective representations or cosmology, whereas "ours" are freely and independently constructed. A key concern here is the persistence and maintenance of the "social persona," or its absence. Less explored, however, are questions about the actual definition of "death," even if more recent analyses have pursued these in relation to biomedical technological advances (see Kaufman and Morgan 2005). My argument here hinges less on the biopolitics of death than on engendering definitions of death that counter the notion that death "kills" life; or that it annihilates it forever. Afro-Cuban religions employ "social technologies" (Refslund, Willerslev and Meinert 2013: 2), which effectively work from a dualistic basis—spirit and body are different substances—to one that transforms this relationship into a non-dualist one. I argued that what Paleros and Espiritistas do is take the materials which death dissolves—spirits from bodies, objects from what they "represent," life from matter—and bring them back together to form *another* kind of life, a "re-death". We should be asking then, following Bloch and Parry (1982), not how a society regenerates *life*, but how it regenerates and recycles *death*. The concept of "perspectives" was used to answer this question, since, in effect, this notion denies "any possible substantial identity" (Goldman 2007: 113) to that of which it is the perspective.

Concluding Remarks: On the Soul

In an article on some cosmological specifics of their North Asian ethnographies, Morten Pedersen and Rane Willerslev begin by noting how common terms such as "hybridity," "montage," and even "cyborg" have become in a postmodern understanding of selves and others, mind and body, individual and world (2012: 464–5). But the real question that can be asked about their Mongolian and Siberian animist ethnographies, respectively, is, what exactly is meant by soul? (ibid.: 466) The animist soul, they say, cannot be treated as a fixed referent but as "an inherently relative or deictic phenomenon, whose form depends on who perceives it and from where" (ibid.: 467). Furthermore, in a Judeo-Christian tradition, the physical body is conceived to be of an entirely different substance to the immaterial soul. But for the Siberian Chukchi there is a sense in which souls *are* bodies; they can eat and drink and be hunted by other creatures. And, for the Mongolian Darhads, souls, *süns*, is best described as the *shadow* of the body (ibid.: 468). Indeed, Pedersen and Willerslev argue that a *perspectivist* ontology makes more sense in their ethnographic contexts, than one that separates body from soul.

As the reader may know, perspectivism is a term-concept used by Eduardo Viveiros de Castro in relation to Amerindian contexts (1992), to describe a cosmos "inhabited by different sorts of subjects of persons, human or non-human, who apprehend reality from distinct points of view" (1998: 469 in Pedersen and Willerslev 2012: 470), subject with a common "soul" and distinct "bodies," thus, the term "multinaturalism." But, Pedersen and Willerslev also argue — through Vilaça (2005) — that the Amerindian "soul," conceived as a quality that identifies the being with all other beings, is also characterized by its connection to the capacity to take on novel bodily appearances (Pedersen and Willerslev. ibid: 471). Thus, "the soul is not simply one body that ego cannot presently see . . .; it is all the potential bodies that ego might take at some future point" (ibid.: 472). This means that the "soul of the soul is *another* body — or, more precisely, *all the other bodies that a body could be*" (ibid.: 472–3). These visions of the (internal rather than external) relation between soul/spirit and body substantially complicate Western notions that divide these into distinct (interventional or non-interventional) spheres. There seems to be a similar logic at play in the Cuban ethnography I have expounded in this chapter, despite the pervasiveness of dualistic-sounding discourses among experts of Afro-Cuban religion.

For instance, Palo Monte appears to furnish an ex-embodied soul, the *perro*, with a new body, the *nganga*. But the *nganga* creates a perspective for the spirit only in as much as it also recognizes this spirit's wish or propensity for "body-ness"; in a sense, the *nganga* is a body of a body, endowing the *perro* with a specific capacity to act and perceive beyond its own already "materialized" dispositions. These spirits are not, in this way, conceived as lifeless, or as inhabiting the realm of the dead, but very much the opposite. The realm of the dead is "reconstructed" *as* "dead" (or "re-dead") among the living, thereby endowing it with vitality. In Cuban Espiritismo, the spirits of the *cordón* are re-created through the materials (bodies) that the spirit medium affords them; however, these spirits are not independent but constitutive of her Self and knowable only through the (internal) relations they sustain with her. In a sense, these *muertos* parallel Pedersen's Darhad's *süns*, souls, in that they "both constitute an inalienable aspect of a person (it is generally held that, if you lose your *süns*, then you will die) and simultaneously be a detachable part of the same person, which can temporarily travel beyond the confines of his physical body (as in dreaming)" (ibid.: 481). In Cuban Espiritismo, the spirits become visible only as they become materialized in and through things; the "bodies," so to speak, pre-exist and determine the "souls." While my feeling is that Palo Monte instigates a more profound re-thinking of matter-spirit dualisms, in Espiritismo we can see a curious process (of development) that goes from many souls (spirits) in one body, to a single soul and many bodies. If the first stage betrays the initial steps in mediumship development—the "implosion" of spirits within the body—the second belies a more productive integration of these spirit "voices" or perspectives through the construction of multiple "bodies" (spirit representations and other materials).

Does all this mean that "death" has many bodies, or souls, or indeed, body-souls? Or that death is somehow immanent in Palo and Espiritismo? Are these concepts even valid for this ethnography? This is a language, according to Todd Ramon Ochoa, which does not really fit the Palo context he works with. In his language for a "new materiality" Ochoa uses words such as "parataxis", "nonlinearity", "turbulence", "influence" (2010: 398) to describe the sea of the dead that constitutes the very bodies that perceive them (ibid.: 390). Palo, he says,

> rests on the understanding that the dead outline the forms bodies assume, and saturate those shapes. By virtue of their persistent turning as eddies in the vast, uncertain sea of the dead, these shapes, or bodies, endure. This is to say that "the body," a human shape or life, is itself a persistent turning and returning within the ambient mass of the dead called "Kalunga" (ibid.: 390).

The dead, and the body, according to Ochoa, are two sides of the same coin.

My analysis in this chapter has been slightly different in that I have argued more from the perspective of people and how they build the means for the dead (or the re-dead) to become present in their material and sensorial milieu. I have argued that constructing the perspectives of the dead in a living setting implicates the use of things—materials, substances, dolls, and one's own body—so much so that these material perspectives produce changes in the souls or spirits who scaffold on them. Indeed, these same "things" do not construct as much as constitute the perspectives of the dead. I have argued that it may be useful to employ the term "re-dead" or "re-death" to think about broader ontological possibilities beyond life-death. These possibilities are generated by creative ritual acts that furnish the "dead" with another kind of death-life. In this sense, these Afro-Cuban religious experts transit from absolutely dualist assumptions—that spirit is in matter, that both dissociate at the hour of death, and that at least one dissolves—to assumptions that reaffirm this dualism by subverting it: positing a logic of ritual assemblages and fabrications that redefines these elements *as a version* (or perspective) *of* death, a peculiarly powerful one too.

Diana Espírito Santo has researched spirit possession and mediation, Afro-Cuban Espiritismo, and African-inspired Umbanda; she is currently examining ontologies of evidence in parapsychology movements and paranormal investigation in Chile. Her interests include personhood, materiality, divination, witchcraft, and technologies. She has published many articles, written two monographs, and co-edited three volumes, including *The Social Life of Spirits* (University of Chicago Press, 2014) and *Making Spirits* (I.B. Tauris, 2013).

References

Barnet, Miguel. 2001. *Afro-Cuban Religions*, trans. Christine Ayorinde. Princeton: Marcus Wiener Publishers.
Becker, Ernest. (1973) 2011. *The Denial of Death*. New York: The Free Press.
Bloch, Maurice, and Jonathan Parry, eds. 1982. *Death and the Regeneration of Life*. Cambridge: Cambridge University Press.
Bolívar Aróstegui, Natalia, and Carmen González Díaz de Villegas. 1998. *Ta Makuende Yaya y las reglas de Palo Monte: Mayombe, Brillumba, Kimbisa, Shamalongo*. Havana: Ediciones Union.
Bolívar Aróstegui, Natalia, Carmen González Días de Villegas, and Natalia del Río. 2007. *Corrientes espirituales en Cuba*. Havana: Editorial José Martí.
Bonelli, Cristobal. 2014. "What Pehuenche Blood Does: Hemic Feasting, Intersubjective Participation, and Witchcraft in Southern Chile." *HAU: Journal of Ethnographic Theory* 4(1): 105–27.
Cabrera, Lydia. 1979. *Reglas de Congo: Palo Monte Mayombe*. Miami: Peninsular Printing.
Calleja, Guillermo, and Ralph Alpizar. 2012. *Nfumbe: El Universo de los Espiritus como Lenguaje Articulado*. Madrid: Ediciones Maiombe.

Cannell, Fennella, ed. 2006. The *Anthropology of Christianity*. Durham, NC: Duke University Press.
Castellanos, Jorge, and Isabel Castellanos. 1992. *Cultura afrocubana: Las religiones y las lenguas*. Miami: Ediciones Universal.
Cohn, Clarice. 2011. "A Criança, a Morte, e os Mortos: o caso Mebengokré-Xikirin." *Horizontes Antropologicos* 16(34): 93–115.
Conklin, Beth A., and Lynn M. Morgan. 1996. "Babies, Bodies, and the Production of Personhood in North America and a Native Amazonian Society." *Ethos* 24(4): 657–694.
Espírito Santo, Diana. 2010a. "Spiritist Boundary-Work and the Morality of Materiality in Afro-Cuban Religion." *Journal of Material Culture* 15(1): 64–82.
———. 2010b. "'Who Else Is in the Drawer?' Trauma, Personhood and Prophylaxis among Cuban Scientific Spiritists." *Anthropology & Medicine* 17(3): 249–59.
———. 2012. "Imagination, Sensation and the Education of Attention among Cuban Spirit Mediums." *Ethnos* 77(2): 252–71.
———. 2014. "Plasticidade e pessoalidade no espiritismo crioulo cubano." *Mana* 20(1): 63–93.
———. 2015a. "Desagregando o espiritual: a fabricação de pessoas e de complexos espírito-matéria em práticas mediúnicas afro-cubanas." *Religião e Sociedade* 31(1): 216–36.
———. 2015b. *Developing the Dead: Mediumship and Selfhood in Cuban Espiritismo*. Gainesville: University Press of Florida.
Espírito Santo, Diana, Katerina Kerestetzi, and Anastasios Panagiotopoulos. 2013. "Human Substances and Ontological Transformations in the African-inspired Ritual Complex of Palo Monte in Cuba." *Critical African Studies* 5(3): 195–219.
Figarola, Joel James. 2006. *La brujería cubana: El Palo Monte*. Santiago de Cuba: Editorial Oriente.
Fuentes Guerra, Jesus, and Grisel Gomez. 1996. *Cultos Afrocubanos: Un estudio etnolingüística*. Havana: Editorial Ciencias Sociales.
Goldman, Marcio. 2007. "How to Learn in an Afro-Brazilian Spirit Possession Religion: Ontology and Multiplicity in Candomblé." In *Learning Religion: Anthropological Approaches*, ed. David Berliner and Ramon Sarró, 103–20. New York: Berghahn Books.
Hertz, Robert. (1907) 2009. *Death and the Right Hand*. Aberdeen: Cohen and West.
Kaufman, Sharon, and Lynn Morgan. 2005. "The Anthropology of the Beginnings and Ends of
Life." *Annual Review of Anthropology* 34: 317–41.
McCallum, Cecilia. 1999. "Consuming Pity: The Production of Death among the Cashinahua." *Cultural Anthropology* 14(4): 443–71.
Miller, Daniel, ed. 2005. *Materiality*. Durham, NC: Duke University Press.
Millet, José. 1996. *El Espiritismo: Variantes Cubanas*. Santiago de Cuba: Editorial Oriente.
Morris, Brian. 1994. *Anthropology of the Self: The Individual in Cultural Perspective*. London: Pluto Press.
Murphy, Nancey. 2006. *Bodies and Souls, or Spirited Bodies?* Cambridge: Cambridge University Press.

Ochoa, Todd. R. 2007. "Versions of the Dead: *Kalunga,* Cuban-Kongo Materiality, and Ethnography." *Cultural Anthropology* 22(4): 473–500.
_____. 2010. "Prendas-Ngangas-Enquisos: Turbulence and the Influence of the Dead in Cuban Kongo Material Culture." *Cultural Anthropology* 25(3): 387–420.
Palmié, Stephan. 2006. "Thinking with *Ngangas:* Reflections on Embodiment and the Limits of 'Objectively Necessary Appearances.'" *Comparative Studies in History and Society* 48: 852–86.
_____. 2013. *The Cooking of History: How Not to Study Afro-Cuban Religion.* Chicago: University of Chicago Press.
Pedersen, Morten, and Rane Willerslev. 2012. "'The Soul of the Soul is the Body': Rethinking the Concept of the Soul through North Asian Ethnography." *Common Knowledge* 18(3): 464–86.
Refslund Christensen, Dorthe, Rane Willserslev, and Lotte Meinert. 2013. "Introduction." In *Taming Time, Timing Death: Social Technologies and Ritual,* ed. Dorthe Refslund Christensen and Rane Willserslev, 1–16. Farnham: Ashgate.
Schieffelin, Edward. 1998. "Problematizing Performance". In *Ritual, Performance, Media,* ed. Felicia Hughes-Freeland, 194–207, London: Routledge.
Taylor, Charles. 2007. *A Secular Age.* Cambridge, MA: Belknap Press/Harvard University Press.
Taylor, Janelle S. 2005. "Surfacing the Body Interior." *Annual Review of Anthropology* 34: 741–56.
Turner, Terence S. 2012. "The Social Skin." *HAU: Journal of Ethnographic Theory* 2(2): 486–504.
Vilaça, Aparecida. 2005. "Chronically Unstable Bodies: Reflections on Amazonian Corporealities." *Journal of the Royal Anthropological Institute* 11(3): 445–64.
Viveiros de Castro, E. 1992. *From the Enemy's Point of View: Humanity and Divinity in an Amazonian Society.* Chicago: Chicago University Press.
Wirtz, Kristina. 2009. "Hazardous Waste: The Semiotics of Ritual Hygiene in Cuban Popular Religion." *Journal of the Royal Anthropological Institute* 15(3): 476–501.
_____. 2014. "Spiritual Agency, Materiality and Knowledge in Cuba." In *Spirited Things: The Work of "Possession" in Afro-Atlantic Studies,* ed. Paul C. Johnson, 99–130. Chicago: University of Chicago Press.

Chapter 5

Sensory Necrography

The Flow of Signs and Sensations in the Corpse

Beth Conklin

The idea of "necrographies" developed in this volume highlights the postmortem existences of the dead. In the Introduction, the editors of this volume propose to trace trajectories of how the bodies, objects and materials, voices and silences of the dead themselves interact with the trajectories and biographies of living people.

The notion of *trajectories*—paths of movement along lines of development—is especially relevant to thinking about the physical bodies of the dead and the corporeal changes that unfold after death. Corpses are anything but static. One of their most distinctive properties is their instability—the inevitability and (under most circumstances) rapidity with which bodies change after death, in ways that are clearly perceptible to living people.

From a Western scientific point of view, the biomaterial transformations that follow a person's death are evidence of the multitude of nonhuman lives that make up the human being. In the wake of the Human Genome Project, notions of the discrete self have been overturned by the oft-cited finding that only ten percent of the cells and DNA in our bodies are human (cf. McManus 2005). The other ninety percent of the body's cells and genes are microbes—bacteria, viruses, fungi, protozoas, and other micro-lifeforms. The trillions of tiny creatures that live in each one of us are not just living alongside us like co-residents in an apartment building. They are a big part of the building itself. Our metabolism, moods, emotions, and many aspects of people's behavior are co-productions between human cells and the much larger number of nonhuman cells that turn genes on and off to regulate enzymes, digestion, immune responses, and even neurotransmitters that influence thought processes and emotions.

What we call "death" ends the life of only the ten-percent-human component of the so-called individual. We-the-Person may die, but They-the-Microbes go on living. In fact, it is the death of the ten-percent-human that makes the independent existence of the other ninety percent most dramatically evident. With cessation of the body's ordinary functions of respiration, circulation, and the oxygenation of blood, the populations of various microbial species change and multiply. Bacteria and fungi break down tissues and release gases. The collapse of the intestines traps these gases in the abdomen, which swells and distends.

These biomaterial transformations are distinct and dramatic. They are prime, empirical evidence of death, and they unfold in a more or less regular trajectory that is perceptible in multiple sensory modes. Visual changes affect the body's color, shape, and size; the abdomen bloats, flesh and organs decay, flesh liquefies as swarms of wriggling maggots take over. The corpse cools to the touch, hardens with rigor mortis, softens as it exudes fluids, and eventually dries out. Olfaction (smell) registers the unmistakable stench of decaying flesh (which could be tasted if one were so inclined). Corpses can even communicate aural sensations (hearing), when pressure from trapped abdominal gases makes bodies explode. (This happened to Henry VIII of England.)

In North America and other parts of the industrialized world in the twentieth century, conventions for dealing with death shifted toward distancing living people from contact with corpses. Bodies now tend to be removed as quickly as possible from the home or hospital where the person died. When people do encounter a dead person, the natural signs of the body's postmortem trajectory usually have been drained away, slowed, and sanitized by the embalmer, covered with makeup and other artifices of the mortician, or burned away by cremation (cf. Hallam and Hockey 2001: 132). The ubiquity of decay-suppressing hygienic regimes means that in these societies, most people have very limited personal experience with dead human bodies. If they interact with them at all, this is often only a fleeting, primarily visual, encounter, such as viewing an embalmed body at a wake or funeral home "visitation," perhaps accompanied by a quick touch or kiss. There is little intimacy with the physical transformations that are the biological facts of life (or, in this case, facts of death) in the postmortem human condition.

Very different sensory regimes accompany death in certain other traditions, however. In this chapter, I examine death rites that press living mourners into close encounters with corpses as they change and decay. My focus is on living people's sensory experiences of the tangible (physical, material) changes that bodies undergo after death. I ask how these sensations interact with the social-emotional dynamics and discursive meanings that surround the cultural managements of death and mourning in particular times and places.

This project of sensory necrography is inspired by what I have learned from the Wari', a population of more than four thousand Chapkuran-speaking people with whom I have worked since the 1980s. Wari' live in the Brazilian rainforest, in the state of Rondônia, on blackwater tributaries of the Mamoré and Madeira rivers that form the border between Brazil and Bolivia[1]. Until the 1960s, they lived almost entirely independent of Brazilian society. In that self-contained, precontact world, their funeral rituals engaged bereaved Wari' and their communities in intimate interactions with the bodies of their dead. From the moment someone dies until the time when the corpse is finally disposed of, close kin gather around, holding their dead loved one in their arms. Day and night, the body is the constant focus of attention, caresses, and ritual action. Relatives hug the corpse and press themselves against it as they cry and keen and eulogize the deceased. People express their grief and honor the deceased with spontaneous, ritualized gestures that involve holding and manipulating the body.

In traditional, precontact funerals, Wari' kept the body intact for three days while the family held it, crying and acting out their grief. With tropical heat and humidity, decay was usually well-advanced by the time it was taken from the arms of its kin to be roasted. Wari' detest unpleasant smells, especially the odor of rotting flesh. But funerals surrounded everyone in a repulsive stench that, elders say, clung to their hair and skin and seemed to lodge in the back of the throat.

At dusk on the third day after death, the male affines the family had chosen as special helpers took the body to prepare it for roasting. Until government agents and missionaries intervened to stop this practice (which occurred in various areas between 1956 and 1969), Wari' disposed of almost all their dead by dismembering, roasting, and eating the flesh, heart, brain, liver, and sometimes the ground bones. In a few circumstances in which eating was considered dangerous (because of contamination) or impractical, they cremated the corpse instead, burning the body and pounding the bones into dust that was buried in a deep hole.

Wari' funerary cannibalism was not motivated by hunger or gastronomic pleasure; indeed, the lapse of time between death and cooking meant the flesh was often so putrid it made people gag. Yet, for reasons summarized below and examined in depth in my book, *Consuming Grief: Compassionate Cannibalism in an Amazonian Society*, Wari' believed it was essential for the body to be consumed. Dying people wanted to be eaten, and their family wanted this to be done, also.[2]

Both cannibalism and cremation ended in the 1960s, when government agents and missionaries coerced and persuaded Wari' to switch to burial instead. By the time I first went to live with them in 1985–87, burial was the universal practice. But every middle-aged adult and elder had personal experience with past funerals in which they had participated, either as eaters or as witnesses to the eating. Their recollections offer the most detailed and extensively-documented information in the world literature on funerary cannibalism as a normative, socially-accepted practice in a particular time, place, and cultural context.

Cannibalism is the aspect of Wari' ritual life that has attracted most anthropological attention, and it has been analyzed in depth by me, my colleague Aparecida Vilaça, and others who have used our work. Wari' themselves are bemused and at times rather irritated with outsiders' apparent obsession with the eating of human flesh. They see cannibalism as only one part—albeit a very meaningful part—of the larger ritual process and complex of mourning practices through which generations of their people have tried to cope with the loss of a loved one.

Sensory experiences loom large in elders' memories of their own experiences of losing and grieving for kin. When Wari' describe the *feel* of precontact funerals, they emphasize the trauma of *seeing* the intact body dismembered, the intensity of the *sound* of collective crying, and the revolting *stench* and *taste* of decayed flesh. Over the years of grappling with the meanings of their practices, I have come to understand that these visceral sensations were not just epiphenomena, but integrally entwined with the discursive (cognitive, symbolic) meanings, social logics, and emotional trajectories of Wari' mourning. The visceral experiences constitute a kind of parallel, sensory-emotional vocabulary deployed along with the ritual symbols and ideas. Sensations and symbols weave together, shaping and reshaping subjective memory-experiences. My project of rethinking Wari' funerary rites as visceral, sensory experience begins with taking seriously these aspects of their experiences that Wari' themselves emphasize.

This is an exercise in what anthropologist Michael Jackson (2004) calls "existential anthropology": taking up the challenge to understand the fundamental cares and concerns that humans face, asking how people are both acted upon by others and the world, how they make their lives more viable by continually, imaginatively, reworking their relations with the resources and possibilities they find in themselves, in the world, and in others. The resource on which this essay focuses is the human body in the tangible immediacy of its postmortem physical changes. What existential problems, what relations and possibilities, do people rework through ritual processes that press them into close encounters with the biological "facts of death" and decomposition?

The Existential Challenge in the Corpse

In his 1871 *Primitive Culture*, Edward B. Tylor theorized the that the earliest religion was born from human confrontations with the corpse. Tylor proposed that people developed the concept of spirit or soul to explain the difference between a living body and a dead body. Among Wari', for example spirit, *jamixi'*, is the principle that animates individual consciousness. Any loss of consciousness, such as fainting, is considered to be a kind of death in which the spirit has left the body.

Julia Kristeva (1982) saw the corpse as a different kind of challenge to cognitive order. The dead body, she argued, is a prime embodiment of abjection, the threatening breakdown of distinctions between subject and object. In an interpretation that drew heavily on Mary Douglas's (1966) ideas about purity, danger, and "matter out of place," Kristeva emphasized that the abject is located outside the symbolic-social order. This, she asserts, is inherently traumatic. We know that the corpse was once a subject similar to ourselves, and in the ordinary scheme of things, a body should be alive. But as a corpse, it is not. The dead body transgresses normal boundaries: it is "death infecting life," (Kristeva 1982: 4).

In Tylor's and Kristeva's models, the problems people confront in encounters with corpses are primarily intellectual: the cognitive dissonance of a human body rendered lifeless, inert; the violation of subject–object distinctions. But the dissonance that dead bodies comprise is not just intellectual, nor related only to inanimacy. Corpses challenge people's sensibilities with their tangible instability and (often quite rapid) transformation into forms and substances unlike any living body. In doing so, they evoke powerful *visceral* responses.

The existential challenge that Wari' address in their death rituals is the age-old question of how to turn loss into a renewal of social life. How to help bereaved survivors regain some emotional tranquility, so they eventually will be able to remake their lives, do productive work, and re-engage with others? In the ritual processes with which they structure mourners' embodied experiences, Wari' have drawn on the power of intense sensory experiences, including intimate, immersive encounters with the tangible trajectories of dead bodies as they move through states of decay and transformation. Cannibalism was a first step in this process.

Cannibalism as Memory-Work

Multiple meanings and motives converged in the former Wari' practice of consuming their dead. This began with the fact that cannibalism offered a positive alternative to the barbarism of burial. Wari' considered cannibalism to be the most respectful and loving way to treat a human body. They think of the ground as cold, wet, and polluting; no self-respecting adult would sit directly on the earth. The idea of abandoning a loved one's body to lie alone and rot in the dirt was unthinkable. Consuming the body saved the dead and their families from that indignity.

Eating the dead was a matter of duty, not desire. Death puts Wari' kin relations and social commitments on display like no other event. The main social distinction at play in funerals is between the dead person's close, blood relatives (consanguines, called *iri' nari*), and their in-laws (affines, called *nari paxi'*), that is, the people related to the deceased by marriage. The dead person's spouse is considered to be *iri' nari*, made into a blood relatives by the merging of blood and body substance that married couples develop over time in exchanging sexual fluids. At funerals, others who are not related to the dead person by either blood or marriage participate alongside the affines.

In the traditional funerals of the past, grieving *iri' nari*, the blood kin and spouse, cried and watched as male affines (*nari paxi'*) whom the family had chosen as special helpers carefully dismembered the corpse and placed the body parts on an open grill. Female affines prepared the dense, unleavened maize bread Wari' call *kapam* (*pamonha* in the regional Portuguese). When these were well-roasted, the close kin (*iri' nari*) took the body parts, separated the flesh from the bones, and offered pieces to the affines and other nonrelatives. They insisted that the others eat as the family watched.

Wari' think of cannibalism as a service that affines performed to help the dead person's close blood kin. One of the prime obligations that came with marriage was the responsibility to eat one's in-laws when they died. Wari' regard this service of eating the body as a practice of care for the person's living survivors. They recognize that the loss of a loved one leaves a wrenching wound that cries for healing. They mobilize social support for the bereaved family, beginning with the funeral where everyone cries and keens in sympathy with the dead person's kin and their suffering. The overall trajectory of Wari' rites of death and mourning is a year-long process whose explicit aim is to help mourners eventually return to productive social life. To achieve a healthy resolution to mourning, Wari' believe that emotional attachments must gradually be attenuated and replaced with new images of a transformed relationship with the spirit of the deceased. Over the course of the year of formal mourning, this process of detachment and transformation is acted out, first on the dead person's physical body, then on other tangible elements of the person's former life, and finally on imagined images of the person's spirit integrated into the underworld where the Wari' ancestors dwell.

Wari' have a well-developed theory of how sensory stimuli interact with memory and emotion to affect bodily states and health. They emphasize the power of sensation—a sight, the sound of a name, a familiar fragrance, a posture or gesture—to evoke memories that spark sadness. They say that when people dwell in their memories, thinking constantly about lost loved ones, this prolonged sadness constricts their heart and weakens their blood. The person grows thin, weak, and pale; they waste away and may even, as Wari' say, "die of sadness."

To help bereaved individuals gradually detach from their memories of the dead, Wari' try to eradicate tangible reminders of the dead person from the social and physical environment. Traditionally, this began with the erasure of the body itself, which is the most direct and tangible reminder of who the person was in life. In the past and continuing today, they burn the dead person's house, all of their possessions, and any crops they planted or harvested. They change the appearance of neighboring houses and reorient village paths so the place "looks completely different." And in the months after a death, senior kin perform a solitary ritual called *ton ho'*, sweeping, which is like a kind of walking meditation. In *ton ho'*, the person makes a series of trips to the forest, seeking out places that bring back memories of the deceased. This might be a log where the dead person liked to sit, a tree that a woman chopped down to harvest fruit, a Brazil grove where a family camped. At each memory-rich site, they think intensely about their lost loved one, honoring his or her life as they slowly cut the vegetation in a broad circle. Later, they return to burn and ritually sweep over the site, "finishing" the memories.

For Wari', the work of mourning is primarily memory-work, based in recognition of the inseparability of emotion and embodied experience. As Nadia Seremetakis observed in a very different context, "Memory cannot be confined to a purely mentalist or subjective sphere. It is a culturally mediated practice that is activated by embodied acts and semantically dense objects" (1996: 9). Wari' emphasize how embodied sensation shapes subjectivity. An indigenous theory of how sensory stimuli affect emotion and health undergirds their emphasis on destroying and transforming tangible reminders of the dead. In traditional funerals, seeing the body be consumed impressed upon the dead person's kin the finality of the death and the irreversibility of their changed relations with the deceased.

Dissonance, Decay, and Transformation

If we think of Wari' death rites as Wari' themselves do, as social tools or technologies for shaping mourners' emotional responses by controlling and structuring their exposures to sensory stimuli, this helps make sense of an unusual aspect of their traditional (precontact) funeral practices: the purposeful immersion in decay. Wari' explain the three-day delay in disposing of the corpse as a matter of both respect and practicality. They say the family needed time to fully remember, eulogize, and honor the dead person and his or her life. And this also allowed time for messengers to carry news of the death to relatives in distant villages, and locate those who were away in the forest hunting or foraging. Wari' did not use canoes precontact, so everyone had to travel on foot. To see (*kerek*) is to know. Wari' say it is essential for all close kin to arrive at the funeral and have the opportunity to *see* the body of their deceased relative. If someone was unable to attend the funeral, a male affine would sometimes save a body part to carry later to the absent kinsperson, then eat it in front of their eyes, so the kinsperson could witness this.

The sights and smells of bodies decaying, being dismembered, and roasting, loom large in Wari' memories and accounts of traditional funerals. This drawing (Figure 5.1) is a Wari' artist's portrait of the moment when the corpse has been removed from its relatives' arms to be prepared for disposal. This drawing was made by Wem Quirio' Oro Eo' in 1987, when he was twenty-two years old. He was too young to have witnessed precontact funerals himself; he based his drawing on the stories he had heard from his parents, grandparents, and other relatives. As I have described elsewhere, we showed his drawings to older people in the community to elicit their comments and critiques (Conklin 2001a). Aside from the ersatz loincloth (which his mother insisted he add for modesty's sake) and the over-use of red feathers (which he added because he likes how they look), everyone we consulted approved of the details in Wem Quirio's rendition.

His drawing highlights several features that Wari' emphasize when they describe how bodies change after death: the jaundiced color of the flesh (represented by his use of yellow), the involuntary evacuation of the bowels (shown in the brown heap on the mat), and the gross bloating of the abdomen which is filled with foul-smelling gases. (The man standing in the middle holds a palm-leaf fan to waft away the stench.) Wari'

Figure 5.1 A drawing by Wem Quirio' Oro Eo' of Posto Indígena Santo André, based on elders' accounts of precontact funerals. From the author's collection.

also describe internal changes, such as the way blood separates into clear serum and the dark, viscous substance they call *tarakixi'*, which Western medicine recognizes as the clotted coagulum of red blood cells.

The swelling of the corpse's abdomen that is so prominent in Wem Quirio's illustration is an image that resonates through several, linked domains of Wari' biology, cosmology, ritual, and symbolism. These include the swelling bellies of pregnant women; of warriors undergoing the health-enhancing ritual disciplines after killing an enemy, which are analogous in certain ways to female fertility and gestation (see Conklin 2001b); and images of human spirits when they are first received in the underworld and pass through a state called *itam*, which is analogous to the warriors' belly-swelling ritual transformation. Wari' see the bloating of the corpse during the funeral as a sign that in the underworld, the person's spirit is undergoing the perfecting transformation that warriors' undergo in the post-homicide ritual. In life, the warrior's ritual belly-swelling bestows health, growth, and longevity. In the underworld, the spirit's analogous ritual transformation bestows immortality. The earthly putrefaction of the corpse is the sign that this is happening in the underworld. It is a negative mirror to the simultaneous, parallel process in the spirit world from which the newly-made ancestor emerges as a perfect, beautiful, immortal being in the prime of youth and health. In funerals, the trauma of dismemberment and disgust of immersion in decay were preludes to the promise that the dead person's spirit would be reborn as an immortal being.

Smell

When older Wari' describe their personal experiences of participating in traditional funerals, it is the stench of decaying flesh they recall most viscerally. People talk about how the foul odor permeated their hair, clung to their skin, seemed to lodge in the back of the throat. They describe the smell as invasive, penetrating—images that express the sense of a force emanating from the corpse and invading the bodies of living individuals.

In decomposing, bodies impose themselves on the living. In contrast to unwelcome sights, which can be avoided by averting one's eyes, odor is unavoidable. Death-odor permeates its surroundings. As Monica Casper and Lisa Jean Moore (2009: 16) observe, although bodies are social objects—created, maintained, and thoroughly enmeshed in human relations—they also retain corporeal agendas of their own. Similarly, while Alfred Gell's (1998) well-known model describes how objects come to have agency through their embeddedness in social relations, the experience of agency in the corpse derives also from people's sensory interactions with its biological properties—the tangible effects of the ongoing lives of its microbial co-constituents.

In traditional funerals, when it came time to eat, the flesh often was so rotten that people could barely stomach it. Teenage girls and women were allowed to excuse themselves from eating and "help" the family by crying instead. Adult men could not. Male elders recall how they would slowly eat a little, then excuse themselves to go to the forest and vomit in private. Then they would return to the funeral and force themselves to swallow a bit more.

The ideal was for all the flesh be consumed by dawn. In practice, it often was so rotten this was simply not possible. When the sun rose, whatever remained uneaten was burned, scooped into a hole in the floor of the house where the funeral was held, pounded into dust with a log, and covered over with earth swept smooth. The goal was to leave no trace of the funeral nor of the dead person's former presence.

Regardless of whether they participated as eaters or as witnesses to the eating, everyone present was immersed in the overwhelming odor of decay. When the funeral ended and they could leave, Wari' say they were careful to walk slowly, with dignity, out of the village. As soon as they were out of sight, they ran to the nearest stream to bathe and bathe, scrubbing their skin and hair, pouring water over themselves, rinsing their mouths to try to get rid of the nauseating smell and taste.

The immersion in revolting exposures to decaying corpses that seems like such an odd aspect of Wari' practices reflects practices found elsewhere in some parts of native lowland South America. In one pattern, associated mostly with small, relatively egalitarian groups, the cultural management of death emphasizes creating emotional and metaphysical distance between the dead and the living by acting upon tangible traces of the dead[3]. Commonly, people burn the dead person's house and possessions and avoid speaking their name. In some societies, people say they do this to drive away the dead person's spirit or ghost. Others, including the Wari', give more psychological explanations. They say material destruction and transformation help ease the pain of bereaved kin, by eradicating tangible reminders that provoke sorrow.

Like Wari', other Amazonian systems that emphasize letting go of attachments also use decaying corpses as a symbolic focus. Anne Christine Taylor (1993) observes that one common approach is to emphasize how the visual appearance of the spirit changes after death, so that the ancestors look different from how they looked in life—either more beautiful and physically perfect, or changed into terrifying ghosts. Another approach is to bombard mourners with detailed accounts of bodily decomposition, in death-songs and chants that go into gruesome, repetitive detail about rotting corpses. Still another strategy is to place mourners in direct encounters with decaying corpses, or with remains exhumed to be cleaned or painted for secondary reburial. The Wari' approach was even more direct: dismembering, cooking, and eating or burning the corpse before the eyes of the person's kin.

Of all the signs that differentiated human flesh from animal meat in Wari' praxis, putrescence was most definitive. Wari' value meat highly; they always roast game quickly and would never let meat spoil. And they detest bad smells. Yet, allowing corpses to decay immersed everyone in the polluting stench of death. This was a radical inversion of ordinary daily life, a clear marker of the fact that this was no ordinary act of eating. It also guaranteed that no one ate with gusto or pleasure, which was a prime concern.

In the symbolism and scripted performances of traditional Wari' funerals, a host of practices, gestures, and verbal statements highlighted parallels between the human body and animal meat. Close relatives, the *iri' nari*, invoked kinship and meat-sharing to persuade affines to consume the flesh: they spoke as if the flesh was *not* human but ordinary meat. Yet at the same time, the personhood and social connections of the deceased were highlighted throughout the funeral. This cognitive/sensory dissonance—the contradiction of flesh that both is and is not like meat—is the well-spring of the symbolic trajectory along which their dead move out of the world of living meat-eaters and into the otherworld of ancestor spirits that become animals. The ancestor-animals offer themselves as food for the living, continuing the bonds of care and feeding that are the essence of Wari' family life.

Sound

Vision, hearing, and smell are the senses Wari' emphasize most, as sources of knowledge and shapers of subjectivity. Funerals are replete with intense, prolonged, immersive exposures to stimuli in these registers—dissonance and sensory overload—that are then followed by their cessation and a return to normalcy.

Sound is a powerful element in Wari' funerals that amplifies emotional intensity and the sense of separation from ordinary daily life. When someone is dying, people crowd around the deathbed, crying and keening loudly in high-pitched, repetitive melodies. After they die, there is a cacophany of voice-sound that never stops during all the days and nights of mourning. The collective tumult rises and falls as individuals express their personal grief and people join in gestures and performances that express the intensity of their feelings.

The noise level is proportional to the social status of the deceased, since the number of people who gather for a funeral reflects the extent of his or her social networks. Young children's funerals are smaller and quieter; relatives who live elsewhere often just send a representative rather than taking the whole family. Funerals for respected adults require wider attendance. Once, when I returned after having been away for several years, I went to see Maxun Kwarain, the most powerful shaman of the last generation of Wari' shamans. The first thing he wanted to tell me was about a recent illness in which everyone thought he was dying. People came from communities far away to crowd around his deathbed. "There were so many Wari', the floor broke!" he said, pointing to a sagging section of his porch. "The sound was huge!" he bragged, chuckling with satisfaction. "And I didn't die, I'm still here!"

Aside from funerals, the only other event in Wari' social life that approaches this level of sonic immersion is *hüroroin*, the most elaborate of Wari' festivals. Like funerals, *hüroroin* ideally unfold over the course of three days, with the culminating ritual transformation taking place between dusk and dawn on the third night.[4] In both funerals and *huroroin* festivals, the village air is filled with loud, repetitive sound that continues, never stopping, for three days and nights. It is difficult to convey the hypnotic power of this ceaseless rhythm that echoes off the surrounding forest and river, pulsing through the days and nights of the ritual. At the end, when it suddenly stops, there is an unnerving void, a visceral sense of silent throbbing. The world feels different.

Sight

Disturbing, dissonant sights were another sensory dimension of traditional funerals. Elders say that for the bereaved kin, the most traumatic moment in the funeral came when the male helpers came to take the body from the family's arms. The crying, keening, and expressions of grief mounted to a fevered pitched as relatives clung to the body, refusing to let go. After they finally gave in, the helpers cut the body into parts in public view. Wari' say that the most emotionally difficult part of a funeral was watching the loved one's body being cut into pieces (not the sight of it being eaten). The family had to sit there for hours, seeing the body on the grill, turning brown, dripping fat, progressively looking less and less human and more and more like animal meat.

In highlighting their pain at seeing the bodies of their loved ones dismembered, and their revulsion at the stench of decay in their funeral rituals, Wari' challenge anthropologists' tendencies to sanitize our representations, our desire to play down unsavory aspects of indigenous people's practices. This is doubly true in writing about cannibalism, which has been so badly used and abused to stereotype native people as savages or exotic primitives. The dilemma is to write about such practices in ways that do not contribute to the "othering" of the people we write about.

Most anthropologists, myself included, who have written about cannibalism as an actual social practice have tended to deal with this by muting or erasing its violence and trauma, by prioritizing semantic meanings and encompassing it in disembodied symbolic-ritual schemes. As the literary critic Frank Lestringant noted, "culturalist" interpretations of cannibalism in general, and structuralist analyses in particular, tend "to idealize the violent act of eating, to shift the noise of teeth and lips towards the domain of language" (1997: 12).

In contrast to the sanitizing, harmonizing tendency in much of our scholarship, Wari' speak of disturbing, visceral realities. It is not so much the "noise of teeth and lips" that they emphasize. Rather, it is the sights, sounds, smell, and taste that are so vivid in people's memories. These sensory experiences were as integral to each death's social trajectory as the discursive meanings attached to the ideas and symbols that surrounded it. Sense and sensibility meshed in the body's tangible trajectory of decomposition and transformation.

Sensory encounters with fragmentation and decay occurred in counterpoint to other intense visual, aural, olfactory experiences that seem to imprint deeply. Although they no longer consume their dead, Wari' funerals and rites of mourning still foreground bodily disciplines and the particular postures and gestures for crying, keening, expressing empathy, carrying news of a death, and protecting mourners from self-injury. Funerals continue to be intense, immersive sensory experiences of a press of bodies and pulsing cacophonies of ceaseless crying and keening.

Sensory triggers evoke connections across time, locating an individual's loss in long chain of other times when other Wari' have keened the same melody, leaned together in the same posture, suffered the same wrenching sorrow. Many times, I have seen Wari' suddenly moved to tears by hearing the distinctive melody of death-keening begin, by seeing a dead game animal, or by leaning into the posture used to express sympathy for another person's sorrow. When asked why, they invariably say they are crying because they were reminded of a loved one they themselves have lost.

Revulsion and Revitalization

Wari' see the bloating of the decaying corpse as the earthly counterpoint to the simultaneous process in which the person's spirit in the underworld is undergoing a perfecting transformation that bestows immortality. This pairing—in which a repulsive sensory experience of the dead body is linked to a positive image of the person's spirit in a purified, transformed state—is a pattern that runs through Wari' death rites. It recurs in the dynamic tension in funerals, between the trauma of dismemberment and disgusting immersion in decay, and the positive promise that the dead become immortal spirits who will bring meat to feed the family they love and left behind.

In Wari' cosmology, dead people's spirits return periodically to the world of the living. When ancestor-spirits return, they are re-embodied in the form of white-lipped peccaries, a kind of wild boar. Individual ancestor-peccaries seek out hunters who are their own relatives. The ancestor-peccaries present themselves to their kinsman, offering their animal body to be killed. They thus ensure that their meat will go to feed the family members they remember and love.

By cooking and eating (rather than simply burning) the corpse, Wari' evoked potent analogies to meat-eating and relations with animals (see Conklin 2001a). This reframed the individual death as a renewal of cosmic cycles of reciprocity between humans and animals. Cannibalism overlaid the death with new meanings and reshaped images of the deceased in ways that, elders say, made it a bit easier to come to terms with the loss.

In treating the body as if it were animal meat, the death rites that included cannibalism identified the dead and human death with powerful meanings associated with Wari' relations to animals, meat-eating, and the nurturant exchanges of feeding and being fed that are the essence of family life, and of ties among living Wari', their ancestors, and animal spirits.

The preference for cannibalism rather than cremation reflects the positive value associated with these human–animal relations and the role of feeding and being fed as the essence of family relations. Consuming the body at the funeral was the first step in a year-long series of mourning rituals that culminated in a collective hunt and meat-eating celebration that marked the formal end of mourning and the transformation of relations with the deceased into a renewal of generative exchanges with the ancestor-animals. In sensory terms, the ritual process moved from the funeral's immersion in putrescence, bodily fragmentation, and the sonic and tactile intensity of collective grief, through the relative silence and isolation of the months of withdrawal into mourning. Eventually, it drew to a close with a return to hunting and feasting, in which the bereaved family once again sat surrounded by an abundance of good-smelling, smoked animal meat and the conviviality of communal singing and celebration.

Philosophical Reflections on Decay and Fragmentation

Wari' funerary traditions may appear extreme in the intimacy of direct contact with bodily fragmentation and decay to which they exposed mourners. But other religious also use close encounters with corpses and decay as a resource for philosophical reflection and spiritual growth. In Buddhism, for example, there is a specialized practice of meditation on corpses and filth. Alan Klima (2001) offers a stunning ethnographic account of how, guided by ancient texts, monks and nuns in a Thai monastery live with corpses and spend long periods staring at every detail of their decay. As part of this meditative practice, they flayed, dismembered, cooked, and displayed the corpse of a fellow nun. Carried out over many years or a lifetime, this spiritual practice aims to foster insights into the impermanence of existence.

In a different set of practices in Tibetan Buddhism, a dead person's family members engage in rituals that graphically show that the deceased's physical body is no longer an object of a relationship. Bodies lie at home, decaying, until they are disposed of four to ten days after death. Most commonly, this is done with "sky burial," in which the corpse is dismembered and fed to vultures (Goss and Klass 1997: 382–84). Like native South American uses of graphic images of decaying corpses, these Buddhist practices encourage people to accept the finality of a kinsperson's death and let go of past personal attachments. In Buddhism, pedagogies built on textual exegesis to link these uses of corpses to spiritual teachings.

Wari' practiced their own version of a kind of pedagogy of the corpse. In allowing the flesh of the deceased to decay and forcing mourners into intimate, visceral encounters with bodily decomposition, they made visible and sensible a fundamental, existential tension in the human condition. The paradox of the body is that it is simultaneously subject and object, person and bio-substance, both like and unlike animal flesh. This paradox is experienced most forcefully after death, when the loss of consciousness/spirit/subjectivity puts the corpse's status as biomatter on display, showing it to be material with the same properties as other biological materials, destined to decay and dissolve.

Intellectually, abstractly, we know we are material beings. We know that our physical selves are composed of substance similar to that of nonhuman animals. And we know that after we die, our bodies eventually will break down into elements that can be food for other creatures. Yet we live our lives, and experience each other, primarily as *persons*, in bodies generally felt to be something *other than* or *more than* just biological matter. When death ends someone's life, the Wari' work of mourning aims to help bereaved kin recalibrate their emotional focus to the lifeworld of living people. In pressing mourners into visceral entanglements with the decay and fragmentation of the physical remains of the person who is no more, Wari' found potent symbolic material to shape mourners' inner worlds. The flow of signs in rotting bodies highlights the necessity to move forward, to re-engage with the ongoing life of the human community in which growth and thriving, decomposition and dissolution, are timeless dynamics in the ever-renewing entanglements of bodies and beings in the trajectories they trace through a more-than-human world.

Beth Conklin is a cultural and medical anthropologist specializing in the ethnography of indigenous peoples of lowland South America (Amazonia). Her research focuses on the anthropology of the body, religion and ritual, health and healing, death and mourning, the politics of indigenous rights, and ecology, environmentalism, and cultural and religious responses to climate change. She teaches courses on anthropological theory, medicine and healing, indigenous peoples, and environmental issues. Her publications include *Consuming Grief: Compassionate Cannibalism in an Amazonian Society* (University of Texas Press, 2001),

"Body Paint, Feathers, and VCRs: Aesthetics and Authenticity in Amazonian Activism," (2001) "The Shifting Middle Ground: Brazilian Indians and Eco-Politics" (with Laura Graham, 1995), "Ski Masks, Nose Rings, Veils and Feathers: Body Arts on the Front Lines of Identity Politics" (Sean Kingston Publishing, 2007), and "Environmentalism, Global Community, and the New Indigenism" (Routledge, 2014).

Notes

1. Until the mid-twentieth century, Wari' lived largely independent of other human populations: they had no trade, no intermarriage, and no peaceful relations with members of Brazilian national society, nor with other indigenous people. This autonomy ended between 1956 and 1969, when a series of government-sponsored expeditions contacted various regional subgroups and infected Wari' with diseases that killed sixty percent of the population within two or three years after contact. The mass deaths and trauma of this period made Wari' dependent on government Indian agency workers and Protestant and Catholic missionaries to get food and medicine. The outsiders used this to pressure Wari' to change their behavior: putting an end to cannibalism was a first priority (see Conklin 2001a).
2. For more information and analysis of Wari' ethnography and history related specifically to mortuary practices, see Conklin 1997, 2001a, 2007, 2008, and Vilaça 2000, 2002, 2005, 2010.
3. For insightful overviews of diverse mortuary practices in native lowland South America, and critiques of anthropological scholarship on death, see Chaumeil 2007 and Course 2007.
4. *Hüroroin* enacts a scenario of death and rebirth that in the warriors' ritual is mediated by a belly-swelling transformation. On the last night of the *hüroroin* festival, some male guests lie unconscious in a ritual state called *itam*, in which their spirits are said to go off to shoot birds. In symbolic resonances that link multiple life-transforming states, Wari' liken *itam* to the health- and growth-enhancing transformation warriors undergo as their bellies swell in their ritual seclusion ... which has many analogies to female pregnancy (see Conklin 2001b) ... and is the same transformation that a dead person's spirit undergoes in the underworld while the person's corpse swells on earth.

References

Casper, Monica, and Lisa Jean Moore. 2009. *Missing Bodies: The Politics of Visibility*. New York: NYU Press.

Chaumeil, Jean-Pierre. 2007. "Bones, Flutes, and the Dead: Memory and Funerary Treatments in Amazonia." In *Time and Memory in Indigenous Amazonia: Anthropological Perspectives*, ed. Carlos Fausto and Michael Heckenberger, 243–83. Gainesville: University Press of Florida.

Conklin, Beth A. 1997. "Consuming Images: Representations of Cannibalism on the Amazonian Frontier." *Anthropological Quarterly* 70(2): 68–78.

_____. 2001a. *Consuming Grief: Compassionate Cannibalism in an Amazonian Society*. Austin: University of Texas Press.

_____. 2001b. "Women's Blood, Warriors' Blood, and the Conquest of Vitality in Amazonia and Melanesia." In *Gender in Amazonia and Melanesia: An Exploration of the Comparative Method*, ed. Thomas Gregor and Donald Tuzin, 141–74. Berkeley: University of California Press.

_____. 2007. "Cannibalism and the Work of Culture in Bereavement: Commentary on Gottlieb." *Journal of the American Psychoanalytic Association* 55(4): 1253–64.

_____. 2008. "Revenge and Reproduction: The Biopolitics of Caring and Killing in Native Amazonia." In *Revenge in the Cultures of Lowland South America*, ed. Stephen Beckerman and Paul Valentine, 10–21. Gainesville: University of Florida Press.

Course, Magnus. 2007. "Death, Biography, and the Mapuche Person." *Ethnos* 72(1): 77–101.

Douglas, Mary. 1966. *Purity and Danger: An Analysis of Concepts of Pollution and Taboo*. New York: Praeger.

Gell, Alfred. 1998. *Art and Agency: An Anthropological Theory*. Oxford: Clarendon Press.

Goss, Robert E., and Dennis Klass. 1997. "Tibetan Buddhism and the Resolution of Grief: The Bardo-Thodol for the Dying and the Grieving." *Death Studies* 21(4): 377–95.

Hallam, Elizabeth, and Jenny Hockey. 2001. *Death, Memory, and Material Culture*. London: Bloomsbury Academic.

Jackson, Michael. 2004. *Existential Anthropology: Events, Exigencies, and Effects*. Oxford: Berghahn Books.

Klima, Alan. 2001. "The Telegraphic Abject: Buddhist Meditation and the Redemption of Mechanical Reproduction." *Comparative Studies in Society and History* 43(3): 552–82.

Kristeva, Julia. 1982. *Powers of Horror: An Essay on Abjection*. New York: Columbia University Press.

Lestringant, Frank. 1997. *Cannibals: The Discovery and Representation of the Cannibal from Columbus to Jules Verne*. Berkeley: University of California Press.

McManus, Rich. 2005. "More Microbe than Human: Relman's Investigations Prove We Are Never Alone." *NIH Record* LVII(24). Retrieved 12 July 2012 from //nihrecord.od.nih.gov/newsletters/2005/12_02_2005/story03.htm.

Seremetakis, C. Nadia. 1996. *The Senses Still: Perception and Memory as Material Culture in Modernity*. Chicago: University of Chicago Press.

Taylor, Anne Christine. 1993. "Remembering to Forget: Identity, Memory, and Mourning Among the Jivaro." *Man* 28(4): 653–78.

Tylor, Edward B. 1871. *Primitive Culture: Researches into the Development of Mythology, Philosophy, Religion, Art, and Custom*. London: John Murray.

Vilaça, Aparecida. 2000. "Relations Between Funerary Cannibalism and Warfare Cannibalism: The Question of Predation." *Ethnos* 65(1): 83–106.

_____. 2002. "Making Kin out of Others in Amazonia." *Journal of the Royal Anthropological Institute* 8(2): 347–65.

_____. 2005. "Chronically Unstable Bodies: Reflections on Amazonian Corporealities." *Journal of the Royal Anthropological Institute* 11(3): 445–64.
_____. 2010. *Strange Enemies: Indigenous Agency and Scenes of Encounter in Amazonia*. Durham: Duke University Press.

Chapter 6

Unanchored Deaths

Grieving the Unplaceable in Samburu
Bilinda Straight

Samburu pastoralists of northern Kenya refer to death by the action it provokes: *lkiye,* from the verb *aya,* to throw down. The explanation Samburu have invariably offered me is that this is because the living person is taken away and the mourners must throw the corpse down. The fact that corpses will be "thrown" is automatically, fundamentally poignant for Samburu. It constitutes a universal dimension of death in a society that in most other respects treats corpses and the memory work associated with deceased persons differently depending on the multiple axes of age, gender, generation, marital and parental status, as well as manner and location of death. This differential treatment can be linked to death's contagious aspects—it can cling to objects and persons—and the belief that some corpses are more dangerous than others and must be positioned and treated accordingly. It can also be linked relationally: in Samburu, parents and grandparents may bless or curse their relatives even after their deaths while young and childless deceased persons cannot engage in exchanges with the living. After dying, their personhood is annihilated in the realm of the public, the social.

This chapter bears the experiential entailments of my attempts to understand for myself, rather than solely explain, why Samburu ritually annihilate certain deceased persons. In the course of explicatory understandings, or understandings seasoned with explanations, I will alternate the personal and the scholarly analytic so that the emotional force of my topic will be preserved, because scholarly writing is always personal even when scholars perform with delicacy and panache the striking-through of their own personhood (see Briggs 1970; Rosaldo 1989; Van Hollen 2003).

As a result of the alternation between the personal and the analytic, and based on my personal experience with grief, I have come to the realization—and this is the nutshell of my scholarly argument—that individual grief is complicated, even amplified in the case of deaths that cannot be anchored in a cultural community's memorialization repertoire whether because the causes of those deaths are stigmatized, the deaths are premature, or for other reasons. In the anthropological literature, these are typically glossed over as "bad deaths," and then culturally specific examples are offered. I would like to offer a language for more precise cross-cultural comparative descriptions that might enlarge our understanding of the ways in which these deaths complicate grief for mourners, and the cultural responses to those complications.

The existential fact of unanchored deaths is visible in culturally scripted responses to such deaths, in the treatment of the corpse and their possessions, and in the immediate as well as enduring prognosis for these dead. The intersection between biographies and necrographies in these cases is likewise challenging in both experience and analyses whether attempted by cultural outsiders or insiders. All of these aspects of unanchored deaths are experientially simultaneous for the mourners. These are shocking deaths, and the grief they cause is overwhelming. In what follows, I will offer a brief theoretical interlude to further orient us, and then I will focus specifically on two categories of unanchored deaths in Samburu: child deaths and the death of unmarried persons.

Disenfranchised Grief

Within the North American field of death education and grief counseling, Kenneth Doka (1989) describes what he labels disenfranchised grief, "the grief that persons experience when they incur a loss that is not or cannot be openly acknowledged, publicly mourned, or socially supported. The concept of disenfranchised grief recognizes that societies have sets of norms—in effect, 'grieving rules'—that attempt to specify who, when, where, how, how long, and for whom people should grieve" (Doka 1989: 4; see also Doka 2002). Doka's notion of disenfranchised grief helpfully situates the dilemma of the mourner with respect to the sensibilities of their community, whether related to stigma associated with the dead person, the manner of their death, their social status, or their relationship to the mourner.

I will not attempt an exhaustive comparative discussion of cases of disenfranchised grief, but I will offer a few illustrative examples. For the US context, in her moving account of the loss of her stillborn child, Cecilia Van Hollen comments that "A generation ago in America it would not have been culturally acceptable for us to name this baby or to utter her name in public. We would not have been able to hold her and stroke her fingers. We would not have a photo album by which to remember her and grieve" (Van Hollen 2003: 216). In other words, stillborn children have transitioned from nonpersons for whom grief is disenfranchised, publicly unacceptable, to persons who can be family members, as Van Hollen notes of her stillborn daughter Charlotte. As persons, stillborn children in the United States can be *necrographically emplaced*—by way of photo albums, public memorialization statements, and even in some cases, burial monuments.[1] That is, in order to be necrographically emplaced, living, biographical entailments are necessary, and in the case of stillbirth, ultrasound has permitted us photographs of the unborn living. Charlotte's personhood has been achieved through naming, unborn photography, and other traces that culture change has empowered Van Hollen and her family to create.

In contrast, some infant and child deaths resist necrographic emplacement. In his book on the anthropology of childhood, David Lancy (2015) discusses cross-cultural practices and grief management surrounding the deaths of fetuses, stillborns, infants, and abnormal births. He notes, "societies have developed an elaborate array of 'cover stories' to lessen grief and recrimination" (2015: 109). Among these is to delay full personhood (e.g., children are not yet fully human) or to categorize some infants and children as not human at all. In the latter category, Lancy notes the practices of the Bhils (central India) and the Toradja of Sulawesi who bury these corpses head down in a tree—both sets of practices intended to protect the living (Adriani and Kruijt 1950; Lancy 2015; Nath 1960).

With respect to grief, Lancy's reference to Denham's work on the Nankani (northern Ghana) is notable; they have a category of "spirit children," children "not meant for this world," who are blamed for "mother or infant death in childbirth and/or chronic infant sickness and, eventual, death" (Lancy 2015: 110, discussing Denham 2012). In Nancy Scheper-Hughes's (1989) classic book *Death Without Weeping*, she similarly discusses children whom their families describe as "little angels" destined for death. She argues that this classification reduces or eliminates mothers' grief, although this aspect of her argument has its critics (e.g., Einarsdóttir 2004; see also Nations and Rebhun 1988).

In her own discussion of nonhuman children (*iran*) in Guinea-Bissau, Jónína Einarsdóttir (2004) argues that mothers and fathers do grieve these children, and that mothers especially resist the categorization of their children as *iran*. Similar to other cases of "nonhuman" or "spirit children," the Papel mothers Einarsdóttir worked with were publicly instructed not to mourn these children. To be clear, Papel mothers are exhorted to forget all dead children over time, but in the case of *iran*, they are also denied external signs of mourning in the initial hours and days after the death. Nevertheless, just as they could not and did not forget any of their dead "human" children privately, they could not avoid grieving their children designated as *iran*.

Important for an understanding of the relationship between the *iran* distinction and necrography, mortuary practices for *iran* differ significantly from those for deceased "human" Papel children:

> When an *iran* child dies no funeral shrouds are wrapped around the body and no funeral rites are performed. In addition, no crying is allowed, though mothers are expected to grieve. The reason for these prescriptions is that the *iran* who occupied the child's body will become delighted with beautiful shrouds and aggrieved weeping and, consequently, be eager to repeat the whole event. It is important to extinguish the body; thus it is preferable to bury it in an ant heap and burn it. (Einarsdóttir 2004: 148)

In Papel understandings, *iran* are spirits from natural springs that may enter a pregnant woman's body and displace the soul of the infant growing in her womb. As bodies without human souls then, *iran* have no place in human lineages; mortuary practices are calculated to annihilate them or send them back to where they came from. They are fundamentally without place, without legitimate living biographies and thus without necrographies. They cannot be cried for or connected to the human world of the dead. Parents nevertheless privately grieve them.

I would suggest that the category of *iran* may culturally displace blame from living communities for congenital abnormalities and chronic diseases (Denham 2012) and protect the living and lineage continuity from "matter out of place," but it does so at the cost of the human need to mourn in the context of social support. As Doka notes, "the very nature of disenfranchised grief precludes social support. Often there is no recognized role in which mourners can assert the right to mourn and thus receive social support. Grief may have to remain private" (2002: 18).

In some cultural cases, deaths may lack necrographic emplacement temporarily, but dynamic cultural practices may accord, or eventually accord, routes to emplacement. These practices offer families relief in their grieving processes. Ellen Schattschneider (2001) has provided an excellent example of this process for unmarried persons in the Tsugaru region of Japan. Those who die unmarried in this cultural context have been denied certain obligations of the living towards them, dying "without knowing the comforts of marriage and without leaving behind a tangible posterity in the form of children" (Schattschneider 2001: 855). Importantly for their eventual destination, if left (unmarried) as they died, these dead will find it difficult or impossible to "attain the transcendent state of Jôbutsu (Buddhahood)" (ibid.).

Schattschneider's essay discusses a cultural solution to this poignant dilemma through the evolving practice of purchasing a bride doll for these deceased persons. Bride dolls are placed into a shrine for the deceased, and other items can likewise be purchased and placed there that the deceased request through spirit mediums or dreams. This practice pacifies these potentially angry dead who had been deprived of full lives, children, and "tangible posterity." After thirty years,

> the soul of the deceased is expected to depart the earthly plane and attain Buddhahood, a spiritual state that transcends individual identity or the need for such human comforts as marriage. The doll spouse, having fulfilled its function as companion and guide, is respectfully burned in a ritual fire or floated out to sea. (ibid.)

As with the dead who married in life, these dead will eventually attain the "generic status of benevolent ancestors" (ibid.: 866).

In the meantime however, unmarried deceased persons provided with bride doll marriages are accorded a retrospective, or fictionally extended biography and simultaneously an emplaced necrography. Loved ones, particularly parents, can enact their grief over time at publicly-endorsed shrines, consoled that their child is "living" in death, the full life they were deprived in life.

> A human-like material substitute into which sacral forces are summoned allows for safely elongated relations between mortal and divine, or between living and dead. At the same time, miniature material images of the human form allow for (and almost seem to demand) intimate physical contact with human bodies, who may touch or hold them. (ibid.: 875)

Loved ones periodically remove the dolls and their belongings from the shrines, touch and caress them, and return them to their cases. "The doll effectively fixes and grounds the restless child spirit, providing a tangible home" (ibid). Eventually, parents can let go of their dead children and simultaneously, of the doll in the shrine. While parents may still grieve, they attain sufficient detachment to let their children go, reassured that those children have become transcendent.

Other cross-cultural examples surrounding solutions to the dilemma of deceased unmarried persons are plentiful. "Ghost marriage" is so well known as to be an anthropological trope.[2] A central emphasis of many analyses of the practice (of African ghost marriage especially) has been (rightly) on the importance of ghost marriage practices for lineage continuity and, relatedly, exchange practices between the dead and living. I would like to also emphasize the importance of these necrographic emplacing practices for the grieving process of the mourners. Schattschneider's essay offers excellent material for this. With respect to African case examples, John Burton's essay on Atuot (Sudan) ghost marriage offers a hint. He shares the tendency in the classic African literature on ghost marriage not to discuss grief, but nevertheless he relates that "Atuot explain the practice by saying 'it is done so a man's name will be heard tomorrow,'" and "so he will 'stand' or be remembered" (1978: 402).

The fact that Atuot memory work for unmarried deceased persons centers on important aspects of Atuot social life such as marriage, children, lineage, and cattle rights, supports rather than distracts from my argument here. A fully socially supported grieving process requires public sanction for grieving, publicly endorsed mortuary rites, and necrographic emplacement that is culturally specific—enacted through the social institutions that constrain the living and also bind them to the dead. When the dead have no place, grief does not become private over time as in cultural scripts for appropriate mourning; it is always already limited to the private and moreover, the mourner becomes linked with the dead to placelessness, disenfranchisement, and a grief without boundaries.

Samburu Children: Annihilating the Unanchored Dead

I relate here a child death from March of 2002:

> It was late in the evening and someone knocked on our door. I opened it and was disoriented for a moment because I didn't recognize the Samburu man on the other side even though he clearly recognized me. Then suddenly I knew it was my friend and research assistant, whom I will call Michael,[3] but he looked wild and distraught. And in that instant of recognizing him I knew that something was terribly wrong, and it was. Someone had just reached him from his other settlement a few miles away to say that the nephew he had fostered for years had fallen into a well sometime that afternoon and drowned. Michael was so wracked by the horror of this that I was utterly overwhelmed. My then-husband left to drive him to where the boy was lying and returned almost as transformed as Michael. He told me how, as they had walked towards the well, Michael stopped every few feet crying loudly, uncontrollably, and then he started vomiting as he walked while the elders accompanying him exhorted him compassionately saying, "*Kogol nkosheke lewa. Kogol nkosheke lewa*—A man's stomach is hard. A man's stomach is hard." In other words, Michael

needed to bear this. But he couldn't. He didn't. He continued stopping, continued to cry his anguish out loud. By the next day, he had exhausted himself into a state of wretched calm.

The experience of that death was so awful, I still cried a week later when I finally tried to write about it. I remembered in particular how we had been called upon to lend a rope to hoist the boy into the grave with, and how afterward, my husband and I were both afraid that they would return it to us. We too, had feelings about death clinging to things. And this death of a child was terrible, the texture of Samburu grief touching us, entangling itself so thoroughly around the somewhat different shape of American grief that I cannot say even now where one kind of cultural grief begins for me, where the other ends. I do remember how grateful I was to cleanse my hands with fat, together with the others. And I remember the insaneness of my feelings before that cleansing as the elders picked the child up with our ropes. I was completely overcome with emotions I can only partly identify because part of his face was exposed in that movement, and he looked so alive. I could feel intensely that this little boy had just been herding his goats, alive in joy, playing like all these others in the settlement, when he had just mysteriously slipped in the mud down into the water hole. And no one was there to see or assist. I was overcome as well because I had experienced a child's death before,[4] of a little girl who—unlike this boy—was surrounded by people as she left us but that fact did not lessen her panic, and I felt her terror move into me. I felt that haunting creep into me right then, and she is still lodged there in my memory, her little fingers frantically reaching for me.

When the burial was complete, we drove back with my friend Michael. As we approached the river crossing, Michael told us to slow the car down, as we knew he would tell us. At that moment, with the car moving five miles per hour across the ford, an elder reached his hands out of the open car window and threw a bundle into the moving river. That bundle contained every single object Michael's young nephew had possessed. Even the calabash he drank milk from was thrown away. And since Samburu do not speak the names of the dead, the child was already being socially erased before my eyes, even as the aunt (foster mother) who had been parenting him was still in her darkened house emotionally incapable of getting out of bed. I knew that the throwing of the bundle was necessary, but it was terrible too, throwing what his hands had held yesterday into rushing water, where I saw them disappear immediately, irretrievably. And his aunt had been left behind at the settlement, with nothing to hold onto aside from her own memory and grief.

Insofar as death impinges on *things*, such as that young boy's possessions, grief and memory may be uneasy partners, as Elizabeth Hallam and Jenny Hockey tell us in their discussion of death, memory, and material culture:

Memories are therefore crucially double edged, facilitating both the sensation of a recovery of whoever has been lost to the past but simultaneously restimulating the painful feelings evoked by that loss. Further, as accounts of the enduringly visceral nature of grief suggest, memories do not simply call pain to mind along with lost presence; rather, they stimulate grief in the present for that which remains "lost" to the past. (2001: 102)

What does it mean to stimulate grief in the present? What sort of grief are we talking about? My mother has told me that when my father died (in a car accident, a sudden and we might say, "bad death"), she reached into the laundry basket and pulled out one of his shirts, breathing his scent into herself. That his smell could linger in that way, even though his corpse was in the morgue awaiting burial, made her hysterical. She soon gave or threw away every single thing that belonged to him, and I was eight years old before I saw so much as a photograph of him, because of that moment when his smell had lingered. My mother had been caught in that terrifying period during which a person has died but everything that marks their presence as persons remains: shirt in the laundry, hair in the brush, coins on the dresser. He had lately touched them all, and in the evidence of that touching, he hovered uncannily.

The grief surrounding Michael's nephew was wild grief, as desperate as my mother's, the sort of grief that makes people cry hysterically, and for Samburu, exceeding the bounds of how men ought to comport themselves. It was also the sort of grief that provoked hard questions. Why should this child die? Something must be wrong somewhere: why else would a person die before having descendants, before their presence could endure beyond life?

In the coming days, as Michael regained his composure but remained fresh in his grief, he wondered aloud about what could have led to this boy's death, particularly given that the boy's brother by another wife of his father had also drowned recently. Michael is an educated Samburu and local politician, but he nevertheless had to ponder: *why* did this boy drown? For a young child to die is already unpropitious, but to drown is even worse, and two drownings in the same family? Children should not die. No one should die childless. There is no way by which dead Samburu children (as well as teens and childless adults) can have meaningful impact on the living—the present is fundamentally imagined without them. As a category, deceased children are referred to as *nkiyo*—something only heard about, not seen.

As I mentioned at this chapter's beginning, the treatment of deceased Samburu differs, in almost every way possible, according to social status and manner of death. That is, social status and manner of death dictate the spatial placement of the corpse, the term by which they are referred as corpses, whether the corpse is given offerings, how the corpse itself is handled, what happens to their possessions, and finally, whether in the future, anyone will remember them. When Christian conversion and Kenyan legal statutes do not intervene, there are only two categories of deceased persons who are buried within or alongside the settlement—small babies and grandparents. Babies whose umbilical cords have not been cut or who have not been weaned are buried in the settlement because they have not sufficiently differentiated as persons to attract unpropitiousness.[5]

At the other end of the spectrum, grandparents have lived long enough to indicate "sweetness," as Samburu put it. Their age is blessing enough, and Samburu want to bury them within the compound where flesh will slip away until their remains smell as sweet as their lives did. Everyone in between will be buried or left exposed in the "bush," well beyond the confines of sociality.[6] People dying violent or even accidental deaths are left where they fell because of the strength of the unpropitiousness signaled by that death. Otherwise, children, young girls, and childless adults are left under a tree for hyenas to consume, while warriors must not even die within the settlement—and subsequently their bodies will stay in the bush where they died. Parents on the other hand, may be either buried or left for hyenas, but even if left for the hyenas, their corpses will receive more elaborate treatment than children and childless adults. While children and childless persons are forgettable—in some cases their clothing and ornaments left on them and their other possessions always discarded—the corpses of parents and grandparents are offered fat, their bodies are fully stripped before being wrapped in a mortuary shroud, and their possessions are distributed according to flexible, but fairly codified rules (see Straight 2007).

There are two intersecting logics governing this highly differentiated treatment of the deceased and their corpses, one relating to unpropitious hazards and the other relating to exchange between the living and dead. Thus, on the one hand, Samburu seek to protect the living from the unpropitiousness associated with what anthropologists often refer to as "bad" deaths, although I am shifting in this chapter towards discussing them more specifically with respect to the ways in which they are unanchored, lacking a properly emplaced necrography, and in doing so, I am addressing the complicated dimensions of grief in these deaths. In the Samburu case deaths may be unanchored due to dying too soon, or because of stigma stemming from their manner or location of death. Something clings to these corpses, and it can infect the living if not handled properly. On the other hand, and in contrast to unanchored deaths, Samburu expect to maintain a connection with their deceased parents and especially grandparents. Since deceased parents and grandparents can harm their descendants as readily as they can bring them blessings, it is important to treat them with as much respect after death as during life.

To sum up, the youthful and childless dead pose a hazard not merely because their deaths disrupt the social order, but also because their corpses threaten the health of their families and neighbors. In contrast, the corpses of deceased parents and grandparents pose much less hazard, and do not need to be handled nearly as carefully. Indeed, a grandparent's corpse is so "safe," that if the person dies in the evening, s/he can be left to rest in the house until the next day before mortuary procedures begin. Important for these dead is that their corpses are fed during the mortuary rites and that offerings are given regularly at their gravesites. These then, are the structural and cultural understandings shaping the differentiated treatment of the Samburu dead.

With respect to grief, while the death of an elderly parent is always painful, Samburu experience that death in markedly different ways from the death of a young person, and I think the way they do so both shapes, and is shaped by, the social status and associated meanings of the deceased. As Samburu get old, they begin to give away their possessions to children, grandchildren, and neighbors who willingly receive them (see Straight 2002). At the same time, they demand tobacco and other pleasurable things because their age entitles them to it—and note that tobacco is a gift that must also be given to dead parents and grandparents. Children and grandchildren readily comply, hoping to get blessings from these morally "sweet" grandparents during life and beyond it. In giving away their possessions, these grandparents are beginning a transition into the passing on of their *nkishon*—their blessed life, behavior, and personal wealth—that will continue after they die. They are already preparing to extend their personhood beyond their corporeal lifetimes. Men and women cherish the belongings they have from their deceased parents and grandparents, keeping objects long after they have worn out, while they simultaneously hasten to pour libations on a grandparent's mortuary site if too many disasters seem to be striking.

What I am suggesting is that the willingness to handle the corpses of grandparents and the relative collective calm attending these deaths—even as people do cry and mourn—is symptomatic of the cultural shaping of a differentiated grief. Grandparents are morally righteous, signifying the moral order at its most exemplary. As such, they closely resemble *Nkai*—Samburu divinity—serving, as *Nkai* does also, as powerful exemplars who intervene in the affairs of the living. These are the memorable dead, the dead who must and *can* be collectively remembered and respected. Causing no surprise, posing little or no hazard, their lives extending beyond death, these are the dead who are grieved with calm tears and nostalgic recollection. The human texture and shape of grief, memory, and the habitus are thoroughly entangled here. These dead are fixed in place, on the landscape where their mortuary rites were performed and offerings continue to be given long after their deaths, in the lineage and clan, and in the memorialization practices accorded "sweet" parents and grandparents. Some Samburu believe moreover, that some portion of the soul of their parents and grandparents is reincarnated, in the form of birds for example, giving the living yet another anchor for their memory practices.

Yet what of the more youthful dead? What of those dead whose existence beyond death is uncomfortably marked and for whom the mere fact of their death may be a moral reproach to the living? For Samburu, as for all of us I suspect, the loss of a child is always horrific, and the moment of the loss overwhelming and terrifying. Comparative examples, including those I discussed earlier in this chapter, suggest that there are different ways to address the wracking loss of what is undoubtedly a universal sense of stolen life.

Unfortunately, in many cultural contexts, beliefs associated with certain dead—such as "spirit children"—do more to amplify and disenfranchise grief than to reassure the mourners. Like the Papel *iran* that Einarsdóttir (2004) discusses, Samburu have a concept of nonhuman children, and infanticide is sometimes practiced in these cases (Straight 2007). However, in Samburu, *all* children are annihilated in death and thus no deceased child can be necrographically emplaced, with the emotional comforts that might offer. The dread and panic Samburu experience simply in handling the corpses of young people and those dying violent and tragic deaths is notable and inexpressibly sad. More difficult than this sense of panic however, is Samburu parents' lingering grief for their dead children, especially in the form of nightmares. My engagement with Samburu cultural practices suggests that nightmares are the most typical dreams possible for the dead who lack necrographic emplacement, for whom no settled, peaceful afterlife can be imagined.

The Young, Unmarried Adult Dead

I move now to my second case example, the loss of Musa, a young Samburu man on 16 October 2009 with whom I had worked since 1992, frequently lived with in the field, and with whom I had a more than typical friendship. Put simply, we loved each other. When he succumbed to AIDS, he was unmarried, thirty-eight years old, and in a car on the way to a Catholic mission hospital his brother hoped would save his life.

How many things can I tell you about the unbearableness of this death and the way in which it occurred? In 1993, he and I had transported the dying girl in my car I mentioned earlier in this chapter, hoping we could save her life.[7] We failed. Afterwards I learned that the child's father owed me, the car owner, a fine for the unpropitiousness of this death that had taken place in my car. Her death clung to my car, and ordinarily, it would require a fine and a cleansing to sort it out. For the person who loves the dying person, there is the additional grief of knowing how painful and disorienting it must be, to die in movement on a rough dirt road. Every bump, every jolt, must be torturous, must make the body into a balloon, stretched taut with pain. And we, the living, think about this. Moreover, if dying on the road, in a car, like the little girl whose death we painfully witnessed together, were not unpropitiousness enough, Musa died of AIDS, a disease that still provokes horror and causes stigma in northern Kenya. Finally, and this was perhaps my breaking point, he died unmarried. In Samburu, a deceased unmarried man is called *lmaasha*, something that has no place.

There is so much tied to these moments of grief, so much at stake, and such indefinable mourning. I consider this both analytically and as one who has emotionally partaken in Samburu grief in ways that integrate American and Samburu cultural understandings because, after twenty-three years, I have forgotten how *not* to think with Samburu sensibilities. Thus, I am left thinking that Samburu practices of collective forgetting in this instance do not necessarily restore the social order (see Rosaldo 1989; Seremetakis 1991 on the potential failures of mourning practices). Nor do I think they necessarily do an adequate job of helping in the mourning process. Rather, the act of categorizing these young people as unpropitious creates a doubling of horror.

I can still remember the sound of my own screaming on the day of Musa's death, "He hasn't married—where will he be? Where will he be?!"

I needed him to be married, to be propitiously interred according to his own Samburu cultural logic, a logic which, in my grief, I had internalized. I did not need him to be buried, memorialized in American style. I needed him to be propitiously Samburu. I needed him to be *somewhere*. Grief had ripped from me the illusion of choice, created of me a creature vulnerable to unevenly following and defying multiple cultural logics by necessities I could only partially intuit. In Kristeva's terms (1980), I had become abject. I was not simply liminal, I had entered the Platonic Chora, the space before distinction but which creates distinction as possible. Grief had made of me a flicker—culture on/culture off, follow/resist.

That Samburu parents sometimes resist their own cultural scripts is evident in the story one mother told me, and which I have recounted elsewhere (Straight 2007), about overcoming her terror and disgust sufficiently in order to touch the son who had just been pronounced dead. She knew she was transgressing when she saw the face of a kinsman watching her, but she could not stop herself from reaching out and touching her son anyway. Likewise I remember the gentleness with which the father carried that small girl from my car and placed her under a nearby tree, crumpling down near her in his grief immediately afterward.

In the case of my beloved friend Musa, when I visited in 2012, his uncles were still trying to organize a ghost marriage for him, a marriage to a young woman who would bear children in his social name. As one uncle reassured me, "Don't worry. We won't leave our young man like that." They too, felt the pull of placing him, so that he could stop being *lmaasha*, a placeless one, and become instead, *lkimaita*—one who has fire. Elders kindle fire, and in so doing, prepare the world for the life that women nurture into being.

The Samburu landscape is enlivened with the sweet old dead—close enough in time that the living remember them—by the long ago, ancestral dead, and by incarnations of divinity that take up residence in trees, caves, mountains, and springs. The landscape is a place by which the dead as well as important events are remembered: stones tossed on cairns marking major events such as when stolen cattle were won back and redirected towards home; tobacco and fat poured under the tree where this particular loved one was placed after death.

In the case of the unplaced dead however, ghostly voices in bushy places can repeat songs that hover in the air eerily, and pathways once trod with one's deceased loved one can become emotionally painful. Samburu recognize this difficulty associated with the unanchored dead and, in addition to discarding their belongings, surviving kin move the settlement a month after premature deaths (even sooner if the death is too unpropitious) to avoid unpropitious contagion but also to ease grief by eliminating triggers. The increasing trend towards building permanent houses complicates these grief practices however, ensuring that the landscape will be a source of enduring sorrow for the living, most forcefully for the unplaceable dead. The fact that I have a permanent research house led one close Samburu friend of mine to say sympathetically, "This house is *mabati*.[8] Can you really move from here? No, you can't. So it will take you years to heal from this death." He was right.

Conclusion

In posing the concept of anchoring, and consistent with this volume's theoretical priorities, I have brought attention to the relationship between the biographic and the necrographic in Samburu mourning experiences. As I have described, Samburu socially annihilate their deceased children. They throw their possessions into moving rivers, offering as explanation that these objects are *tolo*—a mild form of unpropitiousness. These random personal objects are tangible reminders of the kinds of dead who merely haunt the living without offering them anything good. They may wander as voices, but they are irretrievably lost as persons biographically and necographically and thus even the place where their corpses are "thrown down" will not receive offerings. Their deaths untimely and in some cases violent, these dead are likewise reminders of moral and social failure, of collective immorality and the failure to properly take care. Young people are not typically morally responsible for their own deaths,[9] and to the extent they may share some portion of blame if dying in their teens or later, this is secondary to unpropitiousness stemming from earlier moral wrongdoing in the family. Thus, a loss of footing that leads to drowning is never merely a loss of footing.

No wonder—as I am arguing—that Samburu are disgusted by the thought of touching the unpropitious dead and feel a need to rid themselves of objects that would cause visceral shock if left to be found later. While the unpropitiousness attached to their belongings is mild, the corpses of the unanchored dead are hazardous enough to bring more death, in direct contrast to the "sweet" old dead. To touch an unanchored corpse risks contracting a contagion that is irreducibly physical and spiritual. The cultural particularity of grief *demands* that memory and forgetting be accomplished in carefully prescribed ways. Where it concerns the unanchored Samburu dead, social erasure would seem to be a logical response to cultural perceptions of moral disorder and its tragic consequences in ways that merge moral contagion with the shock of grief.

Yet, there are loose ends here, as the raw experiences and emotions of individuals poke into the present despite collective attempts to forget unbearable, unspeakable, irreconcilable loss. *Ketolo*. Little bundles of unpropitiousness. It is better to throw these tiny things into a moving river, and formally annihilate the meanings and implications of certain deaths by erasing the dead themselves. Yet this *does* not and *cannot* erase them from the memories of those who grieve, as any bereaved Samburu can tell you.

Bilinda Straight is Professor of Anthropology and Gender & Women's Studies at Western Michigan University. She works with pastoralists in northern Kenya and is author of *Miracles and Extraordinary Experience in Northern Kenya* (University of Pennsylvania Press, 2007), editor of *Women* *on the Verge of Home* (State University of New York Press, 2005), and has published numerous articles relevant to ontology, emotion, health, and what it means to be human.

Notes

1. See the editors' discussion of necrographies in the Introduction to this volume. I am indebted to the Introduction for the inspiration of my term necrographic emplacement.
2. See pages 855–57 of Schattschneider's (2001) essay, discussed here for several examples of "ghost marriage" in East Asia. For African examples, see Burton (1978), Evans-Pritchard (1945), Singer (1973), and Verdon (1982).
3. Michael is a pseudonym.
4. See Straight 2007.
5. Their lack of separation also means that it would be hazardous for the living if these corpses and their substance were to be consumed by hyenas. For example, if hyenas consumed the corpse of a fetus or infant who died before the umbilical cord was cut, the hyena would be literally consuming the mother's fertility.
6. This has already changed in the highlands, where Kenyan statutes are enforced and universal burial is practiced. Here, the location of burial marks the status of the deceased. In the lowlands, traditional exposure burials are practiced in some cases but change is underway there as well.
7. See also Straight 2007.
8. *Mabati* are the corrugated iron sheets used as roof material for permanent houses. It is used metonymically to refer to permanent houses.
9. The exception is completed suicides. See Straight et al. 2015.

References

Adriani, Nicolaus, and Albertus C. Kruijt. 1950. *The Bare'e-Speaking Toradja of Central Celebes*. Amsterdam: Noord-Hollandsche Uitgevers Maatschappij.

Briggs, Jean. 1970. *Never in Anger: Portrait of an Eskimo Family*. Cambridge, MA: Harvard University Press.

Burton, John. 1978. "Ghost Marriage and the Cattle Trade Among the Atuot of the Southern Sudan." *Africa* 48(4): 398–405.

Denham, Aaron R. 2012. "Shifting Maternal Responsibilities and the Trajectory of Blame in Northern Ghana." In *Risk, Reproduction, and Narratives of Experience*, ed. Lauren Fordyce and Amínata Maraesa, 173–90. Nashville, TN: Vanderbilt University Press.

Doka, Kenneth. 1989. *Disenfranchised Grief: Recognizing Hidden Sorrow*. Lexington: Lexington Books.

———. 2002. "Introduction." In *Disenfranchised Grief: New Directions, Challenges, and Strategies for Practice*, ed. Kenneth Doka, 5–22. Champaign, IL: Research Press.

Einarsdóttir, Jónína. 2004. *Tired of Weeping: Mother Love, Child Death, and Poverty in Guinea Bissau*, 2nd ed. Madison: University of Wisconsin Press.

Evans-Pritchard, E.E. 1945. "Some Aspects of Marriage and the Family Among the Nuer." Rhodes-Livingston Papers, No. 11. Northern Rhodesia (now Zambia): Rhodes-Livingston Institute.

Hallam, Elizabeth, and Jenny Hockey. 2001. *Death, Memory and Material Culture*. New York: Berg.

Kristeva, Julia. 1980. *Desire in Language: A Semiotic Approach to Literature and Art*. New York: Columbia University Press.

Lancy, David F. 2015. *The Anthropology of Childhood: Cherubs, Chattel, Changelings*, 2nd ed. Cambridge: Cambridge University Press.

Nath, Y.V. Surendra. 1960. *Bhils of Ratanmal: An Analysis of the Social Structure of a Western Indian Community*. M.S. University Sociological Monograph Series I. Baroda: Maharaja Sayajirao University of Baroda.

Nations, Marilyn, and Linda-Anne Rebhun. 1988. "Angels with Wet Wings Can't Fly: Maternal Sentiment in Brazil and the Image of Neglect." *Culture Medicine and Psychiatry* 12: 141–200.

Rosaldo, Renato. 1989. *Culture and Truth: The Remaking of Social Analysis*. Boston: Beacon Press.

Schattschneider, Ellen. 2001. "'Buy Me a Bride': Death and Exchange in Northern Japanese Bride-Doll Marriage." *American Ethnologist* 28(4): 854–80.

Seremetakis, C. Nadia. 1991. *The Last Word: Women, Death, and Divination in Inner Mani*. Chicago: University of Chicago Press.

Singer, Alice. 1973. "Marriage Payments and the Exchange of People." *Man* 8(1): 80–92.

Straight, Bilinda. 2002. "From Samburu Heirloom to New Age Artifact: The Cross-Cultural Consumption of Mporo Marriage Beads." *American Anthropologist* 104(1): 7–21.

_____. 2007. *Miracles and Extraordinary Experience in Northern Kenya*. Philadelphia: University of Pennsylvania Press.

Straight, Bilinda, Ivy Pike, Charles Hilton, and Matthias Oesterle. 2015. "Suicide in Three East African Pastoralist Communities and the Role of Researcher Outsiders for Positive Transformation: A Case Study." *Culture, Medicine, & Psychiatry* 39(3): 557–78.

Van Hollen, Cecilia Coale. 2003. *Birth on the Threshold: Childbirth and Modernity in South India*. Berkeley: University of California Press.

Scheper-Hughes, Nancy. 1989. *Death Without Weeping: The Violence of Everyday Life in Brazil*. Berkeley: University of California Press.

Verdon, Michael. 1982. "Where Have All the Lineages Gone? Cattle and Descent Among the Nuer." *American Anthropologist* 84(3): 566–79.

Chapter 7

The Sociality of Death

Life Potentialities and the Vietnamese Dead

Marina Marouda

In contemporary Việt Nam, the landscape of the dead is an overgrown one marked by a plethora of departed whose posthumous fate preoccupies the everyday lives of the living. This plethora includes benevolent ancestral spirits, malevolent ghosts, and national heroes and kings of the past, with whom the living ritually engage on a number of instances marked in the lunar calendar. Focusing on Huế, central Việt Nam, this chapter is concerned with how different categories of dead are made and remade by the ritual actions and/or the manifest neglect of the living. It is particularly concerned with the makings and un-makings of "ancestors" and "ghosts" that have long dominated the anthropological imagination (Wolf 1975; Scott 2007; Cannell 2013). Ancestors and ghosts are considered here not as untransformable or impenetrable states of being, fixed in permanent opposition. Rather, this chapter shows that the boundary separating ancestral spirits and ghostly entities is fluid and flexible. Ancestors can become ghostly entities and equally neglected souls can be recovered from the depths of disremembrance into the realms of ancestry. The changing historical trajectories of the city of Huế and its inhabitants from imperial capital (1802–1945) to postsocialist tourist market place via the horrors of the battlefield are underscored by the fact that categories of the dead exhibit fluid boundaries and transformable attributes in equal measure.

In recent years, ghosts have been increasingly overtaking the space of anthropological work (cf. Morris 2008). Much of this work points to a sharp rise in ghostly apparitions in the wake of momentous shifts in political economy (cf. Mills 1995). In Việt Nam, a body of recent work points to the proliferation of religious practice and rituals for the dead since the introduction of market reforms (đổi mới) in the mid-1980s (Fjelstad and Nguyên 2006; Taylor 2007; Leshkowich 2008; Malarney 2007; Tai 2001). In this context, ghosts served anthropologists as enchanted vehicles through which to explore how the living come to terms with the memory and trauma of war, past animosities, and the challenges of neoliberal economics. Focusing on the ritual commemoration of the victims of civilian massacres which took place during the recent war, Kwon points to the infiltration of unfortunate dead and ghostly entities into the realm of ancestor commemoration (2006), and highlights the potential for the ritual emancipation of "ghosts of war" (2008), and the role of market reforms in creating the conditions for this emancipation to be effected (2007). Bringing together history and cosmology, Kwon eloquently discusses the historical makings of ghostly entities and the changing fates of the "ghosts of war" in the market-driven present, offering glimpses into enduring histories of collective trauma and current ritual efforts in reconciliation (see also Feuchtwang 2011).

Anthropologists' insights on the significance of war for understanding ghostly existence as well as the importance of shifts in political economy for charting the dynamics of change in spirit realms are rightly credited for their relevance across a range of disciplines. As Morris points out, the "ranks of specters are densest" and "more likely to arise" in the "places where war has ravaged the landscape and claimed the lives of individuals" (2008: 231). However, the rich diversity of historic specters and ghostly entities that populate Việt Nam's post-conflict cosmological landscape remains seriously understudied. This chapter acknowledges the importance of history in the makings of Vietnamese ghosts but seeks to move beyond the legacy of the Cold War, which has often dominated pertinent discussions, and bring attention to a multitude of historic specters in operation in contemporary central Việt Nam. Most notably, it highlights the place and relevance of ghosts-victims of earlier conflicts such as those related to the anti-colonial struggle as well as those of the indigenous Cham who were displaced over the centuries by the advancing Việt forces. Both ghost-victims are equally present and relevant today, haunting the lives of ordinary Vietnamese. Moreover, by moving beyond the analytical category of "war dead," I seek to draw attention to an array of additional ghostly entities and unfortunate dead acknowledged and propitiated by the inhabitants of Huế, such as the souls of infants and aborted fetuses, locally known as "maiden aunts" as well as other unfortunate souls who died "unmarried" or "childless" and thus, as locals put it, "without someone to care and provide for them" (không có ai lo cúng).

Attention to disparate ghostly entities that swarm the cosmological landscape in post-conflict and post-revolutionary Việt Nam allows for an appreciation of the lack of relations with caring others as a crucial dimension of the ghostly existence. According to local understandings the fundamental predicament faced by all ghostly entities, be it infants, victims of conflicts and accidents, or childless dead, is the acute lack of material and emotional support by living kin and intimates, as their connections to the latter have become severed or untraceable. This disconnection and ensuing deprivation pervades all aspects of the ghostly entities' destitute and wretched existence. In what follows, I examine the proliferation of ritual practices pertaining to ill-fated souls not only as symptomatic of shifting histories, changing political projects and uncertain transitions but further as intensive efforts to establish connections and institute exchanges across the ontological divide that death forms. Exchanges and relations between the living and the dead I argue here, are crucial for the makings and un-makings of ghosts and ancestors, and for turning the fates of the dead, marking the difference between well-cared-for familial spirits and disengaged restless souls. Without losing sight of current economic and political developments, this chapter sets these practices within the context of a distinct cosmology and a distinctive realization of kinship that include other-worldly entities as integral presences in the actualization of relations and the unfolding of the social.

This chapter is thus concerned with a case of death as a transformative process, with transformation being the effect of rituals, which serve among other things, as exchange vistas in which the living act as intimate hosts and interlocutors of the dead (see Vitebsky 1993; Ladwig 2012).

Death and the Social

In his seminal essay first published in 1907, Hertz pointed to death as not merely an "instantaneous act" or "physical event" (1960: 48, 76). Since then, scores of ethnographic studies have examined the social implications of death, highlighting the significance of mortuary rites for the reproduction and regeneration of social and cosmic realms (Metcalf and Huntington 1979; Bloch and Parry 1982; Parry 1985; Watson and Rawski 1988; Foster 1990; Conklin 1995; Lohmann 2005). Undertaken in a diversity of contexts, ranging from India and China to Melanesia and Amazonia, such studies describe death as a long transformative process, a transitory journey into the other world. However, this journey is often bound to inevitable endings and a definitive *telos*. Though death is presented as one of many transitions experienced in life it is understood as the ultimate transition, punctuated by the passage of the deceased to the world of the dead and their incorporation to an "eternal (ancestral) order" (Metcalf and Huntington 1979: 111). This emphasis on definite endings and socially constructive closures inevitably threads through a teleological narrative.

Understanding death as the ending of all life has much to with a focus on the destruction of the biological body as a devastating and irreversible process. Ethnographic reflections on death often focus on the observable materiality of the deceased that is, the corpse, and its meaningful signification. This resolute emphasis on the physical remains of the deceased hints at a sociological understanding of death whereby "biological" death takes analytical primacy. In some cases, mortuary practices have been understood merely as cultural responses to this physical death (Cederroth, Corlin, and Lindström 1988). Despite a wealth of seminal studies and due critiques of the "punctual view of death" (Bloch 1988), the momentous eventuality and irreducibility of physical death remain largely uncontested. Deprived of a palpable physical form, as the locus of animacy and intentionality the dead have often been treated as "imaginary," "memories" furnished by the anxieties, rivalries, and desires of the living (Ahern 1973; Watson and Rawski 1988). Hence, we are left to contend with a paradox whereby death falls within the domain of the social while the dead are cast firmly outside this domain.

A set of studies shows that mortuary rites do not deal with the destruction of life but rather its articulated fissure and ritual reassemblage (Battaglia 1992; Tsintjilonis 2000). Writing on Papua New Guinea and Indonesia respectively, Battaglia and Tsintjilonis examine mortuary treatment as a constructive process, concerned with finishing the ephemeral body of the deceased and creating its future features. Articulating a sound critique on the implicit ethnocentrism that characterizes much of the work on death, Tsintjilonis suggests that death is not a "natural process of extinction" as "no one can die outside or without ritual" (2000: 5). For the Toraja of Indonesia the "process of death" starts with a particular kind of "feverish illness," which may last for a long time and "one is not seen as dead until the first sacrifice of the mortuary rites has taken place" (ibid). These sacrifices (re)constitute the bodily signs of the deceased, thus pointing to "different forms of substantive embodiment" as well as different ways of dying (ibid: 2).

Viveiros de Castro's (1992) detailed ethnography of a distinct Amazonian eschatology, that of Arawete, discusses death as the ultimate process of becoming that is, becoming-other, through which perishable humans are transformed into immortal divinities. This transformation of humanity into divinity is facilitated by the forceful acts of others, i.e., the gods who kill, eat, and ingest the dead by way of turning them into immortals (Viveiros de Castro 1992: 246). This ethnography advances our understanding of death as a long transformative process, not least by highlighting the complexities, ambiguities, and unknowns involved in this "metaphysical cuisine" of becoming (ibid: 248). Nonetheless, this transformative process remains bound to more or less foreseeable outcomes. The dead—at least the edible ones—are destined to become gods. Much like the Arawete, the becomings and transformations the Vietnamese dead are involved in, very much depend on the actions of their ontological others, i.e., the living. However, the becomings of Vietnamese dead are neither conclusive nor definitive as they are contingent on on-going exchanges with the living.

In Buddhist Việt Nam, death is conceived not as the end of life but rather as a starting point: a generative and formative process that spells the emergence of an entity into new form. Like elsewhere in East and Southeast Asia, Vietnamese funerals seek to bring about the gradual transformation of the deceased from a bewildered potent specter attached to its earthly form to a benevolent and efficacious spirit that takes an interest in the well-being of his/her living kin. However, the funerary process does not simply mark the passage from life to death to ancestorhood and therefore does not merely *represent* given (genealogical) connections. Rather Vietnamese funerary practices seek to create kin anew, striving to induce a shared sense of intimacy and foster affective bonds among kin who are pulled apart by the ontological divide that death ushers in. If the body of the deceased were to be considered key for understanding Vietnamese funerary practices, then it could be said that such practices are concerned with creating an ancestral body; the body understood here as a set of affections and dispositions that instantiates and reveals the relationships upon which it depends (see Vilaça 2005). However, in Huế, funerary treatment does not center on the coffined corpse but rather on the provisional altar set up for the mystified soul of the newly deceased (*bàn thờ linh*). This altar becomes the focus of funerary practices that involve regular offerings of food and votive items. Throughout the funerary cycle that extends up to three years, mourners gather around this altar to take daily meals inviting the soul of the newly deceased to join them. Through these means surviving kin seek to induce a different kind of intimacy with the departed, which falls beyond the scope of everyday and face-to-face encounters. So, the funerary process is marked both by disruption and continuity whereby the corporeality and relationships a person embodies are formed and transformed, re-articulated, and instantiated.

In Huế, funerary treatment extends well beyond burial and the ceremonial disposal of the corpse as a definitive moment of closure. This treatment includes a series of postburial practices which are critical for the deceased's transcendental transformation such as the first- and second-year anniversary after death, known as the "small" and "big clearance" respectively. Soon after the "big clearance" (*đại tường*) the deceased's funeral tablet is ceremonially transferred from the provisional altar that shelters the bewildered soul throughout the funerary cycle to the main ancestral altar alongside other departed kin. However, funerary practices do not mark a final or irreversible transformation but rather form part of a larger process of *becoming*; a signal moment in the existential trajectory of an effectual and affective entity whose existence is impartibly linked with that of their living kin. The transformation of deceased kin into a largely benevolent and responsive spirit (*linh hồn*) is neither conclusive nor unequivocal and the becoming of the dead is continuous, further punctuated by a series of practices for departed relatives, such as periodic rituals and annual anniversaries on the date of death (*ngày giỗ*). Organized as ritual feasts that invite commensal engagements between living and other-than-living-human participants, annual anniversaries seek to sustain ongoing engagements and intimate exchanges across ontological divides.[1] Through these means, living worshippers seek to induce the dead—who are said to be prone to forget all about this world—to remember, engage, and act favorably towards their living counterparts, casting their munificent blessings.

If the needs of the Vietnamese dead for sustenance and assiduous support are not duly met the dead can turn into free-floating malignant spirits, prone to afflict their living relatives. Therefore, the constancy of propitiation for familial dead does not point to ancestorhood as a given, fixed, or eternal condition. Rather the frequency and intensity of rituals for ancestral spirits alludes to the pervasive uncertainty and instability that characterize their posthumous existence, and the constant danger of being turned from a cared-for familial spirit to a neglected restless soul.

Cô Hồn

The English term "ghosts," like the conceptually opposite term "ancestors," fail to describe the diversity and complexity pertinent to the dead in Việt Nam. This diversity becomes evident in the wealth of local idioms used to describe the dead. My interlocutors in Huế scarcely employ the indistinct term *con ma*, commonly used in current literature and translated as "ghost." Instead they use an array of terms depending on the context and presumed circumstances of a deceased's soul, such as *cô hồn* (that can be roughly translated as "neglected soul"), *âm hồn* (souls of the dead), *vong hồn* (drifting soul, especially of a newly deceased) and *oan hồn* (sorrowful soul of a victim of grave injustice). The term most commonly used is *cô hồn*, which signifies a lone or abandoned soul.[2] Below, I discuss the predicaments of *cô hồn* that according to my informants, encapsulate the existential conditions and fundamental difficulties faced by all ghostly entities.

The category of *cô hồn* includes a multitude of souls such as victims of conflicts and accidents, infants and new-borns as well as others who died "unmarried" and "without children." Often born out of unfulfilling, ill-timed, and violent death, *cô hồn* are unfortunate dead that have no one to ritually treat and entomb their body, facilitate their passage to the other world, and duly care for them thereafter. The importance of "violent" and "tragic" death in the makings of Vietnamese ghosts has been duly explored in a number of recent studies (Kwon 2006, 2008; Endres 2008; Gustafsson 2009). However, the significance of neglect and lack of proper rituals in the makings of anguished spirits, though readily acknowledged, remains largely unexplored. Analytical priority is given instead to the "circumstances and manner in which death has occurred" as the most important factor in determining posthumous existence (Endres 2008: 758). As Gustafsson notes, "it is *how* someone dies that most of all determines whether she or he will become an ancestral spirit or an angry ghost" (2009: 55, emphasis in the original).

The distinction between "good" and "bad" death has been seen as key for understanding death in East and Southeast Asia (Ladwig and Williams 2012; Scott 2007; Wolf 1975). Emphasis on this semantic distinction, suggests an understanding whereby "the form of death and not the nature of relationship to the living is the main factor behind ghostly existence" (Scott 2007: 92). However, such relationships should be understood as a constitutive part of the so-called "form of death," and essential for fully grasping what is "good" and "bad" death. In the case of Việt Nam, Kwon foregrounds the meaningful distinction between "dying at home" (*chết nhà*) in familiar settings surrounded by kin and "dying on the street" (*chết đường*) in unsettling circumstances as corresponding to the distinction between "good" and "bad" death in a "house-centered morality of death" (2006: 12). To fully appreciate the significance of *chết nhà* and *chết đường*, one has to engage with the manifold meanings of the term *nhà*, which in turn points to a multitude of relationships on a number of levels, from the family, kin and decent groupings, to the locality and nation. To my interlocutors in Huế, dying away from home is a dislocating and disruptive death not only because it finds one out of place so to speak, but primarily because it disrupts and affects relations with kin and intimates. In their words, *chết đường* means dying "isolated," "without support," "amidst nothing" (*giữa sa*). Thus, ghostly entities suffer not only because of the violent circumstances within which death occurs but primarily because of the consequences and existential implications of this death.

According to my informants, the fundamental predicament faced by *cô hồn* is the acute lack of subsistence and affective support from living kin as a result of their becoming disengaged. In the words of my interlocutors, *cô hồn* suffer because they have "no one to duly care and provide for them" (*không có ai lo cúng*). The most suggestive comment, made by people of all ages, is that *cô hồn* are the ones who died "without children" (*không có con*) and more particularly "without male children" (*vô tử*) to duly care for them in posterity. *Cô hồn* are deprived of the crucial support of spouses, children, and grandchildren or else "people of like body" (*người thân*) who could enable their transformation and journey into the other world and ensure their well-being in afterlife. The potential for these dead to be transformed from drifting souls to cared-for ancestral spirits, and thus their chances at an auspicious afterlife, are wrecked not merely by the fortuitous circumstances of their death but first and foremost by the lack of the support from kin and intimates that could help lift them out of suffering and ensure their ritual deliverance.

The lack of support by living kin is directly associated with the absence of a known identity as *cô hồn* "have no name and age" (*không có tên tuổi*). Name and age are the fundamental elements of a person's identity with the date of death added posthumously. These three particulars (name, age, and date of death) are essential for ritually evoking the dead, and knowledge of these particulars marks the difference between familial dead with whom the living intimately engage in everyday contexts and unidentified dead who are destined to remain unfamiliar. With their name and age left unknown, *cô hồn* are deprived of traceable links to kin groupings and specific localities. *Cô hồn* are often described as having no "house" or "family" (*nhà*), no known "lineage" (*họ*), or "place of origin" (*quê*). Lacking a house, a family, and attachment to kin and local groupings, *cô hồn* are effectively denied what is considered the fundamental conditions of well-being for both living and dead.

Cô hồn are not only without kin or "people of like body" but also without a body. These dead suffer from the loss of their body and thus from the impossibility of its ritual treatment by living kin that could effectively aid their transcendental transformation. Most importantly, *cô hồn* are deprived of the possibility of obtaining a new body that would allow them to re-emerge in this-world and acquire a life anew. Buddhist nuns and monks—who are often charged with the care of unfortunate dead—explained that in re-emerging in this world one acquires a new "body" (*thân*), "house" (*nhà*), and family line (*họ*) and thus obtaining a new body allows for making kin or else "people of like body" anew. Being without a "body to shelter in" (*thân trú ẩn*), a "house" or "access" (*cửa*) to sanctuary of any kind, *cô hồn* are often described by locals as having "no place (or someone) to lean on" (*không nơi nương tựa*).

The lack of the basic means to livelihood and ensuing destitution is another striking characteristic of the ghostly condition. Ghostly entities lead an impoverished existence without the basic means of support. The orphaned souls of those who pass away with no living relations are deprived of the essentials of well-being, such as spirit money, food, and clothing, which are in turn regularly provided to well-cared-for familial dead. In discussing the fates of "neglected" souls an elderly father of seven dutiful daughters—who was however without a male heir—contentedly remarked that there are two kinds of *cô hồn*: the living and the dead ones. He further explained that living in dire poverty, without a house or a firm foothold in a locale, a decent means of livelihood and the support of kin that could lift them out of destitution, *cô hồn* are like the "living dispossessed"; they depend on the charity and generosity of strangers.

Cô hồn is a term used only in reference to unidentified, unknown dead as opposed to familial departed who are commonly referred to by using the appropriate kinship term. Regardless of the circumstances of their death and often troubled existence, the souls of kin and intimates are described as *linh hồn*, a term signifying an efficacious spirit responsive to the prayers of the living. To my informants, many of whom lost fathers, brothers, and uncles in the course of recent conflicts—some viciously killed in the sanctity of their own house—dead kin are by no means *cô hồn* or ghostly entities (*con ma*) for that matter; they are revered mothers, fathers, and grandparents. In his paper on the commemoration of the victims of a Cold War incident in a community in Taiwan, Feuchtwang (2011) remarks that despite suffering a violent and ignominious death, the people who perished in the incident are identified as "ghosts" only by outsiders. To their families and people of the locale they are "ancestors" and familiar dead. This observation is relevant for understanding practices relating to the dead in Huế. That is not to say that the difference between ghostly entities and ancestral spirits is merely a matter of perspective, a perspective no less that pertains exclusively to the living. Rather the significance of this observation rests in alluding to affective connections across the ontological divide as the defining aspect of posthumous existence. For Huế inhabitants, *cô hồn* are not the souls of familial dead but unidentified dead who are destined to remain foreign and unfamiliar. In the words of my elderly male interlocutors, *cô hồn* are "the ones who came from afar and died here," marching in from different provinces and countries in the course of successive wars. Most interestingly, *cô hồn* are those arising from distant historical settings, like the indigenous Cham as discussed in the next section. Therefore, *cô hồn* are those emerging from unfamiliar milieux, be it in temporal or spatial terms.

Charity for *Cô Hồn*

Recent conflicts and the current proliferation of religious practice have brought about upsurges and considerable commotion among the populations of *cô hồn*, as the dead of bygone eras become relevant in the present. Today, the likes of *cô hồn* that swarm localities around Huế, include an array of historical or more contemporary ghostly entities: from the Cham populations that fell in the course of the expansion of the Đại Việt kingdom from the fifteenth century onwards, and the imperial soldiers that resisted the French (1885) to more recent victims that fell during the second Indochina conflict that ended in 1975.

The presence of disparate historic ghosts can be traced all around the physical landscape of the province in countless dedicated shrines found atop trees, on sidewalks, and outside shops and businesses. The influence of such eerie presences further becomes apparent in a series of periodic rituals. Tending to beleaguered souls is an integral part of the auspicious inauguration of the Lunar New Year cycle, whereby the living turn their attention to unfortunate souls, both living and dead. Throughout the first month of the annual cycle, the living engage with an array of dead both related and unrelated, in prescribed order. First, they tend to related dead, taking care of ancestral graves and altars, and subsequently they engage in charitable activities for the benefit of unfortunate souls. More specifically, the first days of the year are dedicated to related deceased, especially in the context of houses where enshrined kin are invited to "return home" (*về nhà*) and join in festivities before being ceremoniously "sent off" on their way back to the other world (*đūa ông bà*). Subsequently, men turn their attention to the ritual treatment of *cô hồn* that hover in the environs of the house while women venture further afield to organize rituals for the deliverance of unrelated dead with the help of Buddhist clergy and provide relief to unfortunate living in orphanages and care homes run by pagodas.[3]

Communal rituals for *cô hồn* are also organized as part of propitiously launching the New Year (*cúng đầu nam*) at village (*làng*) and neighborhood (*xóm*) levels. *Xóm* is described by locals as a group of "interrelated families" (*liên gia*), which "share the same street or pathway" (*có một đường đi*), a space frequented by ill-fated souls of those who died in the environs. *Cúng xóm* or neighborhood rituals for free-floating malignant influences are organized by groups of families in urban as well as rural localities all around Huế during the second week of the first lunar month. I attended such rituals in semi-rural as well as in urban neighborhoods on three occasions, in 2005 and 2006 and again in 2011. In both contexts, participants consistently explained that the outdoor makeshift altars loaded with food and votive offerings sought to appease the neglected souls of those who died in the vicinity but had no one to care for them and with whom worshipers shared their living space.

From city to village and across different localities there was considerable agreement on the purpose of neighborhood rituals, as tending to incongruent assemblages of ill-fated dead. However, there was significant variation in the groups of dead addressed and certain historical ghostly entities emerged as more relevant in specific localities. Prominent among the disparate *cô hồn* evoked in city neighborhoods were the masses of unidentified dead that fell during the recent "battle for Huế" that took place during the so called *Tết* offensive (1968).[4] Launched by the northern Vietnamese forces, the *Tết* offensive entailed a series of coordinated attacks across the territory of the then southern Republic and Huế, a mainstay for American-led forces was a principal target. During the long and fierce battle for Huế, the city's residential and commercial quarters were turned into battlefields, including the imperial enclosure, as opposing forces were stationed within its perimeter. Although the events of 1968 marked a turning point in the war in favor of the revolutionary forces, the battle for Huế is today neither glorified nor explicitly commemorated and the events of this battle remain open to speculation. What is certain is that this month-long battle generated masses of dead. It is these masses of unfortunate souls that the neighborhood ritual held in 2005 at the barracks of the citadel sought to engage and appease. As Phương,[5] a young female but knowledgeable participant explained, this is a ritual in memory of those who died when "a formidable battle took place in the citadel and countless people died, among them many women and children who were crushed by the crowds as they tried to flee the fighting." The prevalence of women and children among the disparate crowds of ill-fated dead was apparent in the context of rituals in the city and the village alike. In the village, civilian victims addressed in neighbourhood rituals emerged from a different and long-gone era, but were no less present and relevant to living worshipers.

In Lưỡng Nghi, a village lying a few kilometers outside Huế, rituals for *cô hồn* are held by neighboring families whose houses edge on the banks of the local rivulet. In Vietnamese cosmography, rivers and watercourses are auspicious elements but are also overflowing with the tormented souls of flood victims, infants, fetuses, and other prematurely dead.[6] Among the disparate crowds of ill-fated souls addressed in village neighborhood rituals was a particular group of historic specters, the indigenous Cham. Previously settled along the central and south coast of what is today Việt Nam, the flourishing Austronesian kingdom of Champa was gradually annexed and eventually eliminated by the Austro-Asiatic Việt who advanced from the north (see Po 2001). In the course of this southward advancement Cham populations were eliminated and forcibly removed from their homesteads and native land. In recounting the history of Lưỡng Nghi, local elders stressed that the founders of the village "came from the north" along with the advancing forces of the Đại Việt kingdom and thus were an integral part of the fifteenth century military campaign that spelled the beginning of the end for the Champa kingdom. Today villagers extol their pioneering forefathers for their meritorious feats (*công đức*) of "opening new lands" (*khai cảnh*) in a series of communal rituals. At the same time, villagers turn to the defeated Cham that "previously inhabited this land" and ritually acknowledge their misfortunes and troubled existence. The relevance of the angst-ridden souls of the Cham in the present became further apparent when a young female friend wavered at the prospect of visiting the Đà Nẵng museum of Cham antiquities. Reluctant to admit the reason she wouldn't join me on a visit to the museum—out of fear that as a foreigner I might misconstrue this as "superstition"—she eventually explained that while for a foreigner the Cham statues were just an interesting exhibit to locals they were evocative of "people who lived and died viciously in Huế." The Cham are today counted among the multitudes of anguished influences prone to afflict the living in the locality. The menacing influence of these historical specters is unlikely to vanish so long as their troubles in the afterlife remain unresolved. Unlike other ghostly entities the difficulty in resolving their troubles is that they remain alien and unfamiliar to the Vietnamese populations of today.

Ritual efforts to engage the troubled souls of the Cham have intensified in recent years, serving to turn strange anguished souls to less ill-disposed influences. In the words of a war veteran, who led rituals in a village neighborhood in the year of the pig (2006), "if we get to be acquainted with them they will get to know us too." Engaging these beleaguered souls necessitates a distinct set of food offerings that locals maintain are alien to them and their ancestries but were rather common for ordinary Cham, notably steamed rice balls. Another striking addition on makeshift altars for Cham souls set along the river bank is knives, resting on chunks of cooked meat and whole chickens. Knives are also offered with sacrificial animals in the context of village rituals for apical ancestors and guardian spirits. These knives allow spirits to enjoy the offerings according to their preferences, "cutting the bits they like" as my informants put it. Yet unlike the metal blades provided to regularly cared-for and largely benevolent ancestral spirits the knives made available to ill-fated Cham are made of bamboo. Ritual participants explained that metal knives are unfamiliar to the "ancient Cham" who used instead bamboo knives. Most importantly, taking into account "what goes without saying" (Bloch 1992), bamboo knives make for a less sharp and dangerous tool to be made available to unfamiliar spirits that admittedly might have grievances against the locals.

Another group of historical ghosts acknowledged and propitiated in present-day Huế are the victims of the "fall of the capital" to the French (*thất thu kinh đo*) (1885). Marking a pivotal moment in the unfolding of the French colonial project in Indochina, the events of 1885 are today noted in local and national histories. The soldiers that fell defending the imperial capital are propitiated in a "shrine for the dead" (*miêu âm hồn*) situated at the heart of the city's commercial district. This shrine is caringly maintained by traders and street vendors operating in the vicinity, who make offerings and hold pertinent rituals for masses of anonymous beleaguered dead. The unnamed victims of the French siege, both combatants and civilians, are also propitiated in the context of grand rituals organized on the anniversary of the events all around the province.[7] These lavish ritual feasts are held in local and central markets by traders who form groups of pilgrims on the basis of their trade specialization (e.g., garment traders, food vendors, and votive item sellers). Markets are closed for the day as traders engage in preparations for the ritual, cooking a variety of dishes on site, setting large tables with food offerings and bundling up votive items. In Huế, appeasing *cô hồn* necessitates copious amounts of food and votive offerings. According to participants in a village market ritual, the enormous quantities of offerings made to *cô hồn* underscore two things. First, the profusion of offerings underscores the large and wide-ranging crowds of unfortunate dead addressed in these rituals, whose age and gender and identity and therefore particular needs remain unknown to living worshippers. Secondly, *cô hồn* are described as lowly entities who are perennially "hungry," "gluttonous," and "greedy." Unlike ancestral spirits, who are regularly provided with food in the form of well-portioned selected dishes, *cô hồn* are treated as entities with insatiable needs and desires. Rituals for masses of hungry dead are held in marketplaces precisely because markets are considered sites of profusion and abundance, and are therefore susceptible to attacks by voracious influences.

Aside from an astounding variety of cooked dishes , *cô hồn* are catered to a set of uncooked offerings that are distinctive of and exclusive to ghostly entities, that is rice grain, salt and unrefined sugar (*gạo, muối, đường*).[8] The rough and unprocessed nature of these offerings points not only to the uncouthness of *cô hồn* but further to their detachment from domestic hearths and familial settings, and their ensuing penury. Denied access to familial settings and attachments to kin groupings, *cô hồn* are starved of regular provisions and support, which are in turn enjoyed by familial dead enshrined in houses and ancestral halls. As female traders organizing the ritual in the city's central market explained, these three items (grain, salt, and sugar) are meant as elementary provisions "that *cô hồn* can use to cook for themselves." The lack of access to domestic hearths and familial warmth, so characteristic of ghostly existence, also becomes manifest in the wood fires burning next to makeshift altars for *cô hồn*. According to female traders, these fires provide relief to *cô hồn* who are always "feeling cold" (*cảm lạnh*).

The manner in which food offerings are served and consumed in market and neighborhood rituals for *cô hồn*, further denotes detachment and disassociation between propitiated spirits and living worshipers. Ancestral rituals are organized in an atmosphere of convivial commensality. In this context, food offerings are first offered to deceased kin enshrined in domestic altars, which in turn are set as dinner tables for these purposes, and offerings are subsequently transferred to tables for living participants to consume. In rituals for *cô hồn*, living participants abstain from consuming the food on offer in the presence of the summoned spirits. Instead foodstuffs are distributed among participants to take back to their homes and consume with their families.

The votive offerings burned at the end of the market worship further bespeak of differences in the ways in which related and unrelated dead are ritually treated and engaged. The essential set of votive offerings (*đốt mã*) for all human spirits includes gold and silver (*vàng bạc*), money (*tiền*), and garments (*áo quần*). Familial dead are most commonly provided full outfits complete with accessories such as hats, umbrellas, and shaving sets for men, and jewellery and make-up for women. At the market rituals I attended, *cô hồn* were instead presented with sheets of paper-made "fabric" (*vải*). Male ritual participants explained that *cô hồn* are presented with fabric instead of tailored outfits because their "age, gender, size and thus particular needs" are unknown to living worshipers. In the words of a man with a young family who was arranging the votive sheets, "*cô hồn* can use this fabric to make outfits tailored to their specific measurements and needs."

Bundles of spirit money are another essential offering for all human spirits, and variations in currency provide further insights into the needs and ritual treatment of different categories of dead. Ancestors are most commonly presented with "ancient money" (*bạc cũ*) which is evocative of an illustrious yet distant imperial past and has long been out of circulation in this-world. Ghostly entities on the other hand, bound with this-world and keeping up with latest developments, are offered ever increasing amounts of US dollars (*đô la*) issued by the "bank of the netherworld" (*ngân hàng âm phủ*). In his engaging article Kwon (2007) discusses the "dollarization" of the ghost economy in recent years, suggesting that such developments point to the emancipation and empowerment of disadvantaged ghostly entities vis-à-vis ancestral spirits, and thus the "democratization" of the nether realm. The article offers significant insights, pointing to the instrumentality of money in transforming moral and social worlds. Nonetheless, as Kwon observes it is important not to "confuse money in this world with money in the other world" and hence construe the latter realm merely as a reflection of the former (ibid: 87).

In Huế, dollars are by no means unfamiliar to ancestors of near generations, many of whom lived in the dollar-infused economy of the southern Republic. Furthermore, they are by no means unfamiliar to their living descendants many of whom have siblings and close kin living in the United States. Dollars are an important part of reciprocal exchanges among kin across national boundaries and more often than not are channelled towards the care of common ancestors, funding the construction and restoration of ancestral graves and halls. While in recent years the flow of US dollars has contributed to the well-being and prosperity of both living and dead kin, this particular foreign currency is largely considered by my interlocutors as unsuitable as a direct offering to ancestral spirits.[9] Such potent foreign currencies might be part of ancestors' lived experiences, yet they remain alien to their divine essence as *linh hồn* or munificent spirits. Offering copious amounts of dollars to ancestors risks an unwelcome association with the existence of destitute ghostly entities and their insatiable desires, not to mention the risk of drawing too close an association between ancestors and former so-called "foreign aggressors." Furthermore, offering unwarranted amounts of votive dollars to ghostly entities serves not merely to improve their wealth in monetary and commemorative terms but further to underscore their needy and precarious condition.

Generous hand-outs are meant to provide destitute souls with a means to subsistence and brief relief from suffering rather than a means to attain transcendental transformation. Spirit money is only part of the resources required in order to liberate a soul from ominous netherworlds. The most important resource, and essential means for effecting transcendental transformation, is the affective capital and earnest support of scores of caring others. Ghosts and spiritual entities are highly active entities who can act upon their own will. However, unfortunate souls can only escape adverse existential circumstances with the support of committed others, both living and dead. The bountiful rituals discussed above seek to acknowledge and assuage the suffering of unrelated unfortunate dead. These rituals and occasional hand-outs from the living, however generous, cannot bring about release from suffering in afterlife. This release can only be effected by means of mobilizing a group of living pilgrims that identify with the predicaments of ill-fated souls and act ritually upon them.

Movements and Transformations

In Huế, unfortunate death does not fix entities into an eternal condition but rather prompts intensive ritual efforts for their release from distressing life-worlds. A case in point is the rise of a female spirit from the depths of the local rivulet, where she lurked unidentified for three generations. This was the spirit of a "maiden aunt" (*bà cô*) who died ominously in water, aborted while still a fetus.[10] Her appearance mobilized a group of related families on the basis of their shared responsibility towards this suffering soul and prompted the formation of a new lineage sub-group. The spirit made its predicament known by afflicting a junior descendant with illness, causing him to suffer unusually strong headaches. As doctors could not establish a cause for ill health, relatives turned to a female spirit medium that in turn pointed to the anguished spirit as the root of the ailment and revealed the spirit's identity and genealogical connections with the victim's family. Previously inactive in terms of holding communal ancestral rituals, the victim's descent grouping organized a grand ritual to recover the spirit from the river, resolve its grievous fate, and facilitate its transformation into a cared-for ancestral spirit. The unfortunate spirit was liberated with the help of a populous group of kin most notable among them a male affine who lent his expertise as a Taoist priest and an elderly widow whose body was momentarily seized by the spirit in its effort to rise from the river.

Ancestral figures can also become "neglected" souls as links and communication with their living kin are severed due to lack of or detachment from descendants. The passing of generations does not only enhance the existence of forebears prompting their advancement in ancestral seniority, but it can also result in forgetting and neglecting. The changing posthumous fates of Huế's former royal and mandarinal elite provide with an interesting example. In the course of the two Indochina conflicts, many of the former elite fled the country abandoning in the process ancestral houses, graves, and shrines and relinquishing at best the care of ancestral spirits to lateral relatives and associated Buddhist monasteries. Today many of those who fled, return to Huế to join forces with residual relatives in ritually recovering the troubled souls of dead kin and transforming them to munificent ancestral spirits. In the winter of 2011, I attended a grand ritual in Huế that sought to "resolve the grievous fates and injustice" (*giải oan bạt độ*) that had been inflicted on deceased kin. The ritual was organized by an eminent descent grouping with royal connections that is well-known across the province. The leading members of this lineage, now living in the US and France, were briefly reunited with remaining relatives in Huế to organize pertinent rituals. The ritual was primarily concerned with the plights of a young relative who drowned at sea in 2005 at the age of fourteen, and ever since tormented his older sisters with recurring nightmares and disturbing apparitions. However, the ritual sought to collectively address the troubles of a host of related souls who have died in adverse circumstances, some in the course of recent conflicts. The gravity of the task at hand required the involvement and expertise of Buddhist abbots and monks from the nearby associated pagoda that had undertaken the collective care of the family's troubled dead. Summoning the aid of merciful Bodhisattvas, the Buddhist monks ceremoniously petitioned to the custodian of the netherworld (*Địa Tang*) to release the suffering souls and allow them to settle on the family altar where they were already enshrined alongside other less-distressed ancestral souls.

Thus, in specific contexts and under certain forces, ancestors can become ghostly entities, and vice versa. The nonbecoming ghost is brought about by the attentive care of the living who recognize a dead person as a relative. Similarly, nonbecoming an ancestor is precipitated neither by chance nor by the premature coming of death but rather by the neglect of the living to acknowledge a death as the loss of a relative. Within this set of dynamics that are far-from-in-equilibrium, the actions of living kin are the crucial dimension of posthumous existence, a case of becoming being partly determined by the agency of others located across the divide that death forms.

Oan Hồn: Infant Souls

Ethnographic material presented so far highlights the importance of relations and exchanges across the ontological divide for (re)constituting, and transforming the lives of the dead. But what happens when there are severe difficulties in engaging the dead in meaningful interactions? The case of a particular set of ill-fated dead, namely *oan hồn*, a term that refers to the sorrowful souls of victims of injustice, is rather illuminating. To my informants, *oan hồn* are the ones who die without fulfilling their destiny and potential (*chết lục chưa đế số mạng*), thus falling victims to a "grave injustice." In the words of a retired teacher, *oan hồn* include those who died before or soon after birth, such as aborted fetuses (*sạ say*) or else those who left this world before "acquiring a name" (*chưa có tên*), as well as others who died in accidents (*tai nan*) or in war (*chiến tranh*). The latter category has been examined in a set of recent writings focusing on Cold War victims (Kwon 2006; Endres 2008; Gustafsson 2009). Here, I turn my attention to another set of *oan hồn*, namely infants and newborns, who are crucial for understanding the ghostly condition in contemporary Việt Nam.

In Huế, fetuses and newborns are among the most fear-provoking *oan hồn*. Considered unblemished in nature while alive, these infantile souls are transformed by way of their premature and unjust death into vicious eerie perpetrators, who engage in a consuming quest to avenge the wrongs inflicted on them and escape their suffering by means of claiming a substitute victim. The most likely victims are healthy newborns, who are often given an unattractive or "ugly" name by way of prophylaxis from malicious influences. In Huế, infants and young dead make for a particularly problematic category of ghostly entities and transforming their fates presents the living with a set of challenges. One of the difficulties pertaining to infants' souls is that they died "unmarried," and therefore have been denied the emotional and social fulfilment that comes with marriage and procreation. With their relational potential curtailed and emotional state unhinged premature dead are in effect "difficult to engage, deal and reason with," as elderly men and women put it. Deceased infants are said to be of a mischievous and malicious disposition because they are unable to prevail over their grievances and feelings of distress. This is primarily because deceased infants remain in many ways, corporeally, perceptually, and emotionally, "undeveloped" (*chưa phát triển*). A most evocative comment pertaining to deceased infants is that their sensory and perceptive faculties and the vital spirits (*via*) that animate these faculties, remain unformed and underdeveloped. Their sudden, unexpected, and premature death interferes with the development of their elemental human capacities and hinders their maturation to the extent that it renders them unable to achieve their full potential as a human being and relatable entity.

In the case of infants, premature death afflicts what is construed in Việt Nam as an essential human capacity on the basis of which sociality is enacted that is, the ability "to eat" (ăn). The verb ăn has a number of meanings including "eating," "receiving," "taking," and is often used as synonymous to "living." Participation in a series of convivial events in everyday as well as in ritual contexts is marked by using the verbal form "to eat" (ăn), and my friends in Huế literally eat their way through sociality by partaking in a series of life cycle and social events, e.g., weddings (ăn cưới), death anniversaries (ăn giỗ), and peer gatherings (ăn tiệc). Like elsewhere in Southeast Asia, food and commensality are essential for creating a sense of intimacy and relatedness in everyday contexts (Carsten 1997). However, in Việt Nam exchanges of food among kin and neighbors further instantiate a different kind of sociality, realized across ontological divides and implicating not only living humans but also spirits and divinities. The difficulty the living face with deceased infants is that the premature coming of death affects the latter's capacity to eat. Dead children are said to be "unable to chew food" and thus in ritual feasts their needs are often accommodated by means of offering rice gruel (cháo thành). The inability of infantile souls "to eat" makes them unable to receive and appreciate the painstakingly prepared ritual offerings that in turn, instantiate the heart-felt emotions of living hosts. This inability of infantile souls to cordially engage with caring others, adversely affects the former's potential in transformation and their chances in release from ghostly existence.

The posthumous fates of those who die in infancy, childhood, and adolescence are a matter of increasing concern for the inhabitants of Huế. Their growing presence and relevance are traced in outdoor shrines, locally known as am thờ, featured on the edges of domestic gardens, yards, and balconies all around the province. These outdoor shrines shelter little-known kin who have perished before or soon after birth while deceased mothers, fathers, and other intimate dead are duly enshrined inside the house. In recent years, am thờ have become more visible and elaborate often taking the form of lavishly adorned miniature temples, where small offerings are placed in the context of regular rituals for ancestral souls. Most importantly, ritual responses to related prematurely dead have changed remarkably. Previously, infants and adolescents received little or no funerary treatment—hastily buried in unmarked graves. Today a number of Buddhist monks advocate that deceased infants merit the same funerary treatment as mature dead. Such shifts in ritual engagement with young dead became evident on my recent visit to Huế (2011) as I joined again families who had lost teenage sons and school-age daughters. During my initial fieldwork in Huế (2004–2006), I encountered families grieving young dead but at the time the death of young kin was an issue rarely discussed and respective funerals were small quiet affairs.

Currently, bereaved families are at pains to provide care and support to their young dead by means of organizing lengthy funerals, enlisting the help of Buddhist abbots in praying for the deliverance of the newly deceased, and planning for the construction of elaborate graves at the end of the mourning cycle. Previously relinquished to pagodas, today the care of young "unmarried" dead is performed in both domestic and Buddhist settings.

This was the case of a family who lost their only son, Bình, to rapidly advancing cancer at the tender age of fifteen. Upon Bình's death the family redefined their domestic and living arrangements by means of shifting the focus of the house from the main ancestral altar that sheltered the grandparents and founders of the house to the newly set up altar for the deceased teenage son. This rearrangement allowed the surviving family members to sleep, take meals, and entertain in the proximity of the new altar, and thus share daily activities with their newly deceased member. Through a series of ritual and everyday acts this family, as well as other households that had lost young members, strived to (re)institute relationships and exchanges with their little-known dead kin and prepare their unquiet souls for transcendental transformation or rebirth (see also Schattschneider 2001). More so, through these acts the said family responded to the ambiguities and uncertainties intrinsic to the posthumous fate of its recently deceased member: through sharing meals and daily acts of affection, Bình was integrated into the house group as a benevolent spirit responsive to the prayerful appeals of living kin while periodic rituals further tended to his needs as a restless spirit.

Conclusion

The material presented here points to a multitude of ghostly entities in operation in contemporary Việt Nam. This multitude includes not only those who died in war and conflicts but encompass a host of unfortunate dead. In recent years, considerable research has been conducted on Vietnamese ghosts, focusing in particular on victims of the recent war and their changing fates in the market-driven present. This focus needs to be complemented by and expanded in two distinct directions; on the one hand, by including those untimely dead that fall short of explicit anthropological treatment and comprise infants, fetuses, and "people without a spouse and children," and on the other, by reaching further back into the past and bringing into view other historical periods that contemporary Vietnamese are also anxious about and which resulted in droves of untimely dead.

Engaging with the diversity of beleaguered souls that swarm the cosmological landscape of post-conflict societies allows for an appreciation of the complexities of the ghostly condition. More particularly, attention to deceased infants and other prematurely dead reveals that their wretched existence relates not only to the violence and injustice implicated in the process of dying but further to the ensuing loss of intimate connections with caring others. Infant souls serve as a edifying instance through which to explore the plights of ghostly existence. Their premature death adversely affects their development into relatable entities, capable of forming bonds with others. Ill-equipped to form affective connections they are less likely to escape their solitary anguished existence and join the ranks of well-cared-for spirits sheltering in ancestral altars. And so, the case of infant souls, more than any other, highlights that ongoing relations and exchanges with the living are a crucial dimension of posthumous existence, upon which the makings and un-makings of ghosts and ancestors depends. Recent anthropological discussions have overstated the transformable potential of ghosts as opposed to ancestors, who have in turn been consigned to the planes of certainty and stasis. The material presented here demonstrates that movements and transformations are an intrinsic part of post-death existence, pertinent as much to ancestral as to ghostly entities. In contemporary Huế, "ancestors" and "ghosts" are not rigid categories fixed in permanent opposition nor impermeable and unchanging states of being. Rather, *linh hồn* and *cô hồn*, are categories involved in reciprocal implication with the boundary separating them being fluid and flexible. That is because the difference between *linh hồn*, or "munificent spirits responsive to the prayers of the living," and the wrathful souls of *cô hồn* or *oan hồn* rests largely on their ability to engage with and relate to their ontological others, namely living humans.

Marina Marouda is currently a Research Fellow in the Department of Anthropology, University of Sussex. She has conducted extensive research in Việt Nam on topics relating to death and animacy, kinship and ways of relating, as well as to the entanglements of history, ritual and power. Her publications include "The Neglected Side of Philanthropy: Gifts to Hungry Ghosts in Contemporary Việt Nam" (*South East Asia Research*, 2017) and "Potent Rituals and the Royal Dead: Historical Transformations in Vietnamese Ritual Practice" (*Journal of Southeast Asian Studies*, 2014).

Notes

Research for this chapter was supported with a doctoral scholarship from the ESRC [PTA-030-2003-01415] and a grant from the Evans Fund, University of Cambridge (2011). Writing was undertaken during an ESRC postdoctoral fellowship [PTA-026-27-2840].

1. On intimacy between the living and the dead in South East Asia see also Tsintjilonis (2004).
2. In kinship terminology, *cô* refers to father's younger sister, and it is also used to address non-kin, usually a young woman who might, by implication, be unmarried. *Hôn* can be roughly translated as "soul."
3. For more on Buddhist practices relating to ghostly entities see Marouda (2017).
4. *Tết* is the abbreviation of *Tết Nguyên Đán* (Lunar New Year).
5. All names used here are pseudonyms.
6. According to local accounts "in the old days" miscarriages would often incur in rivulets, while women bathed.
7. Like all practices relating to spirits, the "fall of the capital" is marked on the lunar calendar and specifically on the 23rd of the 5th lunar month.
8. Ancestors are commonly offered glutinous rice (nếp), which is considered of superior quality, in cooked or distilled form, e.g., sticky rice (xôi) or rice wine (rượu) (see Nguyễn 2007).
9. On a recent visit to Huế (2011), I observed that in some ritual occasions, small amounts of votive dollars were tucked under piles of votive gold and silver offered to enshrined familial dead but this move was often controversial.
10. *Cô* denotes here an unmarried female relative (see endnote 2). *Bà* refers to "grandmother" and it is used here to denote antecedent generation.

References

Ahern, Emily M. 1973. *The Cult of the Dead in a Chinese Village*. Stanford: Stanford University Press.

Battaglia, Debbora. 1992. "The Body in the Gift: Memory and Forgetting in Sabarl Mortuary Exchange." *American Ethnologist* 19: 3–18.

Bloch, Maurice. 1992. "What Goes without Saying: The Conceptualization of Zafimaniry Society." In *Conceptualizing Society*, ed. A. Kuper, 127–146. London: Routledge.

Bloch, Maurice. 1988. "Introduction: Death and the Concept of Person." In *On the Meaning of Death*, ed. S. Cederroth, C. Corlin and J. Lindström. Uppsala: Almquist & Wiksell International.

Bloch, Maurice, and Jonathan Parry, eds. 1982. *Death and the Regeneration of Life*. Cambridge: Cambridge University Press.

Cannell, Fenella. 2013. "Ancestors and Ghosts in Western Kinship." In *A Companion to the Anthropology of Religion*, ed. J. Boddy and M. Lambek, 202–222. London: Wiley-Blackwell.

Carsten, Janet. 1997. *The Heat of the Hearth: The Process of Kinship in a Malay Fishing Community*. Oxford: Clarendon Press.

Cederroth, S., C. Corlin, and J. Lindström, eds. 1988. *On the Meaning of Death: Essays on Mortuary Rituals and Eschatological Beliefs*. Uppsala: University of Uppsala/Almqvist & Wiksell.
Conklin, Beth. 1995. "'Thus Are Our Bodies, Thus Was Our Custom': Mortuary Cannibalism in an Amazonian Society." *American Ethnologist* 22: 75–101.
Endres, Kirsten W. 2008. "Engaging the Spirits of the Dead: Soul Calling Rituals and the Performative Construction of Efficacy." *Journal of the Royal Anthropological Institute (N.S.)* 1: 755–73.
Feuchtwang, Stephan. 2011. *After the Event: The Transmission of Grievous Loss in Germany, China, and Taiwan*. Oxford: Berghahn Books.
Fjelstad, Karen, and Nguyên, Thi Hiên, eds. 2006. *Possessed by the Spirits: Mediumship in Contemporary Vietnamese Communities*. Ithaca, NY: Cornell University.
Foster, Robert. 1990. "Nurture and Force-Feeding: Mortuary Feasting and the Construction of the Collective Individual in a New Ireland Society." *American Ethnologist* 17: 431–48.
Gustafsson, Mai Lan. 2009. *War and Shadows: The Haunting of Vietnam*. Ithaca and London: Cornell University Press.
Hertz, Robert. (1907) 1960. *Death and the Right Hand*, Translated by R. and C. Needham. Glencoe, IL: The Free Press.
Kwon, Heonik. 2006. *After the Massacre: Commemoration and Consolation in Ha My and My Lai*. Berkeley: University of California Press.
_____. 2007. "The Dollarization of Vietnamese Ghost Money." *Journal of the Royal Anthropological Institute (N.S.)* 13(1): 73–90.
_____. 2008. *Ghosts of War in Vietnam*. Cambridge and New York: Cambridge University Press.
Ladwig, Patrice. 2012. "Visitors from Hell: Transformative Hospitality to Ghosts in a Lao Buddhist Festival." *Journal of the Royal Anthropological Institute* 18(1): 90–102.
Ladwig, Patrice and Williams, Paul (eds). 2012. *Buddhist Funeral of Southeast Asia and China*. Cambridge: University Press.
Leshkowich, Ann Marie. 2008. "Wandering Ghosts of Late Socialism: Conflict, Metaphor, and Memory in a Southern Vietnamese Marketplace." *Journal of Asian Studies* 67(1): 5–41.
Lohmann, Roger I. 2005. "The Afterlife of Asabano Corpses: Relationships with the Deceased in Papua New Guinea." *Ethnology* 44: 189–206.
Malarney, Shaun Kingsley. 2007. "Festivals and the Dynamics of the Exceptional Dead in Northern Vietnam." *Journal of Southeast Asian Studies*, 38 (3): 515–540.
Marouda, Marina. 2017. "The Neglected Side of Philanthropy: Gifts to Hungry Ghosts in Contemporary Việt Nam." *South East Asia Research* 25 (3): 251–267.
Metcalf, Peter, and Richard Huntington. 1979. *Celebrations of Death: The Anthropology of Mortuary Rituals*. Cambridge: Cambridge University Press.
Mills, Mary Beth. 1995. "Attack of the Widow Ghosts: Gender, Death, and Modernity in Northeast Thailand." In *Bewitching Women, Pious Men: Gender and Body Politics in Southeast Asia*, ed. Aihwa Ong and Michael G. Peletz, 244–73. Berkeley: University of California Press.

Morris, Rosalind C. 2008. "Giving up Ghosts: Notes on Trauma and the Possibility of the Political from Southeast Asia." *Positions: East Asia Cultures Critique* 16: 229–58.
Nguyễn, Xuân Hiên. 2007. "Glutinous Rice, Kinship and the Tết Festival in Vietnam." In *Kinship and Food in Southeast Asia*, ed. Monica Janowski and Fiona Kerlogue, 242–65. Copenhagen: NIAS.
Parry, Jonathan. 1985. "The Symbolism of Food and Eating in North Indian Mortuary Rites." *Man (N.S.)* 20(4): 612–30.
Po, Dharma. 2001. "The History of Champa." In *Cham Art*, ed. Emmanuel Guillon, 14–27. Bangkok: River Books.
Schattschneider, Ellen. 2001. "'Buy Me a Bride': Death and Exchange in Northern Japanese Bride-doll Marriage." *American Ethnologist* 28(4): 854–80.
Scott, Janet Lee. 2007. *For Gods, Ghosts, and Ancestors: The Chinese Tradition of Paper Offerings*. Seattle: University of Washington Press.
Tai, Hue Tam Ho (ed). 2001. *The Country of Memory: Remaking the Past in Late Socialist Vietnam*. Berkeley: University of California Press.
Taylor, Phillip, ed. 2007. *Modernity and Re-enchantment: Religion in Post-Revolutionary Vietnam*. Singapore: ISEAS.
Tsintjilonis, Dimitris. 2000. "Death and the Sacrifice of Signs: 'Measuring' the Dead in Tana Toraja." *Oceania* 71: 1–17.
_____. 2004. "Words of Intimacy: Re-membering the Dead in Buntao," *The Journal of the Royal Anthropological Institute*, 10(2): 375–393.
Vilaça, Aparecida. 2005. "Chronically Unstable Bodies: Reflections on Amazonian Corporalities." *The Journal of the Royal Anthropological Institute (N.S.)* 11: 445–64.
Vitebsky, Piers. 1993. *Dialogues with the Dead: The Discussion of Mortality among the Sora of Eastern India*. Cambridge: Cambridge University Press.
Viveiros de Castro, Eduardo. 1992. *From the Enemy's Point of View: Humanity and Divinity in an Amazonian Society*. Chicago: Chicago University Press.
Watson, James, and Evelyn Rawski. 1988. *Death Ritual in Late Imperial and Modern China*. Berkeley: University of California Press.
Wolf, Arthur P. 1975. "Gods, Ghosts and Ancestors." In *Religion and Ritual in Chinese Society*, ed. Arthur P. Wolf, 131–82. Stanford: Stanford University Press.

Chapter 8

"Enlightened" Spirits

Modern Exchanges between the Living and the Dead under Spiritism

Raquel Romberg

> ... if I understand Dr. du Prel's letter aright, he does admit that there are phenomena which imply the agency of "other subjects"—that is, of what we term "spirits."
>
> —Alfred Russell Wallace, 1892[1]

Introduction: A Modern Threshold to the Afterlife

Rather than an inevitable and final end, death has been conceived in some societies at various periods of human history as a passage or threshold to another, often higher, realm of existence. This passage has been imagined in many cases as the transformation of spirited matter into dematerialized spirit, which then may find ways to manifest itself again in the material world (cf. Pels 1998). Spiritism, as encoded by the French Allan Kardec by mid-nineteenth century, is a case in point.[2] This research shows that Spiritism, defined as a cosmopolitan progressive, humanistic moral philosophy, not a religion, has been shaped by the ethos of modern science, social positivism, and evolutionism. As aptly characterized in *Secular Spirituality* (Sharp 2006), this philosophy assumed a world of disincarnated spirits of the dead in a relentless process of evolution that interacted with the incarnate world of living individuals, who by virtue of their free will could follow their directives in order to create a spiritually enlightened world.[3] Its global history includes orthodox forms that have been institutionalized at Spiritist centers, and vernacular, heterodox forms that have merged, in Latin- and Luso-American Caribbean societies, alternative Catholic, native American, and African religious practices. Tensions between orthodox and heterodox forms of Spiritism in Latin America and the Caribbean (see Amorim 1994) have been crucial in elucidating and situating class- and ethnic-based viable forms of exchange between humans and spirits of the dead in different sociocultural contexts. I discuss these issues extensively elsewhere (Romberg 1998, 2003a, 2003b, 2005a, 2005b, 2007, 2015, 2016), and thus will refer to them only tangentially here.

Instead, this chapter provides extensive ethnohistorical evidence for launching a critique of theories of modern death and modernity predicated on the "disenchantment" of the world, which, I wish to argue, disregarded the very modern forces that have reframed previous orthodox and later heterodox religious enchantments within new scientific, progressive enchantments. In this sense, the critique of modern forms of exchange with the dead apply equally to orthodox and heterodox Spiritist practices. What I suggested only briefly here is that various kinds of modernist esoteric philosophies (not just Spiritism), inspired by Enlightenment ideals of reason, science, development, and progress, have been operating *coevally* in modern practices, such as those of Spiritism not only in centers but also in home-altars of vernacular Spiritists. Modernity theories of death have disregarded for the most part such coeval modernist forces in the West, which rejected dogmatic religious explanations of death and the afterlife in favor of progressive, secular, scientific explanations of the afterlife that were both "modern" and "moral." For example, the magisterial treatise on the mentalities informing death and dying in the West by Philippe Ariès (1974) presents evidence scripted around a predetermined modern mega narrative that disregards differences of class, ethnic, regional, or religious affiliations, precluding concurring alternative scripts of death in the nineteenth century, such those of Spiritism (cf. White 1973; Latour 1993). The latter, if examined in detail, shows that the predictions of modern theories of death, predicated on the break with cosmic relationships between self, community, and spirits of the dead, failed to materialize. The same could be said of Jean Baudrillard's ([1976] 1993) overarching modern nostalgia of the "symbolic order," the loss of which underlines his argument about the loss of exchanges with death both in its material and figurative (transformative) significance, as a result of the assumed alienation of modern, capitalist societies.[4] In theoretical characterizations of both death and modernity that stress their disjuncture (Bauman 1992), either an alternative epistemology of modernity and death that does not reject the symbolic order but rather reinforces it or a combined ontology based on the agency of human beings and spirits (as in Spiritism) are inconceivable; any empirical realities that attest to the contrary have been thereby ignored.

Disenchantment is no doubt one of the more enchanting tropes of social theory, a mega narrative that has produced its own evidence, as suggested above (Saler 2006). In the words of Gianni Vattimo: "Disenchantment has also produced a radical disenchantment with the idea of disenchantment itself; or, in other words, demystification has finally turned against itself, recognizing that even the idea of the elimination of a myth is a myth" (quoted in Latour 2001: 5). Indeed, since roughly the 2000s historians have not only ceased to buy into the sociological prophecy of modern disenchantment but have also set out to uncover the enchantments of modernity or the specters and phantoms of modernity (Meyer and Pels 2003; for the African continent, see Comaroff and Comaroff 1999, 2001). Reviving the scholarly interest in European Spiritism and Anglo-American Spiritualism they have unraveled their rich cultural, political, and religious significance for critical reassessments of theories of modern death, as will be further discussed below. My work should be assessed in these terms.

A similar revisiting can be traced within anthropology. Whereas evolutionary anthropologists differentiated between their alleged own disenchanted societies and the still enchanted world of "primitives," the relativist conception of the uncanny by no means meant the exploration of the uncanny in their own societies—even though the evolutionist E. B. Tylor was a habitué at Spiritist séances. Even before the institutionalization of anthropology as a discipline, evolutionist anthropologists Alfred R. Wallace (see Pels 2003) and Edward B. Tylor (see Stocking 1998: 15) debated the possible, if problematic, relation between material and spiritual evolution. After his conversion to Spiritualism, Wallace envisioned a form of human evolution that would include morality as an addition to what he and Darwin figured as natural selection (Oppenheim 1985: 322; Pels 2008: 275). But for classic anthropologists, in general, the idea that "spirits" (in the plural) might concern their own societies, not just that of exotic distant others, was highly problematic. Indeed, Malinowski begins his discussion of magic among the Trobriand Islanders with a short but poignantly dismissive reference to the "stale revivals" or survivals of magic in his own society, mentioning colleagues whose "scientific mind" did not prevent them from being fascinated by the occult, the mysteries of esoteric truths, and "half-understood ancient creeds dished up under the names of 'theosophy,' 'spiritism' or 'spiritualism'" ([1925] 1948: 69). Facts such as these are crucial to my research here, for they help to explain the relative, and until recently almost total, omission of anthropological research about the quest after fluid, continuous connections between the living and the dead within Western modern societies—research that would have helped dismantle the "modern us vs. premodern others" rhetoric implicit in classic ethnographies. This revision would have also highlighted the very inconsistencies of "modern disenchantments" in the West and would have promoted the exploration of selective continuities instead of ruptures with the rest of the world (cf. Coudert 2011; Knauft 2002; Gaonkar 2001; Hanegraaff 2003).

Concomitantly, evidence about the intense, variegated exchanges between spirits and human beings, embodied, for instance, in oral, written, oneiric, and somatic forms, advances the idea that the agency of spirits should be considered in tandem and in relation to the agency of humans (cf. Latour 2013; cf. Parkin 2007). Recently published work such as the *Social Life of Spirits* (Blanes and Espírito Santo 2014) and articles that elaborate on the unique ontology of spirits, their presence and materialization, have challenged both traditional conceptions of agency and modes of anthropological research and writing about nonhuman agency, not only among distant, exotic societies (Goslinga 2012; Romberg 2012, 2014, 2017; Scheper Hughes 2012; Straight 2006).

Drawing on recent revisionist scholarship on Spiritism and the history of science and religion, this chapter begins with a brief history that traces the philosophical premises of Spiritism, as they were constituted in England, Spain, and France.[5] The purpose of the historical section is to identify the various Enlightenment philosophical streams converging within Allan Kardec's codification of Spiritism in the nineteenth century, and to show how the workings of the spiritual world and its hierarchical organization reflect on enlightenment ideals, scientific discoveries, evolutionism, and social positivism, providing a grounded critique of modern theories of death. The second and third sections are based on my ethnographic research of Spiritist centers in Brazil and Puerto Rico and extensive participant fieldwork with vernacular *espiritistas-brujos* in Puerto Rico.[6] These materials show how enlightened spirits have first been institutionalized in Spiritist centers and then have moved from Spiritist centers to the home-altars of vernacular healers, articulating more ethnically varied necrographies of spirits of the dead and of light. Operating in urban centers, these home-altars as well as some contemporary Spiritist centers are attended by a variety of urban, secular, professional, and white- and blue-collar followers whose daily interactions with spirits of the dead defy the dichotomous portrayal of modern theories of death, which relegate such intimate interactions with the dead to anachronistic rural folk practices. A number of ethnographic vignettes will illustrate the visceral and affective ways in which the lofty ideals of nineteenth-century Spiritism—reviewed in the historical section—have been materialized in forging both a modern and moral Spiritist way of life. These vignettes vividly convey everyday convivial, sometimes exploitative, but always influential relationships of spirits of the dead and entities or spirits of light with mortals.

"Enlightened" Necrographies in Historical, Political, and Philosophical Contexts

A revisionist historiography of Spiritualism and Spiritism unravels the ubiquitous appeal of spirits of the dead in entertainment shows in the nineteenth century and the dramatic modes in which mediums communicated with the dead (Bennett 2005; Herman 2006; Leonard 2005; Noakes 2000, Washington 1995). Due to space limits, the fascinating history engaging "dancing tables," "automatic writing," and "spirit cabinets" will be omitted here. Worthy of mention, albeit briefly, is the impact that technological and scientific discoveries in telegraphy, photography and cinema had in bringing material "proof" of the existence of spirits of the dead in the form of "spirit photography," "ectoplasms," and spirit-moving images (see Bruce 2005; Collins 1994; Cadwallader 2008; Herman 2006; Krauss 1995; Natale 2010, 2011; Noakes 1999, 2004, 2005, 2007; Schoonover 2003). This search drove many well-respected scientists to be publicly discredited—Sir Conan Doyle, being one of the most notable for falling for the obvious hoax behind Griffith's Cottingley Fairies, tiny fairies appearing miraculously hovering on spirit photographs (Doyle 2003; Lycett 2007).[7]

In contrast to such flashy hopes and disappointments, the cultural history of Spiritism suggests routine yet more enduringly ongoing interactions of spirits of the dead and humans for the last century and a half, as a consequence of what Bret Carroll aptly termed "the ministry of spirits" (1997). Such ministry has shaped a Spiritist way of life in great measure via the implementation of practical procedures and subjectivation processes informed by the various principles of the Enlightenment, scientific discoveries, evolutionism, and social positivism—detailed below. Such subjectivation processes were implemented by Spiritist centers in four major areas of social intervention: education, publication, healing, and philanthropy, providing pragmatic, rather than dogmatic, moral charters for spirit–human exchanges.

The nineteenth century has witnessed the emergence of various Spiritualist and Spiritist movements in Europe and the Americas. A brief mapping of the place that spirits acquired in socio-political predicaments in these places aims at illuminating the ideational processes that constituted the particular moral agency spirits. For example, American Spiritualism emerged in Antebellum North America in response "to the widespread perception that American society was descending into atomistic particularity"; to fight against this grim outlook, Spiritualists aimed at recovering what they perceived as a lost state of communion and harmony by means of a "sympathetic communion" with the dead (Cox 2003a, 2006). In France and Spain, Spiritism emerged at slightly different times as an anticlerical, republican political force (see Abend 2004: 507–508, 512–513; and Romberg 1998, 2003b). Enlightened spirits were recruited in France at the height of the 1848 revolution by republican Romantic socialists in forging a new progressive society (Monroe 2003; Sharp 2006); but by the end of the nineteenth century spirit exchanges left the political arena, becoming, instead, the object of scientific paranormal studies (Abend 2004; Monroe 2008: 38; Staubermann 2001) that would inaugurate the field of parapsychology (Brower 2010, 2013; Lachapelle 2011; for the United States, see Moore 1977). In Spain, enlightened spirits were enlisted, first, by liberal revolutionaries during the Sextenio of 1868–1874, and then by anarchist socialists (Abend 2004: 530). In contrast to European Spiritism, Latin American and Caribbean Spiritism was shaped not only by a liberal and anticlerical impetus for progress but also by the ethos of anticolonial sentiments. For instance, the anti-hegemonic messages of enlightened spirits calling for progress and development based on reason were immediately embraced by Creole independence activist groups fighting against the rule of the Spanish Catholic colonial state in Cuba and Puerto Rico (Romberg 1998, 2003b; Román 2007). Indeed, the colonial state persecuted both Freemasons and Spiritists for what it perceived as subversive organizations, threatening the continuation of colonial rule. Since then, Brazilian Spiritist centers have become the most vocal and activist organizations in the Spiritist world of today (see below).

Philosophically, nineteenth-century evolutionism, materialism, scientific discoveries, and social positivism have shaped the moral and practical sides of Spiritism, especially the cosmological hierarchy of spirits of light and their edifying interventions in human interactions. The passage from spirited matter into dematerialized spirit has been imagined within Spiritism in an evolutionary scheme that would assure—via reincarnation—an ever-evolving enlightened world, striving towards perfection, justice, and equality among all religions, classes, and genders. In a top-down sequence stands God, followed by Jesus and other enlightened spirits or entities (unique individuals who had left a mark in human history), other spirits of light (at various stages of enlightenment), and ignorant, underdeveloped spirits of the dead at the very bottom. The idea was that an enlightened afterlife would assure an enlightened material, incarnate world and vice versa. Alternative conceptions of materialism had been recruited in envisioning the imbrication of the afterlife in this life. Among them, the ideas of Swedish scientist-turned-into-mystic Emanuel Swedenborg (1688–1772) provided rational clues for explaining how matter could be related to spirit (Carroll 1997: 16–34) within a "unified field-theory of the cosmos" or "system in which religion was congruent with modern scientific thought" (Menand 2001: 89). The theory of animal magnetism by German physician Franz Anton Mesmer (1734–1815) provided Spiritists with notions about the invisibility, and unique materiality and attributes of spiritual matter, which were instrumental to the transmission of thoughts, energies, and vibrations between humans and spirits (Monroe 2008). Conjoining ideas of materialism and evolutionism (both reigning at that time within the social sciences and philosophy), Spiritists reinterpreted evolutionism (à la Darwin) in spiritual-materialist terms. Progress of the world towards greater complexity was imagined as a form of "spiritual metamorphosis"—with affinities to Lamarck's (1744–1829) theory of "soft inheritance"—by means of which material and spiritual features acquired during one's lifetime were passed down to offspring (resonating with a current theory of DNA transmission of learned behavior).

Scientific theories and discoveries in physics were also incorporated as evidence for the existence and modes of communication with spirits of the dead. For example, Newton's gravity law (1686) was recruited in explaining the hierarchical layout of the world of spirits and the mediumistic abilities and processes that facilitated communication with that world. Robert Hare (1781–1858)—a Philadelphia mainstream leader in chemistry, electrochemistry, and heat—proposed distinguishing between ponderable and imponderable matter—the latter labeled "ethereal matter" or "ethers" due to its lack of weight. Since spirits were endowed with such imponderable matter, their "moral specific gravity" determined their location in the cosmos: the more morally pure and meritorious the spirit was, the lower its "moral specific gravity" and, hence, the higher it could rise in the spheres of spiritual development, ascending "according to the laws of nature until it came into equilibrium with the atmosphere of the proper sphere" (Hare quoted in Hazen 2000: 104). Also, ethereal fluids explained mediumistic or "mesmeric" phenomena and the possibility of asserting "will power" outside one's own body (2000: 109). In effect, the same scientific explanations of invisible physical forces such as electricity, light, and sound waves provided Spiritists with empirical accounts about the invisible work and influence of spirits in the visible world.

Lastly, the ideals of nineteenth-century social positivism figure in the democratic quests for knowledge, pedagogy, free will, and self-improvement ("know yourself") championed by Spiritism. Justifying the expected moral responsibility of those more enlightened Spiritists to "educate" and "enlighten" others, such principles were to secure a better world and cosmos (similarly to the premises of Manifest Destiny). Drawing a parallel between the certainty embedded in Newtonian laws of nature and the inevitability of spiritual and moral laws of society, various utopian agendas, among them the Saint Simonian socialist program (Darnton 1968: 145) would promote the establishment of enlightened societies based on reason, order, free will, social responsibility, and social justice. For example, Welsh social reformer and Spiritualist Robert Owen (1771–1858) founded the influential utopian urban project New Harmony Vision (1854), and the French utopian socialist Charles Fourier (1772–1837) designed a system of phalanxes or utopian communities.[8] Such activist pedagogical impetus informing social reform and urban planning would influence Spiritist endeavors of "scientific grounding with a spiritual uplift"—resonating with August Compte's (1798–1857) "seventh science" or "moral science" (Treitel 2004: 43). Spiritist centers also founded and funded all sorts of philanthropic programs and institutions, assuring that their activist role was translated into charitable works. These centers were organized into regional federations and national confederations, and then into international councils (the same mode of organization persists today).

Next, I discuss how such scientific and moral quests have been implemented with the agentive intervention of enlightened spirits in the funding and operation of Spiritist centers and their programs of social reform.

Modern yet Moral Exchanges with "Enlightened" Spirits

Material progress, brought forth by science, was seen by Spiritists as congruent with spiritual progress on a cosmic level (Hazen 2000); that is, an enlightened society was imagined in both material and spiritual terms. Since moral laws were likened to natural laws, the fusing of spiritual and social reform as well as science and religion were seen as necessary for society to progress. Most importantly, this progress depended first and foremost on individual spiritual development (see Hess 1991: 74–76; Aubrée 2000; Bergé 2005; Sharp 2006). Stressing the responsibility of individuals, spiritual laws provided the moral charter for everyday life actions. Believed to regiment the world of the living with the same certainty that natural laws did the physical world, the Spiritists spiritual laws are: a) The Law of Progress (mentioned earlier), b) The Law of Love, c) The Law of Cause and Effect, and d) The Law of Reincarnation. Briefly, the Law of Love and Charity states that the law of love supersedes all human-made laws. All actions are to be measured against the life and teachings of Jesus (or other spirits of light), and it is left to the conscience of each person to determine the righteousness of an action. According to this Law, one's *cuadro* (spiritual power and protections) has to be shared in order to assure its further development: the more we share, the more blessings and prosperity we are given back. The Law of Cause and Effect means that every action has a consequence in this world and for generations to come. We pay for our wrongdoing in subsequent reincarnations; through good deeds and charity toward our fellow humans we can compensate for social debts (wrongdoings to fellow humans) acquired in previous existences. Finally, the Law of Reincarnation states that via reincarnation and free will humans are given infinite opportunities to develop towards the highest degrees of spiritual enlightenment. In *The Spirits' Book* (1857) Kardec characterized the steps guiding reincarnation within The Law of Progress, stating that a soul could only advance through an expiatory cycle of reincarnation, which would take the soul from earth (the lowest circle in the planetary hierarchy) towards more advanced planets, such as Jupiter, prohibiting retrograde movements (Monroe 2008: 106). Indeed, knowledge and progress based on science and reason alone was incomplete unless it was combined (following Rudolf Steiner) with spiritual progress. In a booklet published by a Spiritist Center in Puerto Rico in 1913, the following dictates by enlightened spirits illustrate this idea: "Intelligence without morals is like the dawn without the sun"; "The arrogant architect is reminded of foundations laid on sand" (Club Amor y Ciencia 1913: 75–79).

Since the emergence of Spiritism, Spiritists have attested to the agentive power of the spiritual world in directing the human world. They have drawn on the messages delivered by enlightened spirits though the years in order to constitute and instill Spiritist principles. The agency of spirits at different levels of evolution—as they direct, advise, warn, discipline, and punish human beings—is intrinsic to the very basic conception of Spiritism and the various activities of Spiritist centers (and later of vernacular forms of Spiritism, as will be shown below). Allan Kardec's The *Spirit's Book*, written "under the direction of the spirits by whom it was originally dictated . . . is a compilation of their teachings. It has been written by the order and under the dictation of spirits of high degree, for the purpose of establishing the bases [*sic*] of a rational philosophy, free from the influence of prejudices and of preconceived opinions" (1996 [1857]: 19). It is not surprising that this book by Kardec, in its many editions and translations, has become an icon that is usually placed on the table around which mediums sit at public séances. A short quote, presented in a dialogue format between Kardec and a spirit of light, illustrates the overall rationalist and empiricist tenor of Spiritism:

—What is spirit?
The intelligent principle of the universe.
—What is the essential nature of spirit?
It is not possible to explain the nature of spirit in your language. For you it is not a thing, because it is not palpable; but for us *it is a thing*. (My emphasis, Kardec 1996 [1957]: 69)

Historical and literary records reveal that the communication of messages authored by influential spirits for human beings was instrumental to the political and social transformation envisioned by Spiritists. For instance, ghost-written texts, authored by renowned scientists, writers, musicians, saints, Indians, pirates, even Jesus and Buddha, were disseminated for these purposes (Gomel 2007: 189). The social-moralizing tenor of such phantom writers is evidenced in the messages transmitted, for instance, by the spirits of Benjamin Franklin and Thomas Jefferson to Robert Owen in order "to change the present, false, disunited and miserable state of human existence, for a true, united and happy state . . . and to infuse into all the spirit of charity, forbearance and love." Due to the lack of space, recent research tying the content of enlightened messages to specific historical contexts will be sketched only briefly. Depending on the specific context, messages were atemporal and abstract or specific and political (see Abend 2004: 520; Cox 2003b; Kneeland 2008: n12, 247; and Monroe 2008). Most importantly, serving the educative function, necrographic messages were systematically transcribed, published, circulated, and discussed in order to translate lofty ideals into everyday life actions. From the very start, the socialization of Spiritists was conducted via regular collective and individual séances as well as classes and meetings that were held regularly. During these gatherings, participants had an opportunity to learn, ask questions, and discuss the principles of Spiritism following the values of pure inquiry and reason in clear opposition to the dogmatic teaching of religion.

Hundreds and thousands of such centers had been founded for about one and a half centuries in various parts of Latin America, North and Central America, the Caribbean, Europe, and Asia.[9] A quick google search (0.7 seconds) of "Spiritist centers" yielded 264,000 results. Among them, the Spiritist movement in Brazil, for example, is thriving today, with twenty million individuals registered as Spiritists, twelve thousand centers offering classes and services, and a publishing industry that prints four hundred titles a year, selling 38.6 million copies. In addition to the information I gathered when I visited a few centers in Rio de Janeiro in 2002, I also learned from a considerable number of websites I surveyed that their activities follow on the footsteps of nineteenth-century Spiritist centers in terms of the quests to disseminate Spiritist ideas and engage in charitable work. In addition to extending their educational activities to after-school programs in difficult urban areas, Spiritist centers engage in charitable and social welfare activities such as holding community kitchens for the poor and children, and distributing food and clothing in hospices for orphans, women, and the elderly. Recently, Spiritist centers have used the internet for outreach programs in daily radio and televised transmissions that assist people in solving family and work problems. Messages delivered by "enlightened spirits" are relentlessly being published in pamphlets and booklets and circulated to the local public, via radio and internet TV programs, and to the international public via websites, showing the continuous agentive power of spirits of the dead and spirits of light in human affairs. In the next section, ethnographic vignettes will explore vernacular versions of Spiritism and point to the visceral, affective impact of spirits of light on the lives of contemporary Puerto Ricans.

Vernacular Exchanges with Spirits of the Dead and Spirits of Light

Based on "Scientific Spiritism" or institutionalized orthodox forms of Spiritism, vernacular versions have been developing, in private altars among mediums, that merged Kardecean Spiritism with a variety of practices drawn from African, indigenous, and Catholic religious elements. At private altar-rooms, rather than at Spiritist centers, spirits of the dead at different levels of evolution and spiritual entities keep delivering important messages at divination, cleansing, and healing rituals as well as during the performance of magic works. These sorts of exchanges between humans, spirits of the dead, and spirits of light occur during nightly collective séances or *veladas* and private consultations. In both contexts, the purpose is to summon messages by the spirits, delivered by mediums possessed or in trance, and then to act on them as soon as possible.[10] As spirits manifest themselves at *veladas*, or cleansing, divination, and healing events, the emotional level of participants rises considerably, eliciting vivid spiritual dramas in which visceral, sensorially affective interactions between humans and spirits are enacted. Since spirits tend to manifest in this world suddenly, one of the crucial divinatory practices is to define who is the spirit delivering the message in relation to the hierarchical structure of the spiritual world. Since manifesting spirits of light are usually part of the mediums *cuadro* or *protecciones*, their specific identity is usually known. Only lower level spirits need to undergo some form of examination, which is conducted via interrogation sessions between mediums and spirits in a manner that resemble the dynamics of law enforcement questionings, as described by Michel de Certeau in his *Possession at Loudon* ([1970] 1996). These sessions usually end with Hail Marys and Our Fathers, prayed in litany, in order to encourage the spirit to raise to higher levels of spirit evolution—as is usually done during novenas.

One of the important concluding stages of funeral rituals is to ensure the successful departure of the spirits of the dead from this world and their spiritual evolution. Elaborate funerary and waking rituals take place with special attention given to enlighten the spirit of the dead and to cajole it to depart from this world to the world of spirits by means of well attended novenas and prayers. The passage from incarnate to disincarnate spirit is envisioned within Spiritism, as in other cross-cultural cases, as a positive transformation conveyed via the trope of "spirits are birds." For example, when Tonio, a very old Puerto Rican *brujo* (Spiritist witch healer) spoke of his imminent disincarnation, he expressed his wish "to fly over the Yunke," a magnificent rain forest in Puerto Rico believed to be the abode of spiritual entities of light (see Romberg 2011a).[11] A "healthy" departure of spirits of the dead from this world is critical, for it assures the positive influence of their impromptu manifestations—in the form of dreams, and messages given via the possession mediums and all sorts of sensorial signs—as well as their potential evolution into spirits of light.

Albeit operating at the lowest levels of spirituality, below the *entidades* (entities), *los muertos* or spirits of the dead are not only the closest to human beings but also the most mercurial and treacherous. Some individuals have a particularly close relationship with a *muerto* that could be excruciating as in *"causas"* (bewitchments) or *"espíritus de existencia"* (wandering spirits latching onto the body of a victim). But these relationships could be extremely favorable when *muertos* become protectors. *Espíritus de existencia* may become a curse, when everything their victims try to do inevitably fails or ends in tragedy. This is what was diagnosed to Marta during a divination session, when Haydée—the *espiritista-bruja* I worked with intensely for more than a year—told her that a very "possessive" *espíritu de existencia* who "even believes that he owns you, won't let any man approach you." As a proof, Haydée foretold, "Marta, you have seen many nice men get close to you and then watched them leave in a flash for no reason. And unless someone will be able to drive him [the *espíritu de existencia*] out of your life, you will never be happy." In contrast, *muertos* may also intervene mischievously to help their protégées.

Nora, an *espiritista-santera*, braggingly confided in Haydée and me that she doesn't need a husband, because her *muerto* provides her "with everything." Once, she passed by a store and saw a golden chain worth 2,000 pesos, and heard a voice behind her saying, "You'll have it." A few nights later, when Nora was sleeping, she heard, "Get up!" She explained, "this *muerto* doesn't let me sleep! . . . The next morning my uncle won the lottery and said, 'Take these 2,000 pesos.' . . . The *muerto* gives it to you and already, immediately, forgets about it. He only expects you to stay with him, working [the spiritual work]."

A less colorful but equally positive nurturing relationship developed between Dominga and her dead husband's spirit. Following the death of her husband, a family feud emerged in inheritance matters. In consultation Dominga learned that the spirit of her dead husband was making sure no prospective buyer would ever purchase the house. In exchange for his help, Haydée advised her to light a white candle for him in order to feed his positive spiritual energies. As pawns in a huge cosmic army, *los muertos* might also work for *brujos* on a freelance basis in exchange for devotion and care—marked by a symbolic amount of money, candles, flowers, prayers, or other small offerings. In their dual role, they might either promote or thwart the success of magic works performed for or against their clients; but when the summoned *muerto* is a kinfolk of the *brujo* their "work" is guaranteed.

When Puerto Rican Spiritists say they are positive mediums they mean that they are endowed with "good energies" or a "positive *cuadro*" (a set of spiritual guides that become personal shields or *protecciones*). Such *cuadro* not only attracts more spirits of light to "elevate" or "enlighten" individuals guided by negative spirits or having a *causa* (bewitchment); it can also "exorcise" both the victim and the pestering *muerto*, enticing them to develop their respective spiritual levels. Although a *cuadro* is inherited from close kin, it can also be developed according to the Law of Reincarnation in this and later reincarnations. Having a "nice" *cuadro* with spirits of light will promote and be a sign of having prosperity, luck, love, and respect (see Romberg 2011b).

Even though entities or spirits of light are more distant and less readily accessible than *muertos*, their moral interventions in shaping how people act in this world are no less powerful; they can effect real changes, particularly as such vital yet invisible forces are usually invoked and recruited for spiritual guidance and comfort. According to the Spiritist Law of Love and Charity, such positive energies need to be shared in helping others evolve spiritually. In this way, each individual is personally responsible for working toward the spiritual progress of the cosmos. Basi, a Spiritist medium and owner of a *botánica* (store that sells religious paraphernalia), who hosted me for several months, was involved at that time in a court case against one of her tenants. Reminiscing, she told me that when a pregnant woman came several months ago to the *botánica* complaining she was left homeless after her boyfriend had thrown her out on the street, she felt a transcendental need to help her. As this woman spent the welfare aid for rent on alcohol and drugs, Basi brought her to the courts—not for the purpose of evicting her but for forcing the woman by court order to seek help. Basi explained to me referencing the Law of Love and Charity that her *cuadro* and *protecciones* had always helped her in difficult times and now was the time to retribute that goodness: "I'm prosperous, and the more I give, the more I receive."

Exchanges between spirits and humans are also mediated by the moral tenets of the Law of Cause and Effect, which highlight our free will in making the right choices, and the fact that we always pay for the consequences of our actions in this world. Doris, a healer-medium who worked extensively in rehabilitation clinics, mentioned how she was able to heal an adolescent who had trespassed the law by using and selling drugs. She demanded he first makes a commitment to repent and be ready to *"salir del fango"* ("get out of the mud"; slang for lowlife). In subsequent visits she was able to heal him by means of a series of cleansing rituals, in which her own spirits of light were recruited, followed by the gifting of protective amulets during a rebirth baptism at a river in the rain forest. The Law of Cause and Effect also explains the case of Tomasa, who, after several divination sessions, decided to follow the spirits' advice rather than take the money that the courts adjudicated in her favor. Tomasa had won a court case awarding her past-due rent money (plus interest) from a tenant who was a single mother on welfare. During divination, Tomasa heard the following messages from the spirits: *"Lo mal quitado no luce"*—in this context, "whatever is maliciously seized won't shine"; i.e., you won't be able to enjoy anything you've achieved through acts that defy spiritual laws of charity and fairness. She also heard: *"Lo que no es mío no lo quiero* [what's not mine, I don't want]," indicating that she shouldn't accept the interest money plus attorney fees, just the rent money, since the tenant was a poor woman in distress and Tomasa a well-to-do woman. The spirits added the warning, *"La soga revienta por lo más débil* [The rope breaks at its weakest point]"; i.e., you are going to suffer the spiritual consequences—not the lawyer. This was the spirits' last attempt to encourage Tomasa to reject the man-made judgment in favor of a spirits-made judgment determining she should accept the minimum amount of the rent alone; it was reinforced by the moral reproach: *"Cuanto uno más tiene, más quiere* [The more you have, the more you want]."[12]

Conclusion

This chapter has offered theoretical, historical, and ethnographic ruminations about "enlightened" exchanges between spirits and human beings in the West, unraveling, along with current critiques of modernity and agency, the contrived and problematic exceptionalism with which we have learned to apprehend modernity, agency, and modern attitudes to death. Most importantly, the ethnographic section has shown that spirits of the dead and spiritual entities participate in the lives of humans on a daily basis, making sure they follow the spiritual laws that would assure the overall moral evolution of this world and the cosmos. Certainly, these exchanges pertain to modern societies, contradicting the expected "disembedding" (Giddens 1991) and "liquidity" (Bauman 2000) of social relations assumed by most modern social theories. Moreover, rather than being relegated to the private sphere, as modern death theories suggest, the dead appear as active partners in forging the evolution of a just, progressive world both in material and moral terms. The alienation and moral disjuncture between the living and the dead, predicted by such theories, appear to be the result of predetermined theoretical scripts of modernity rather than a reflection of the ongoing, intensely abiding exchanges going on from the nineteenth century until today between the living and the dead under Spiritism.

Sociocultural anthropologist and folklorist **Raquel Romberg** is the author of *Witchcraft and Welfare: Spiritual Capital and the Business of Magic in Modern Puerto Rico* (University of Texas Press, 2003) and *Healing Dramas: Divination and Magic in Puerto Rico* (University of Texas Press, 2009). Her publications focus on ethnohistorical, performative, and material approaches to the modernity and morality of Spiritism and brujería; the affectivity, efficacy, and indeterminacy of healing rituals and possession; gestures and religious subjectivation; the ritual life of altars; and creolization in colonial and postcolonial perspectives. She is currently associate editor of *Magic, Ritual and Witchcraft*.

Notes

1. Excerpt from a "Letter to the Editor," written by evolutionist anthropologist Alfred Russell Wallace after his conversion to Spiritualism and in reaction to the publication of Carl du Prel's *Philosophy of Mysticism* (1889), published in *Light* (London) on 9 April

1892. Retrieved from the webpage of Charles H. Smith, "Alfred Russel Wallace on Spiritualism, Man, and Evolution: An Analytical Essay." Retrieved on 9 March 2015 from https://people.wku.edu/charles.smith/wallace/S446A.htm.
2. The orthodox form of Kardecean Spiritism practiced in Spiritist centers is often referred to as Scientific Spiritism, especially since the early decades of the twentieth century, in order to contrast it to vernacular forms practiced in private home-altars; but here I refer to both as Spiritism. Elsewhere I extensively discuss the politics of this difference (Romberg 1998, 2003a, 2003b).
3. Spiritism and Spiritualism share some premises with regard to spirit communication, with Spiritism including reincarnation in its philosophy. But they are also marked by divergent genealogies: whereas Spiritism developed in France and Spain and later in Latin America and the Caribbean by mid-nineteenth century, Spiritualism emerged in North America and Great Britain by the beginning of the same century. The philosophical background refers to both Spiritualism and Spiritism.
4. Characterizing late modernity, this nostalgia resonates with Anthony Gidden's (1991) notion of "disembedding" of social relations.
5. For recent titles on the intellectual histories of a variety of esoteric movements, such as Occultism, Hermeticism, Theosophy, Rosicrucianism, and Spiritism in Germany, England, France, and North America, see Sharp (2006), Rosenthal (1997), Hanegraaff (2013), and Young (2012), and about their relevance in Western arts, architecture, sciences, therapy, philanthropy, and politics, see Barz (2010), Colbert (2011), Hanegraaff (1999, 2014, 2013), Maurois (n.d.), Materer (1995), and Schoonover (2003).
6. The ethnographic materials are based on my fieldwork in Puerto Rico (1995–96), some of which were discussed extensively in Romberg (2003b, 2009).
7. See also the case of well-known British scientist Sir William Crookes (1832–1919) (DeKovsky 1976; Hall 1962).
8. Several utopian communities, such as the "intentional communities" in the United States and other parts of the world, were influenced by Fourier's utopian model. In Cuba, Antonio Ojeda y Cabral designed in 1908 an urban regeneration project for Havana following the Spiritist theme of republicanism (Román 2006).
9. In Vietnam, for example, the "Caodai pantheon of saints includes not only Asian figures and Jesus, but also Victor Hugo, Jeanne d'Arc, Jean Jacques Rousseau, De la Fontaine, even Lenin" (Hoskins 2014).
10. Elsewhere I discuss spirit possession in detail both as a discourse and performance that articulate the uncanny presence of spirits (Romberg 2014).
11. In this chapter, I refer to *brujos* indistinctively as Spiritists and *brujos*, since they define themselves as *espiritistas-brujos*. Elsewhere I discuss the problematic politics of these categories (Romberg 1998, 2003a, 2003b).
12. A more detailed account appears in Romberg (2003b).

References

Abend, Lisa. 2004. "Specters of the Secular: Spiritism in Nineteenth-Century Spain." *European History Quarterly* 34(4): 507–34.

Amorim, Deolindo. 1994. *Africanismo y espiritismo*, trans. Pura Argelich Mingella. Caracas: Editora Cultural Espírita León Denis, Ediciones Cima.

Ariès, Philippe. 1974. *Western Attitudes toward Death: From the Middle Ages to the Present*. Baltimore: Johns Hopkins University Press.

Aubrée, Marion. 2000. " La nouvelle dynamique du spiritisme kardéciste [New impetus for Kardecist spiritism]." *Ethnologie française* 30(4): 591.
Barz, Christiane. 2010. "Scientific Spirit, Spirituality and Spirited Writing—Spiritualism between Science, Religion and Literature." *Tijdschrift voor Skandinavistiek* 1(31): 121–58.
Baudrillard, Jean. (1976) 1993. *Symbolic Exchange and Death*. London: Sage Publications.
Bauman, Zygmunt. 1992. *Mortality, Immortality and Other Life Strategies*. Cambridge, UK: Polity Press.
_____. 2000. *Liquid Modernity*. Cambridge, UK: Polity Press.
Bennett, Bridget. 2005. "Sacred Theatres: Shakers, Spiritualists, Theatricality, and the Indian in the 1830s and 1840s." *The Drama Review* 49(3): 114–34.
Bergé, Christine. 2005. "Kardec, Allen." In *Dictionary of Gnosis and Western Esotericism*, vol. 2, ed. Antoine Faivre, Roelof van den Broek, Jean-Pierre Brach, and Wouter J. Hanegraaff, 658–59. Leiden: Brill Academic Publishers.
Blanes, Ruy, and Diana Espírito Santo. 2014. *The Social Life of Spirits*. Chicago: University of Chicago Press.
Brower, M. Brady. 2010. *Unruly Spirits: The Science of Psychic Phenomena in Modern France*. Champaign: University of Illinois Press.
_____. 2013. "Investigating the Supernatural: From Spiritism and Occultism to Psychical Research and Metapsychics in France, 1853–1931." *Journal of Modern History* 85(1): 197–99.
Bruce, Susan. 2005. "Sympathy for the Dead: (G)hosts, Hostilities and Mediums in Alejandro Amenabar's The Others and Postmortem Photography." *Discourse: Journal for Theoretical Studies in Media & Culture* 27(2–3): 21–40.
Cadwallader, Jen. 2008. "Spirit Photography Victorian Culture of Mourning." *Modern Language Studies* 37(2): 8–31.
Carroll, Bret E. 1997. *Spiritualism in Antebellum America*. Bloomington: Indiana University Press.
Club Amor y Ciencia. 1913. *Tesoros espirituales: Dictados de ultratumba obtenidos en Arecibo*. Arecibo, Puerto Rico: n.p.
Colbert, Charles. 2011. *Haunted Visions: Spiritualism and American Art*. Philadelphia: University of Pennsylvania Press.
Collins, Matthew. 1994. "Telegrams from the Dead," *The American Experience Series*. PBS. WGBH.
Comaroff, Jean, and John Comaroff. 1999. "Occult Economies and the Violence of Abstraction: Notes from the South African Postcolony." *American Ethnologist* 26(2): 279–303.
_____. 2001. "Millennial Capitalism: First Thoughts on a Second Coming." In *Millennial Capitalism and the Culture of Neoliberalism*, ed. Jean Comaroff and John Comaroff, 1–56. Durham, NC: Duke University Press.
Coudert, Allison P. 2011. *Religion, Magic, and Science in Early Modern Europe and America*. Santa Barbara, CA: Praeger.
Cox, Robert S. 2003a. *Body and Soul: A Sympathetic History of American Spiritualism*. Charlottesville: University of Virginia Press.
_____. 2003b. "Vox Populi: Spiritualism and George Washington's Postmortem Career." *Early American Studies: An Interdisciplinary Journal* 1(1): 230–72.

———. 2006. "Spiritualism." In *Introduction to New and Alternative Religions in America*, Volume 3, ed. Eugene V. Gallagher and William M. Aschcraft. Westport, CO: Greenwood.

Darnton, Robert. 1968. *Mesmerism and the End of the Enlightenment in France*. Boston: Harvard University Press.

de Certeau, Michel. (1970) 1990. *The Possession at Loudun*. With a foreword by Stephen Greenblatt. Translated by Michael B. Smith. Chicago: The University of Chicago Press.

DeKosky, Robert K. 1976. "William Crookes and the Fourth State of Matter." *Isis* 67(1): 36–60.

Doyle, Arthur Conan. 2003. *The History of Spiritualism*. Fredonia, NY: Fredonia Books.

Gaonkar, Dilip Parameshwar. 2001. *Alternative Modernities*. Durham, NC: Duke University Press.

Giddens, Anthony. 1991. *Modernity and Self-Identity: Self and Society in the Late Modern Age*. Stanford: Stanford University Press.

Gomel, Elana. 2007. "Spirits in the Material World: Spiritualism and Identity in the Fin de Siècle." *Victorian Literature and Culture* 35: 189–213.

Goslinga, Gillian. 2012. "Spirited Encounters: Notes on the Politics and Poetics of Representing the Uncanny in Anthropology." *Anthropological Theory* 12: 386–406.

Hall, Trevor H. 1962. *The Spiritualists: The Story of Florence Cook and William Crookes*. New York: Helix Press.

Hanegraaff, Wouter J. 1999. "Some Remarks on the Study of Western Esotericism." *Esoterica* 1: 3–19.

———. 2003. "How Magic Survived the Disenchantment of the World." *Religion* 33: 357–80.

———. 2013. *Western Esotericism: A Guide for the Perplexed*. London: Bloomsbury Publishing.

———. 2014. *Esotericism and the Academy: Rejected Knowledge in Western Culture*. Cambridge: Cambridge University Press.

Hazen, Craig James. 2000. *The Village Enlightenment in America: Popular Religion and Science in the Nineteenth Century*. Champaign: University of Illinois Press.

Herman, Daniel. 2006. "Whose Knocking? Spiritualism as Entertainment and Therapy in Nineteenth-Century San Francisco." *American Nineteenth Century History* 7(2): 417–42.

Hess, David J. 1991. *Spirits and Scientists: Ideology, Spiritism, and Brazilian Culture*. University Park: Pennsylvania State University Press.

Hoskins, Janet. 2014. "From Colonial Syncretism to Transpacific Diaspora: Re-Orienting Caodaism from Vietnam to California." In *Dynamics of Religion in South East Asia (DORISEA) Working Paper Series*, Issue 7. Göttingen, Germany: German Federal Ministry for Education and Research.

Kardec, Allan. (1857) 1996. *The Spirit's Book*. Translated by Anna Blackwell. Rio de Janeiro: Federaçao Espirita Brazileira.

Knauft, Bruce M. 2002. *Critically Modern: Alternatives, Alterities, Anthropologies*. Bloomington: Indiana University Press.

Kneeland, Timothy W. 2008. "Robert Hare: Politics, Science, and Spiritualism in the Early Republic." *The Pennsylvania Magazine of History and Biography* 132(3): 245–60.
Krauss, Rolf H. 1995. *Beyond Light and Shadow: The Role of Photography in Certain Paranormal Phenomena: An Historical Survey.* Munich: Nazraeli Press.
Lachapelle, Sofie. 2011. *Investigating the Supernatural: From Spiritism and Occultism to Psychical Research and Metapsychics in France, 1853–1931.* Baltimore: Johns Hopkins University Press.
Latour, Bruno. 1993. *We Have Never Been Modern.* Cambridge, MA: Harvard University Press.
———. 2001. "'Thou Shalt Not Take the Lord's Name in Vain': Being a Sort of Sermon on the Hesitations of Religious Speech." *RES: Anthropology and Aesthetics* 39: 215–35.
———. 2013. *An Inquiry into Modes of Existence: An Anthropology of the Moderns,* trans. Catherine Porter. Cambridge, MA: Harvard University Press.
Leonard, Todd J. 2005. *Talking to the Other Side: A History of Modern Spiritualism and Mediumship: A Study of the Religion, Science, Philosophy and Mediums that Encompass this American-Made Religion.* Lincoln, NE: iUniverse.
Lycett, Andrew. 2007. *Conan Doyle: The Man Who Created Sherlock Holmes.* New York: Free Press.
Malinowski, Bronislaw. (1925) 1948. "The Art of Magic and the Power of Faith." In his *Magic, Science and Religion and Other Essays,* 69–90. Prospect Heights, IL: Waveland Press.
Materer, T. 1995. *Modernist Alchemy: Poetry and the Occult.* Ithaca, NY: Cornell University Press.
Maurois, Andre. n.d. *The Weigher of Souls.* Retrieved 9 March 2015 from http://www.unz.org/Pub/FantasticMysteries-1950oct-00086?View=PDF.
Menand, Louis. 2001. *The Metaphysical Club: A Story of Ideas in America.* New York: Farrar, Strauss, and Giroux.
Meyer, Birgit, and Peter Pels, eds. 2003. *Magic and Modernity: Interfaces of Revelation and Concealment.* Stanford: Stanford University Press.
Monroe, John Warne. 2003. "Cartes-de-visite from the Other World: Spiritism and the Discourse of Laicisme in the Early Third Republic." *Journal of French Historical Studies* 26(1): 119–53.
———. 2008. *Laboratories of Faith: Mesmerism, Spiritism, and Occultism in Modern France.* Ithaca, NC: Cornell University Press.
Moore, R. Laurence. 1977. *In Search of White Crows: Spiritualism, Parapsychology, and American Culture.* New York: Oxford University Press.
Natale, Simone. 2010. "Spiritualism Exposed: Skepticism, Credulity and Spectatorship in End-of-the-Century America." *European Journal of American Culture* 29(2): 131–44.
———. 2011. *The Spectacular Supernatural: Spiritualism, Entertainment, and the Invention of Cinema.* PhD diss., University of Turin.
Noakes, Richard. 1999. "Telegraphy is an Occult Art: Cromwell Fleetwood Varley and the Diffusion of Electricity to the Other World." *British Journal for the History of Science* 32(115): 421–59.

_____. 2000. "Spiritualism." In *Reader's Guide to the History of Science*, ed. Arne Hessenbruch, 703–4. London: Fitzroy Dearborn Publishers.

_____. 2004. "Natural Causes? Spiritualism, Science, and the Supernatural in Mid-Victorian Britain." In *The Victorian Supernatural*, ed. N. Bown, C. Burdett, and P. Thurschwell, 23–43. Cambridge: Cambridge University Press.

_____. 2005. "Ethers, Religion and Politics in Late-Victorian Physics: Beyond the Wynne Thesis." *History of Science* 43: 415–55.

_____. 2007. "Cromwell Varley FRS, Electrical Discharge and Victorian Spiritualism." *Notes and Records: The Royal Society* 61(1): 5–21.

Oppenheim, Janet. 1985. *The Other World: Spiritualism and Psychical Research in England, 1850–1914*. Cambridge: Cambridge University Press.

Parkin, David. 2007. "Wafting on the Wind: Smell and the Cycle of Spirit and Matter." *Journal of the Royal Anthropological Institute (N.S.)* 13(s1): S39–S53.

Pels, Peter. 1998. "The Spirit of Matter." In *Border Fetishisms: Material Objects in Unstable Places*, ed. Patricia Spyer, 91–121. London: Routledge.

_____. 2003. "Spirits of Modernity: Alfred Wallace, Edward Tylor, and the Visual Politics of Fact." In *Magic and Modernity: Interfaces of Revelation and Concealment*, ed. Meyer, B, and P. Pels, 241–271. Stanford, CA: Stanford University Press.

_____. 2008. "The Modern Fear of Matter: Reflections on the Protestantism of Victorian Science." *Material Religion: The Journal of Objects, Art and Belief* 4(3): 264–83.

Román, Reinaldo L. 2006. "Más allá de la Habana: On Spiritism and Corporate Aggregation from the Late Colony to the Early Cuban Republic." Paper presented at the meeting of the Latin American Studies Association, San Juan, Puerto Rico, 15–18 March.

_____. 2007. "Governing Man-Gods: Spiritism and the Struggle for Progress in Republican Cuba." *Journal of Religion in Africa* 37(2): 212–41.

Romberg, Raquel. 1998. "Whose Spirits Are They? The Political Economy of Syncretism and Authenticity." *Journal of Folklore Research* 35(1): 69–82.

_____. 2003a. "From Charlatans to Saviors: Espiritistas, Curanderos, and Brujos Inscribed in Discourses of Progress and Heritage." *Centro Journal* 15(2): 146–73.

_____. 2003b. *Witchcraft and Welfare: Spiritual Capital and the Business of Magic in Modern Puerto Rico*. Austin: University of Texas Press.

_____. 2005a. "Glocal Spirituality: Consumerism, and Heritage in an Afro-Caribbean Folk Religion." In *Caribbean Societies and Globalization*, ed. Franklin W. Knight and Teresita Martínez Vergne, 131–56. Chapel Hill: University of North Carolina Press.

_____. 2005b. "Ritual Piracy: Or Creolization with an Attitude." *New West Indian Guide* 79(3 & 4): 175–218.

_____. 2007. "Today, Changó is Changó, or How Africanness Becomes a Ritual Commodity in Puerto Rico." *Western Folklore* 66(1 & 2): 75–106.

_____. 2009. *Healing Dramas: Divination and Magic in Modern Puerto Rico*. Austin: University of Texas Press.

_____. 2011a. "Flying Witches, Embodied Memories, and the Wanderings of an Anthropologist." In *Serendipity in Anthropological Research: The Nomadic Turn*, ed. Haim Hazan and Esther Herzog, 157–174. Farnham: Ashgate Press.

———. 2011b. "Spiritual Capital: On the Materiality and Immateriality of Blessings in Puerto Rican *Brujería*." In "The Economics of Religion: Anthropological Approaches," ed. Lionel Obadia and Donald Wood. Special issue, *Research in Economic Anthropology* 31: 123–56.
———. 2012. "Sensing the Spirits: The Healing Dramas and Poetics of Brujería Rituals." *Anthropologica* 54(2): 211–25.
———. 2014. "Corporeality and Discourse in Spirit Possession." In *Spirited Things: The Work of "Possession" in Black Atlantic Religions*, ed. Paul Christopher Johnson, 225–56. Chicago: University of Chicago Press.
———. 2015. "Magic in the Postcolonial Modern West (19th and 20th centuries)." In *The Cambridge History of Magic and Witchcraft in the West*, ed. David J. Collins, 576–634. Cambridge: Cambridge University Press.
———. 2016. "Legitimate and Illegitimate Vernacular Religions in Colonial and Postcolonial Times: Historical and Anthropological Explorations of Ritual Indeterminacy." In *Religious Diversity Today: Experiencing Religion in the Contemporary World*. Vol. 2, *Ritual and Pilgrimage*, ed. Anastasia Panagakos, 189–214. Santa Barbara, CA: Praeger.
———. 2017. "'Gestures that Do': Spiritist Manifestations and the Technologies of Religious Subjectivation and Affect." In "Marching the Devotional Subject: The Bodily-and-Material Cultures of Religion," ed. Urmila Mohan and Jean-Pierre Warnier. Special issue, *Journal of Material Culture* 22(4): 385–405.
Rosenthal, Bernice Glatzer, ed. 1997. *The Occult in Russian and Soviet Culture*. Ithaca: Cornell University Press.
Saler, Michael. 2006. "Modernity and Enchantment: A Historiographic Review." *The American Historical Review* 111(3): 692–716.
Scheper Hughes, Jennifer. 2012. "Mysterium Materiae: Vital Matter and the Object as Evidence in the Study of Religion." *Bulletin for the Study of Religion* 41(4): 16–24.
Schoonover, Karl. 2003. "Ectoplasms, Evanescence, and Photography." *Art Journal* 62(3): 30–43.
Sharp, Lynn. 2006. *Secular Spirituality: Reincarnation and Spiritism in Nineteenth-Century France*. Lexington, MA: Lexington Book.
Staubermann, Klaus B. 2001. "Tying the Knot: Skill, Judgement and Authority in the 1870s Leipzig Spiritistic Experiments." *The British Journal for the History of Science* 34(1): 67–79.
Stocking, George W. 1998. *After Tylor: British Social Anthropology, 1888–1951*. Madison: University of Wisconsin Press.
Straight, Bilinda S. 2006. "Becoming Dead: The Entangled Agencies of the Dearly Departed." *Anthropology and Humanism* 31: 101–10.
Treitel, Corinna. 2004. *Science for the Soul: Occultism and the Genesis of the German Modern*. Baltimore: Johns Hopkins University Press.
Washington, Peter. 1995. *Madame Blavatsky's Baboon: A History of the Mystics, Mediums, and Misfits Who Brought Spiritualism to America*. New York: Schocken Books.
Young, George M. 2012. *The Russian Cosmists: The Esoteric Futurism of Nikolai Fedorov and His Followers*. Oxford: Oxford University Press.

Chapter 9

Channeling the Flow

Dealing with Death in an African-Based Religion

Gabriel Banaggia

The faithful of several different African-based religions in Brazil have a widespread saying that goes somewhat like this: "In our tradition, there is a way out of everything, except death." However, in at least some of these practices and for a few persons, even death can be cheated, albeit to varying extents. Sometimes that happens with help from the dead, other times against their will. This piece brings forth the argument that the ways through which adepts of these religions obviate termination depend on satisfactorily manipulating a vital energy that potentially exists in everything. To achieve that, and since the spirits of the dead may be either composed of this energy or agents of its annihilation, dealing with them is paramount to survival. The dead, nonetheless, behave and operate in lots of ways like the living, so to better understand their manner of being one must first turn to how the faithful channel the force of life to enact and receive healing during ceremonies and also to go about their daily routines, which are also influenced by religion. These points will be gradually made clear throughout the chapter by drawing on ethnographic situations from one of these religions, starting with the vignette that follows.

Dead Man's Hand

The ceremony was about to end. Apparently, it had been a resounding success. The occasion had been sensitive since various groups that did not always get on had turned up at the venue. But when the final entity had left the body of the cult house's most prestigious adept, the initiate did not come around. She remained immobile on the ground, completely still, as though she had fainted—or worse. The religious leader who had conducted the event was obliged to ring the small bell over the adept's head in order for her to come around, completely unaware of what had transpired. Afterwards the rest of the confraternity speculated among themselves about the motives for her collapse. Would she now have to perform a new rite to regain her strength? Had the hand of the deceased that hovered over her head finally turned into a malevolent influence? Or was the spirit of the curer who had initiated the entire congregation now finally demanding payback for his funerary ritual not having been fully concluded?

The event in question was a festivity belonging to *Jarê*, an African-based religion developed in Brazil. Jarê, which can be considered a kind of *caboclo Candomblé*,[1] involves festivals in which practitioners sing, dance, and in general allow the entities closest to them to manifest in their bodies. Frequently they include meals, ritual or not, and occasionally animal sacrifices, when initiations are being held. The ceremonies vary in duration, usually five to ten solid hours on a single day. Occasionally they may be repeated on more than one day, generally two or three in succession, in contrast to what happened in the past when festivities could last up to nine days straight. Over the course of each celebration, people sensitive to the action of the entities usually end up receiving up to a dozen per night. In total, in the houses with the largest number of followers, almost one hundred distinct incorporations may occur at a single festival.

Unlike Candomblé, which emerged on the Brazilian coast, Jarê was developed and perpetuated exclusively in Chapada Diamantina, a mountainous region with a semi-arid climate in the geographic heart of Bahia, a state located in the northeast of the country. The nonindigenous colonization of this inland area began as early as the seventeenth century, but the migratory processes with the biggest impact on the region took place mostly at the end of the eighteenth century and during the first half of the nineteenth with artisanal mining. The principal commodity extracted was diamond, which gave its name to the *chapada* (upland plateau) and marks a historic division of the municipalities belonging to the region, depending on whether or not they contain mineral deposits. Hence the oldest towns belong to the mining region in the center of Chapada Diamantina. The growth of the settlements in the surrounding area was driven by the need to supply agricultural produce to the mining areas, as well as to find a viable economic alternative in the intervals between the peaks of the mineralogical cycles, giving rise to a life based fully around agriculture in place of mining.

Historically Jarê developed in this same direction, outward from the towns of Lençóis and Andaraí, located in the mining region, identified as the religion's birthplace.[2] A huge contingent of slave labor was forcibly transferred to these cities in the nineteenth century. Composed of African people brought directly from the coast and Afro-descendants coming from other regions of Brazil, this contingent subsequently formed the basis of a local population considered primarily *mestiça* (ethnically mixed) due to the influx of prospectors from the interior of the state of Minas Gerais, a region known for gold mining, and from the Recôncavo area of Bahia, the same state but closer to the coast. The fact that Jarê developed in the diamond-mining region means that the religion's history is intrinsically connected to the history of the place, until very recently shaped by the extraction of precious stones through dangerous manual prospecting. Seeking an economic alternative when income from diamond extraction began to wane in the second half of the twentieth century, the residents of Lençóis successfully redirected their activities to the service sector and ecotourism in particular. The town's colonial housing was listed as national historical heritage in 1972, and in 1985 a conservation area was decreed, taking the form of a huge national park encompassing the Serra do Sincorá mountain range. This measure acted as a brake on the depredation of the natural environment that the area continued to suffer due to highly mechanized mining by outside companies that had replaced the traditional artisanal mining. Furthermore, both forms of protection helped place the region definitively on the map of the best global ecotourism destinations (Brito 2005: 299).

The Life of the Land and the Death of the Soil: A Telluric Metaphysics

With the transition of the local economy to ecological adventure tourism, there was a growing demand for guides who knew the treacherous paths of the mountain uplands, capable of taking visitors along trails that sometimes last several days before reaching magnificent waterfalls, deep caves, subterranean lakes and plateaus with fascinating landscapes. The members of the traditional mining population found themselves in some ways already well-prepared to become guides through the woods and mountains, cultivating the habit of walking for hours on end and transmitting knowledge of the Chapada topography, both themes central to Jarê since they are directly connected to the earth, as will be seen later. The work of the diamond prospectors, like that of the tour guides they would become, involved an intimate connection with the land. Their own survival depended on their knowledge of the region's geography and mining techniques, which included altering river courses, undertaking excavations, and prospecting in the *grunas* (submerged caves with air pockets that allow for breathing), information on the different rock residues that needed to be sifted through when searching for diamonds. Similarly, their work required them to trek many kilometers through the mountains and woods of the Chapada, clearing paths, building temporary shelters in which they would sometimes spend the night, or climbing steep rock faces (Toledo 2001: 102–13, 2008: 69–76; Lima and Nolasco 1997: 19).

While the men walked for long distances in their daily work in the prospecting industry, the women also moved about considerably as part of their everyday activities, whether to fish, wash clothes, or fetch firewood. It is no coincidence, therefore, that the population of Lençóis today makes use of numerous expressions and existential considerations linked to walking. Someone trustworthy, for instance, is commonly said to "step safely." Another person's exemplary conduct might be praised with the remark: "I would step where she steps." Copying someone's actions is described as a desire to "walk their path," while obtaining an advantage at someone else's expense is "to trip him up." Applauding restrained behavior or condemning someone else's hastiness might involve the dictum that "the one who runs tires but the one who walks arrives." Not to mention the many references to problems in life as obstacles to be overcome on a journey, as in the saying: "This is not a high wall that cannot be jumped over, nor a deep river that cannot be crossed" (Gonçalves 1984: 115).

The families made up of artisanal miners in the past and trail guides today comprise the bulk of the adepts of the Jarês in the diamond prospecting region. Their dispositions in relation to the earth are connected to the cosmological and ritual elaborations that Jarê similarly nourishes vis-à-vis the land and its composition, in a fairly similar way to the coastal Candomblés in Brazil. Dance steps need to be precise and match the style of the entities that visit the ritual sites at each moment, all of them called "caboclos" practically without distinction. The substances resulting from the ritual offerings should be deposited in the center of the cult houses and absorbed there by the land, becoming part of the force of the place and at the same time putting it in motion. The energy repository concentrated there can never be removed from the site. Around it, are fixed the religious community and above all its spiritual leadership, the people responsible for the procedures involved in the mystical maintenance of the locality.

This series of dispositions in relation to the earth and the land can be seen as part of a "telluric metaphysics."[3] While not in any sense exclusive to Jarê, this metaphysics encounters a particularly fertile soil for its elaboration in Chapada Diamantina. The mystic tellurism of Jarê can be discerned from the outset in the action of the older entities, explicitly linked to the land, like Nanã Borocô and Abaluaê, who after becoming incorporated in followers immediately collapse prostrate on the ground. When people begin to sing to these spirits, all those present customarily place at least the fingers of one hand on the ground, maintaining contact with the earth. When they arrive in the *pagodô* (the largest space in the Jarê temples), these entities crawl towards the drums, pouring water and palm oil in front of them. The liquids mix with the beaten earth making up the floor of the hall, producing a mud that the entities themselves manipulate and spread over their bodies, especially on the back of their hands and arms. This phenomenon amplifies another one evident at every Jarê: people dancing barefoot on the sometimes wet earth floor (soaked with water or sweat) partially erode it, taking care to ensure that the ground does not become too slippery. Just as the gradual melting of the candles—vertical objects that seem to move closer and closer to the ground, as though sucked by it—transmits the idea of the permeability of the earth, so many of the substances utilized and produced in the rituals end up being spilled on the earth of the *pagodô* and assimilated with it, especially blood, but also palm oil, sugar cane rum, honey, water, and sweat. The energy mobilized in and by the rituals, which is simultaneously constituted and transmitted by these diverse substances, penetrates the earth of the cult house and becomes part of it, continually turned over and re-administered by and in other ritual actions, as in the example of the mud.

Similarly, participants should always remove their footwear after being taken over by an entity, since the incorporated spirits refuse to take a single step without their feet being in direct contact with the ground. There are indeed moments, observed with considerable pleasure and attention, when the entities incorporated in a Jarê briefly abandon their connection with the earth, or make other people lose it. Although their choreography is generally performed almost entirely very close to the ground, some men in particular, when manifesting their spirits, add small jumps, sometimes lifting both feet from the ground while bending their knees. These steps are greeted enthusiastically by the onlookers who find them amusing and beautiful. This evaluation also recognizes the risk that was taken, not only of slipping but also of abandoning the safety of the ground for a few instants. Similarly, a greeting made with great pleasure by some entities, generally shown to children but not limited to them, involves lifting someone off the ground with a strong hug, bending their own body backwards as they lift. Jarê adepts remark that this is a form of transmitting health to the person being greeted, emphasizing a particular possibility of channeling that occurs whenever their own contact with the ground comes to depend on, and be made by, an entity. In an inversion of this configuration, participants should avoid jumping over someone lying on the ground, especially during the period of seclusion, lest they open the person's body to harmful influences.

This telluric metaphysics also helps explain the apprehension of the native population of Chapada Diamantina concerning the death of the soil caused by the advance of mechanized mining in the region at the end of the 1990s. People add, however, that when prospecting for precious stones has been undertaken in the vicinity of important Jarê houses, all that was found was coal rather than diamonds. These failures—whether deemed to be the result of the mystic action of the Jarê leaders to protect their territory, or conceived as a response of the land itself in those locations where its force is more concentrated against the attacks to which it has been subject—revealed the importance of the life of the earth. Traditional, less invasive forms of prospecting never led to the radical destruction of the earth shown by the large banks of sand left by mechanized mining or the consequent decline in animal and plant species in the region. The people of Jarê depend on the force that the land condenses not only as a direct source of sustenance but also to maintain their religion.

Forces and Their Forms: Modulating Intensities

All the entities mobilized in Jarê, especially those that become incorporated in the adepts, can be conceived of as forces in a concentrated state, capable of participating in the everyday life of human beings in various ways, including manifesting in their bodies. With the passing of time, cultivation of the habit of receiving the entities in the cult houses, and the emergence of intimate relations between people and their spirits, the forces—which the entities simultaneously are and have—become sedimented in the bodies of those who receive them, concentrated in them: the caboclos manifested by Jarê adepts are like people "precipitated" from force-spirits that are more absolute, in the chemical sense of the term. Various entities of the world, like other animals, plants, and certain objects such as specific stones, also exist as products of a kind of "distillation" of the pervasive forces with which human beings enter into contact, very often assuming specific formats and determined consistencies that facilitate interaction. The Jarê rituals encourage the utilization of innumerable fluid substances—with special attention given to the viscous and cloudy—like perfumes, rum, wine, water, sweat, saliva, blood, palm oil, honey, foods like *vatapá* and *caruru*, talcum powder, *pemba* clay powder, ashes, gunpowder, the sulphur from rockets, incense, and even breath (of the spoken word, of songs, and of the gasp that reveals the effort to persevere despite exhaustion), similarly to what happens in various other African-based religions (Souty 2007: 455). All these forms which the forces of Jarê can acquire on being circulated and transmitted are capable of spreading to the people present, whether daubing, smearing, splattering, or spraying them. On the other hand, other granular substances whose particles are not held in liquid suspension—like flour, sweetcorn, and beans—are reserved to feed unincorporated entities and also for initiation rituals, enabling the bodies of initiates to become open, more porous to transferences, until they become closed once more, protected now by these entities.

Blood, especially sacrificial, is one of the primary substances responsible for transmitting the force mobilized by Jarê, and also its concrete form *par excellence*, precisely on account of its being, by definition, the first vital fluid. The blood spilled on the adepts and simultaneously offered to the entities is and contains the forces that the ritual authority engages in order to perform cures, connecting or separating persons and spirits. People emphasize that after the initiation ritual those who have just become linked to the cult house must sleep that night with their bodies and clothing stained by the coagulated blood from the offerings. This is removed the following morning with the ritual bathing that concludes the works. The remaining blood spilled in the middle of the Jarê halls at the end of the initiation rituals is spread and covered with earth, until it literally becomes part of the force that is and emanates from the ground of the holy site and from the set of ritual objects buried in it. In some cases, the sacrificial blood is also consumed directly by those frequenting Jarê during the ceremonies held in honor of entities venerated by the local leader. Here the blood is left to pour into a special basin and mixed with honey and an alcoholic drink, typically rum. This mixture—which is immediately offered in small cups to those present for them to take a few sips, with the advice that this should be done reverentially—is called precisely *sangue real* (royal/real blood). The sacrificial blood that ideally needs to be spilled during the ritual encapsulates many of the modulations that the forces can acquire on being manipulated: a fluid, transferable, transposing, dilutable, condensable, and sapid substance.

Inversely, blood may also be effectively used in mystic procedures aimed at taking away life, as in the case of the blood resulting from violent acts. In all events, the most common situation in which blood figures as a kind of force opposed to the entities revered in the festivals can be observed in the taboo on menstruating women being present at the ceremonies. The adepts say that women during their menstrual periods should avoid frequenting Jarê festivals, since sometimes the mere proximity of the caboclos to a menstruating woman is enough to drain their energy, making their *aparelhos* ("equipment/devices" — as people are called when they receive entities) collapse unconscious on the ground. Some young women, not wishing to miss a single Jarê, alter the frequency with which they take contraceptive pills so that their menstrual periods do not to coincide with the festival dates, a practice viewed disapprovingly by more cautious people. It is not uncommon to say of menstruating women — with some euphemism used since the topic is viewed as sensitive — that they are "ill" or that they have a "dirty body." The latter designation also applies to anyone who has had sex recently, who should take propitiatory baths prior to the festival so that their state is not harmful to the entities. As in the first case, the bodies of the persons involved are deemed to become "open," especially subject to the influences of pernicious forces due to the proximity established with the vagina. As the adepts assert, even when they are not menstruating, women have a greater propensity and capacity to weaken the entities since their bodies possess a channel through which blood intermittently flows. Menstrual blood is considered an ideal substance for making and breaking sorcery spells, and its obvious connection to death — or, more precisely, non-life — allows it to act as a contradictory force of considerable intensity, doubly abortive. The fact that female urine shares the same passageway with blood imbues it — in contrast to male urine — with a similar potential to neutralize energy, at least in terms of its application against spells. Some people call this force, opposed to that of the caboclos, *abajé* (a term also applied to a woman's state during her menstrual period), capable of toppling entities in the Jarê halls precisely because of its excess of strength.

Necessary Distancings and Risky Approximations: The Mortuary Rituals

The ritual occasions that deal directly and indirectly with the death of people connected to Jarê reveal how even after leaving this world a person can still act on it. The quintessential funerary ritual in Jarê is fairly similar to the one performed in Candomblé (cf. Bastide 1958: 135–137; Elbein dos Santos 1975: 231), called *axexê* or *sirrum*. Whenever an important leader from the religion dies — especially in the case of Jarê masters, that is the people who have initiated others who later founded their own cult houses—one of their peers is called to send away the energy accumulated by the deceased person in order to dissipate it. In the ceremony itself, which can last several days, their vital force will condense one last time, vibrating the chair which in life functioned as a throne in the temple's main hall. As the adepts remark, the clothing and decorations are not just forms that assist in recognizing the entities: they are objects themselves capable of causing transformations and which contain something of the personal force of those who possess them, as well as their spirits. For this reason, indeed, the clothes of spiritual leaders, which may number many dozens of items, are carefully unsewn. Personal objects that belonged to the deceased are also broken, while the leather of the drums in the cult house is slit. These objects are not just forms of intensifying a person's proximity to the spirits: they configure materializations of part of this connection and the forces involved in the process of incorporating them.

The rite in question tends to mark the end of a specific cult house, since it is common for the energy center that feeds it to weaken and disintegrate after the death of the person who looked after the place. This operation may even be performed by the cult house leader while they are still alive, if the person feels that death is approaching and has no wish for there to be a succession at the temple concerned. Properly undoing forces that cannot remain active without the person's presence is also a way of not transmitting these powers freely, preventing them from being inherited by someone who cannot—or should not—receive them. Considerable effort is needed to build a cult house and it is the endeavor of creating it and enabling it to grow that allows the leader to acquire at least some of the knowledge needed to control and tend to the forces involved in the process. An absence of continuity is thus commonplace in the history of Jarê temples, meaning that houses are almost always built from scratch and demolished after the death of their leader. Cult houses with a prolonged existence constitute an exception. As the adepts say, the house itself is alive, as the pulsation of its walls during the ceremonies shows, animated by the sound of the drums. It makes perfect sense, therefore, that the life of the person responsible for the house is very directly linked to the physical structure of the locale, with the solidity of one reflected in the other. Hence any deterioration to the buildings of a religious site may be greeted with concern, a fairly clear signal of the personal weakening of its spiritual leader. The closeness of this connection is another factor that makes the reutilization of the same cult house by another religious leader highly risky—albeit a possibility that, like any risk in Jarê, harbors a potentiality for anyone capable of handling it.

Not holding the ceremony for sending on the deceased person is an alternative sometimes taken, in which case part of their force continues to animate the cult house and protect the confraternity. This force, however, may become coveted by people who wish to mobilize its power in their own favor. In one case, for example, a young and ambitious curer, who had access to the ceremonial attire of a deceased and renowned father in sainthood (*pai-de-santo*) from a neighboring town, put on the clothes and subsequently became mad for a considerable time. The outcome was not just punishment for the young man's unduly audacious attitude: it was a fairly direct effect of the disproportion between his personal force and the force of the late curer, somehow present in—or accessible through—his clothes. In a curious and opposite case, people tell that another young father in sainthood decided to abandon his destiny and perform his own funerary rite while still alive, divesting himself of his ritual objects and clothes. Sometime later the entities decided to punish him for this attempt and force him to return to Jarê. One of the less serious consequences of this process was his complete loss of contact—even after the opening of a new cult house—with one of the most important spirits that he had mobilized in the past.

Another funerary ritual needs to be held after the death of a Jarê leader. This time, though, the rite is performed on those initiated into the dead leader's cult house, since the influence over them does not necessarily end with the leader's death. On the contrary, it may then become involuntarily harmful. The act of "removing the hand of the dead person" from their heads, as the procedure is called, is usually officiated by the leader set to become responsible for the mystic pathways of their lives in a new confraternity, effectively replacing the dead person's hand with their own. The procedure itself consists of a new initiation rite, with the addition of disjunctive stages to mark the separation between the person being initiated and the person who had been responsible for them. People say that not everyone needs to remove the hand of the deceased—older women especially are generally less susceptible to the actions of the dead person—but doing so can prove imperative if someone's problems are diagnosed to be of mystic origin, or if the person wishes someone else to assume responsibility for the continuation of their life in Jarê. This may even result in a change of place of residence to be able to follow the routine of the new cult house closely.

People who have not performed the ritual for removing the hand of the person who initiated them are more liable to suffer from what the adepts call "tumbling over" (*tombamento*). This state can be initially glimpsed in a milder form when the manifestations of the spirits become less stable, dancing with unsure footing, becoming unsteady, tripping and making the wrong steps. In more accentuated cases, a person may collapse to the ground after a possession has ended, generally falling brusquely and violently, remaining unconscious after being disinhabited by the entity that until then the adept had revered in their body. This "brief death" can normally be reverted over time by the head of the temple, who kneels next to the body and plays a small ritual bell in the person's ears. This ritual collapse represents a sign of weakening of both the human being and their entities, generally the result of the absence of a connection with the person who performs initiations. It may also be a kind of punishment inflicted by the spirits on the person who receives them, manifesting their discontent with some behavior or attitude or the failure to fulfill some obligation. The fact that the withdrawal of the entity can prevent the person's return to consciousness, hurling them to the ground, is aggravated by leaving them immobile, in contrast to the precise, well-paced and continuous movement that marks the enjoyment of life and the cultivation of longevity that Jarê so highly values.

Channeling the Flow: Against Death, Movement

As we have seen, the forces with which Jarê constantly deals, and which ultimately comprise specific modulations of a primary energetic monism, assume particular forms in order to be put into circulation properly with the main purpose of maintaining life. The idea of movement as a quality of life is present in the curing processes central to the ritual economy of Jarê. Every initiation process is also potentially a therapeutic—or at least prophylactic—action, regulating the vital flow of initiated followers and mobilizing this flow to keep them healthy. In particular, the aim is to achieve an equilibrium—or more precisely, a less unstable temporary configuration—in terms of the degree of participation of the immaterial entities that accompany and constitute them. Much of the ritual work performed during the Jarê curing and initiation ceremonies can be described through metaphors taken from the natural sciences as a way of elucidating this ritual work for an audience unfamiliar with how it functions. The borrowing of terms like kinetic energy, tension, intensity of flow, facilitated diffusion, is all the more appropriate insofar as the disciplines from which they originate (mechanics, especially fluid mechanics, electronics, and cellular biology) employ them to refer to the exchange of energies and substances. These procedures refer to stabilizations that come about as a result of an initial difference, whether in potential or concentration, existing between two or more subsystems entering into contact. Forces of different intensities communicate with one another and flow from one direction to another, supplying the afflicted person with a new equilibration and establishing a higher level of mutual participation between the parties than at the start.

To a greater or lesser degree, Jarê can be seen as a device for guiding microbeliefs, flows of intentionalities and attentions, oriented towards the establishment not only of communicational channels but also communicating vessels: these feed and keep alive the entities of the world—whose degrees of existence are continually variable—which includes, albeit perhaps far from being the most fundamental part, the people who frequent a cult house and their dead. From this viewpoint, the people linked to the cult houses function above all as relays due to their capacity to redirect particular flows through their actions, either weakening or revitalizing certain entities of the world. Religious leaders, in turn, are responsible for orienting the direction of this force: when directed to one side, it is literally transported, caused to leave its current position, necessarily producing a kind of vacuum as a result. For the forces of Jarê, rather than being just sides, left and right are above all directions: they can be understood to be oriented towards either emptying or filling space. Every transference process, however, involves transitions, generating more emptied spaces and more filled spaces simultaneously. The emergence of these energy vacuums causes weakening and, in the case of human beings, sickness or even death. It is thus up to the ritual authorities to perform cures that re-establish a less deficient situation, regardless of the fact that any equilibrium attained is inevitably provisional. One of the main forms of correcting these energy insufficiencies derives from the entropic quality possessed by this force, which means that it tends to flow from the places where it is most abundant to where it is most scarce: in this case, from the head of the cult house to the members of their confraternity, but equally from entities in general to human beings.[4]

The tensile configuration of this process of energy transfer helps us comprehend the reasons why it is advisable to avoid performing rites for people who, in the expression of the adepts, "were already born made." The rituals conducted by any Jarê leader are premised on the idea that an energy deficiency will be remedied through the abundance of their personal force, including the powers of the leader's entities. Liturgical measures are therefore conducted to this end, to help in the task of transferring their excess energy to the initiate. Generally speaking, religious leaders are more experienced in its handling, knowing how to modulate this energy to obtain the desired effects, possessing it in greater quantity, and mobilizing it more easily. Sometimes, however, this is not the case since on rare occasions people emerge who from birth possess an untamed force of considerable intensity. Even without any kind of ritual work on their behalf, they already display this energy in large quantity. More experienced Jarê leaders can recognize this quality among certain people and are aware of the precautions that need to be taken to deal with them as well as the benefits of potentializing the force of their cult houses which the continuous presence of these individuals can bring. At the same time, they know that such people can perhaps never be initiated, or only with extreme difficulty, precisely because of the excessive force that they possess.

If a ritual authority carries out the customary procedures but comes across someone who, against all expectations, presents even more force than them, the results can be disastrous: a kind of short-circuit is established by an overload in which the transfer of force occurs in an uncontrolled fashion, potentially leaving the leader of the place severely debilitated at the very least.[5] In contrast to what more usually happens, in these cases the affliction that can lead someone to go—or be taken—to a Jarê authority derives not from a lack of energy but its overabundance, precisely one of the main causes of the episodes of madness typical of the behavior of many people destined to later perform cures themselves. It is fairly common for Jarê leaders to become exhausted and even carry some kind of after-effect, temporary or permanent, once the initiatory rites are performed. Indeed it is no coincidence that in many instances this involves an effect on the person's capacity to move about, such as swellings and problems with the feet, legs, and knees. These are anticipated consequences of the work of curing, which is considered therefore a path marked by charity and altruism, and a function of the new configuration established by the ritual.

Cheating Death: Religiosity Turned to Life

Death is a theme that tends to be much less elaborated in Jarê than life and living beings. Indeed for this reason, it would not be accurate to consider death the opposite of life, since it only forms part of its conclusion, in the same way that birth marks its beginning, thus being the true opposite of death.[6] In fact people at times remark that in Jarê, while death is usually considered the last moment of existence for the human being, it is not for all of them. Death—which is occasionally linked to the sea, "because the sea is infinite," people explain[7]—implies inevitability while at the same time provoking speculation about what happens to a person after death. While some believe that the souls of all human beings may live eternally in another domain of existence, a large proportion of the adepts categorically state that nothing exists for people after death. Thus, they continue, there is no reason to be afraid of cemeteries—unlike churches, which are terrifying locations. It can be seen, therefore, that if the soul of someone does not comprise exactly their essence, something that would survive after death, it is still a potential vestige that can inhabit the world for some time and that is not necessarily left by each person on dying, or "disembodying," as people say. In the language most frequently used in the context of Jarê, it amounts to a "shadow," which can be defined here as an amalgam of the person who died and something from the entities that accompanied them in life.

After dying, a person may or may not leave part of themselves in the world of the living—a part which those left alive can access if they possess the ability to deal with these beings, a capacity generally called "mediumship." This can also be developed in Jarê ceremonies and its control tends to signal the person's destiny as a future religious leader. As well as people who died in natural accidents or tragedies, human beings who demonstrated great personal force in life and who continually mobilized it tend to leave their shadow behind, partially surviving the person's death. Not everyone, then, will necessarily continue to exist in the beyond—a place inhabited by the spirits of the dead, sometimes called *eguns*, who occasionally set out to visit the living with a variety of outcomes. The adepts say that it is inadvisable to pay too much attention to these spirits, since they can feed off these flows of intentionalities that are also capable of relaying energy, generating deficiencies that may cause harm that needs to be cured in Jarê. As a result, leaders of the houses instruct those who frequent the ceremonies to ignore strange beings who they may sense or detect, in order to not run the risk of strengthening the spirit of a dead person, encouraging them to remain among the living.

The entities close to a person, who may also become part of their composition, have the same capacity to survive the death of anyone initiated into the cult, possibly at an even more pronounced level. Unlike human beings, the saints never die, people say, however they may vanish over time if they cease to be worshipped. The possibility of not dying is one of the characteristics distinguishing these entities from the bulk of humanity, save for the people who have left the world of the living without dying by becoming "enchanted." By turning into an inhabitant of this other world, this kind of ex-living-person, having never faced death, undergoes a peculiar transformation, acquiring a constitution that approximates the spirit to the entities worshipped in Jarê, many of which may be interchangeably called "enchanted ones" (*encantados*). People who enchant, generally disappearing in the mountains or forests, and whose bodies have never been discovered, point to a phenomenon that can be considered the opposite of being born ready-made: people who will never be unmade by death.[8] These figures and the people who appear among the biggest names of Jarê all display a characteristic that reveals a chromaticism between human beings, Jarê entities, and spirits of the dead. Due to their considerable personal force, both those born ready-made and those who became prepared in a very intense form over the course of life are themselves particularly likely to become entities to be worshipped—just as may have happened in the past, both among the native population from the African continent and among indigenous peoples in the Americas, as some of the adepts speculate. In the same way that they guided the initiated in life, so after abandoning their physical existence these people may continue to provide help to the living who frequent Jarê, in a way perhaps not limited to the action of the entities left behind and that may continue to exist.

The most elaborate process of decomposition of the person is reserved for the great religious authorities of Jarê. These should be given the already mentioned funerary ritual called *sirrum*, generally held some years after their death at the close of a period of mourning. *Sirrum* is usually presided over by another Jarê leader, very often resulting in the complete deactivation of the cult house of the deceased person. As people recount, no drums are played in these ceremonies: they remain covered in white cloths. The destruction or dissolution of the possessions of the deceased forms the main activity of the ritual. Those who frequent the house find it difficult to contain their tears, though one should try to do so. In all events, the fact that not every dissolution of the person needs to be complete is another example of the degrees of continuity between the living and the dead, humans and entities, with the latter also sometimes responsible for carrying out transferences, actualizing fairly direct connections with the domain of death. This was the case of a newborn child, the daughter of a woman who gave birth at a cult house. An entity, Odé—which in Jarê is considered an infantile version of Oxóssi, the patron spirit of hunting—became manifested in the curer responsible for the house and came to greet the little girl, asking the child's mother, apparently in a playful tone, whether she would give him the baby.

Finding the situation funny and ignoring the consequences of her words—as the woman who told this story emphasized—the mother said yes to the entity, which was fascinated with the beauty of the newborn. A short while later the child stopped moving, abandoning the living world. There was little doubt among those who had witnessed the event that she had been taken by the entity. Thereafter she would rest in the City of Joined-Feet (*Cidade de Pé-Junto*), which is how some people refer to the cemetery, the dwelling where everyone now alive will rest one day, as they say. The joined feet cited in the name not only refers to the way in which dead people are laid out in their coffins: it also calls attention to the main characteristic of those who are no longer alive, namely the immobility of their feet, which no longer ascend and descend the mining uplands, no longer cross the rivers and forests, no longer walk or dance.

Every Jarê ends with a homage to a twin entity whom a myth approximates to Ibêji, an African double orisha also linked to twins. According to this history, in an African kingdom long ago there lived a pair of brothers who were absolutely identical and for this reason already deemed very special. One day, during a celebration of the entities, Death arrived in the kingdom saying that it would take with it all the inhabitants as soon as the leather of the drums stopped vibrating. Faced with this nefarious fate, the brothers had an idea. They decided to take turns on the drums, allowing one of them to rest while the other kept the music alive, thereby extending the duration of the festival indefinitely. As they were identical and swapped places when Death was distracted, Death was unable to distinguish them and imagined that it was the same person playing continuously. Tiring of the wait, Death finally gave up and left the kingdom without claiming anyone who lived there. The twins were hailed as heroes and later became divinities themselves. In a way, every Jarê held to this day can be conceived as a reactualization of this clash and this ruse. Like the twins in the myth, the drum players are responsible for keeping the festival running, urging, along with the other people present, the adepts to continue dancing, the entities not to leave the hall, despite the exhaustion to which everyone is inevitably subject. Performing Jarês is a form of ensuring that life continues in all its plenitude. Indeed for this reason ceremonies focus on curing and reviving those who frequent them, mobilizing the entities and forces that compose and are composed by people, and gradually sending away the spirits of the dead and their disturbing influences. Drumming Jarês is above all a means of keeping alive an endless party, a festival that cannot end without running the risk of its conclusion also meaning the end of life as we know it. Above all a festival also is—and needs to be—a happy, animated occasion, even though the circumstances might not always favor joyfulness. Even in the face of a series of obstacles and the possibility that its reality may vanish if their efforts are not renewed, the people linked to the cult opt for an existence full of vivacity. Not only during the ceremonies but also outside them, they thereby testify to the powers of life and movement. Against death, they affirm the forces of Jarê.

Gabriel Banaggia is a postdoctoral fellow at the Pontifical Catholic University of Rio de Janeiro's Social Sciences Graduate School. During his PhD studies at the National Museum in Brazil, he conducted fieldwork in Bahia on *jarê*, a traditional trance religion. He focuses on African-based religions in Brazil and is currently developing a georeferenced database of ethnographies on the topic.

Notes

1. The word "caboclo" in Brazil usually denotes a person of indigenous or mixed ancestry, and in this instance qualifies several different but related meanings of a specific religious variety, as will become clear.
2. I conducted fieldwork lasting almost fourteen months (twelve of these consecutive) in the town of Lençóis, with the adepts of the local Jarês. I take the opportunity to thank them once again. This research resulted in my doctoral thesis, later revised and published as a book (Banaggia 2013, 2015). The only other two works dedicated to the same theme available at the time dealt either panoramically with the Jarês of Chapada Diamantina as a whole (Senna 1998), or in depth with Jarês from a district in the agricultural zone (Rabelo 1990). Recently another doctoral thesis was completed in which Jarê was the subject of a detailed ethnographic inquiry (Pedreira 2015).
3. Term proposed as a transformation of the use given by one of the main chronicler's of the region to the expression "telluric democracy" (Moraes 1983: 19).
4. Even so, it is not a case of completely discarding the existence of an effectively negative force, an "anti-force" — in the sense held by the term "anti-matter" — responsible not just for emptying energy but for completely annihilating it. This anti-force seems to be the exclusive domain of highly dangerous entities, however, beings with whom little dialogue is possible, such as the shadows of the dead, and from which one should always remain as far away as possible. In another African-based ethnographic field, the religious houses in the town of Pelotas in the far south of Brazil, the expression *axé de miséria* (misery force) or the term *inxé* may be used to refer to the symmetric opposite of *axé*, which bears clear similarities to the anti-force described here (cf. Barbosa Neto 2012: 95–98, 106, 226 note 200, 274).
5. One adept, for example, reports, in an apparently unassuming way, how all the people who tried to perform some kind of cure for her ended up dead a short time later (Rabelo 1990: 178–79).
6. This can also be observed from the fact that while heads of cult houses may sometimes invoke and perhaps even receive spirits of the dead, they never do so during Jarê ceremonies, a cult whose "religiosity is turned to the world of the living" (Gonçalves 1984: 131, 134).
7. The association between the sea and death seems to be recurrent in Angolan Candomblé and in other African-based religions, heavily reminiscent, for example, of the Kalunga of the Cuban palo religion, including in the way in which they speak about it, equated with the sea: it comprises a plane of immanence from which subjects and objects emerge to the rhythm of the fluctuations and tides (Ochoa 2004: 42–53; 2007: 482). The term was chosen to form part of the name of a work that collates images produced over three centuries concerning the black population in Brazil (Moura 2000: 15).
8. In Candomblé, the earthly existence of children whose death is claimed before they are even born, called *abiku*, is dependent on a negotiation with the entities, meaning that they should not be initiated: since the initiation replicates a death, one from which

these children are extracted every day, they are unable to bear suffering a still greater permeabilization to its effects (Augras 1994: 77–78, cited in Barbosa Neto 2012: 28 n20). Although the term is not used in Jarê, the episode narrated here shows very clear similarities to this phenomenon, the dramatic development of which took place entirely in front of the living.

References

Augras, Monique. 1994. "Os gêmeos e a morte: notas sobre os mitos dos *ibeji* e dos *abiku* na cultura afro-brasileira." In *As senhoras do pássaro da noite*, ed. Carlos Eugênio Marcondes de Moura, 73–84. São Paulo: Editora da Universidade de São Paulo.

Banaggia, Gabriel. 2013. *As forças do Jarê: movimento e criatividade na religião de matriz africana da Chapada Diamantina*. PhD diss., Universidade Federal do Rio de Janeiro.

———. 2015. *As forças do Jarê, religião de matriz africana da Chapada Diamantina*. Rio de Janeiro: Garamond.

Barbosa Neto, Edgar Rodrigues. 2012. *A máquina do mundo: variações sobre o politeísmo em coletivos afro-brasileiros*. PhD diss., Universidade Federal do Rio de Janeiro.

Bastide, Roger. 1958 (2005). *O candomblé da Bahia (rito nagô)*. São Paulo: Companhia das Letras.

Brito, Francisco Emanuel Matos. 2005. *Os ecos contraditórios do turismo na Chapada Diamantina*. Salvador: Editora da Universidade Federal da Bahia.

Elbein dos Santos, Juana. 1975 (2002). *Os nàgô e a morte: pàde, àsèsè e o culto égun na Bahia*. Petrópolis: Vozes.

Gonçalves, Maria Salete Petroni de Castro. 1984. *Garimpo, devoção e festa em Lençóis, BA*. São Paulo: Escola de Folclore, Prol.

Lima, Carlos César Uchôa de, and Marjorie Csekö Nolasco. 1997. *Lençóis, uma ponte entre a geologia e o homem*. Salvador: Empresa Gráfica da Bahia.

Moraes, Walfrido. 1983 (1997). "Prefácio à terceira edição." In *Jagunços e heróis: a civilização do diamante nas lavras da Bahia*, 19–21. Salvador: Empresa Gráfica da Bahia.

Moura, Carlos Eugênio Marcondes de. 2000 (2012). *A travessia da calunga grande: três séculos de imagens sobre o negro no Brasil (1637–1899)*. São Paulo: Editora da Universidade de São Paulo.

Ochoa, Todd Ramón. 2004. *The Dead and the Living in a Cuban-Kongo Sacred Society*. PhD diss., Columbia University.

———. 2007. "Versions of the Dead: *Kalunga*, Cuban-Kongo Materiality, and Ethnography". *Cultural Anthropology* 22(4), 473–500.

Pedreira, Carolina Souza. 2015. *Tecidos do mundo: almas, espíritos e caboclos em Andaraí, Bahia*. PhD diss., Universidade de Brasília.

Rabelo, Miriam. 1990. *Play and Struggle: Dimensions of the Religious Experience of Peasants in Nova Redenção, Bahia*. PhD diss., University of Liverpool.

Senna, Ronaldo de Salles. 1998. *Jarê—uma face do candomblé: manifestação religiosa na Chapada Diamantina*. Feira de Santana: Editora da Universidade Estadual de Feira de Santana.

Souty, Jérôme. 2007. *Pierre Fatumbi Verger: du regard détaché à la connaissance initiatique*. Paris: Maisonneuve & Larose.
Toledo, Carlos de Almeida. 2001. *A mobilização do trabalho nas Lavras Baianas*. MA thesis, Universidade de São Paulo.
_____. 2008. *A região das Lavras Baianas*. PhD diss., Universidade de São Paulo.

Chapter 10

Of Shadows and Fears

Nepalese Ghost Stories from Classical Texts and Folklore to Social Media

Davide Torri

Introduction

What do we talk about when we talk about ghosts? A ghost is first and foremost a story. It exists in a narrative dimension and through it, or by it, it perpetuates itself. It needs listeners more than it needs witnesses. A ghost is a scary, unsettling story which nonetheless should be recounted. In the form of the unpacified revenant, it is a story coming back from the past again and again, it is the undying, unresolved past itself—a past which refuses to be just memory but lingers on and still needs something from the living, beyond the mere act of listening. To talk about ghosts is an activity which is undoubtedly linked to at least two, intertwined, orders of factors: on one side, conceptions, ideas, and beliefs about ghosts are inextricably tied to local dimensions and discourses pertaining to the afterlife, its conceptualizations, and to a general theory on the fate of the soul/life-energy/subtle body/breath; on the other side, the ghost appears also as a general, almost universal, transcultural concept, immediately recognizable, identifiable, and translatable from one context to the other with very similar connotations. It is also undoubtedly and very obviously, tied to the sphere of death: after all, it is death—the morbid fascination that this phenomenon exerts, with its inexhaustible source of mystery—that is the first and most important source of all ghost stories (Poo 2009: 1). Any discourse related to the existence of ghosts is linked to the ampler topic of life-after-death, a life-like existence which is imagined, or postulated, as: 1) something radically different or 2) in a radically different dimension. Variations on these themes are unaccountable, and diverse human cultures have given different answers to this crucial question. Modern studies on the links between the biological event defined "death" and its meanings for the individual as well as for collectivities could be linked with the first anthropological enquiries on the birth of religion itself (see, for example, Tylor 1871; Frazer 1913; Lévy-Bruhl 1927).

Dead can appear in dreams and visions to the living. On certain occasions, it is possible to perceive them during waking life. These two sets of events, oneiric and encounters during the waking life, constitute the raw materials of ghost stories. And yet, on the normative side, the dead are also safely encountered during calendrical festivities, which often include days devoted to the worship of the dead, and a popular belief holds true that on those days communications between the two sides is easier. On any other days, they can appear as embodied members, through possession. Despite being separated from the community of the living, they still maintain a certain degree of agency over it, be it in form of protective ancestors, restless spirits, or malevolent entities. Every discourse on ghosts must start with a body. The body of the dead and the body of the witness, in South Asia, appears often in relation to each other, whether in the context of possession, illness, or, even before that, in the treatment that the body receives during the *postmortem* phase. A lot of interactions between the living and the dead, in fact, presuppose a mistreatment of bodies.

The body is not a totally bounded entity: it has porous borders, natural openings, and casual wounds that can let life energies and vital forces in and out, blurring the boundaries between self and other, freeing the soul from being bound to its physical vessel, and even making possession possible. A whole set of transformations takes place within and around it, often mirrored in the decay of the mortal spoils, where the basic components of the body itself are going back to their natural constituents, the primary elements. In the Nepalese context, theories about the body and the process of death are usually deriving from two distinct, to some extent interrelated, sets of sources: the Hindu knowledge on one side and the Buddhist, on the other.

"For in That Sleep of Death, What Dreams May Come, When We Have Shuffled off this Mortal Coil . . ."

The decomposing body mirrors the dissolution of the social ties between the individual and the social group to which he or she belongs to.

Moreover, it could be argued that the corpse itself constitutes the link between the individual and the social body: it is its decomposition which sets into motion the complex patterns of ritual exchanges and fulfillment of duties involving relatives and friends. As such, it constitutes a pivotal element of the solidarity system on which the *communitas* is centered. It is starting from the corpse, in fact, that multiple meaningful practices are employed to state, reinstate, or even amplify the social ties. The dead, through proper ritual, is transformed into something different, but still present and to a certain extent still exerting a degree of agency. The wider *spectrum* of postmortem ritual is actually an elaborated process of detachment from the community of the living and incorporation in the same community on a different level: ancestor, if the proper rituals were correctly performed; saint if his or her lifestyle was particularly exemplary according to the group ethical standards and expectations; ghost if restless, due to incorrect funeral rites or tragic, unnatural, inexplicable, unjust, or untimely death.

Postmortem rituals have an effect simultaneously on multiple levels: practically, they constitute the proper way of disposal of the putrefying corpse, deemed highly polluting and inherently dangerous; socially, they placate the anxieties affecting the group deprived of one of its members, activating a solidarity web of compensation; and finally, spiritually or religiously, the dead acquires a new status or a new life. These different levels are naturally interwoven, as amply demonstrated by funeral rites themselves: the diverse techniques employed to take proper care of the corpse are in fact directly related to the notions about the specific afterlife as conceived by the group. These rites constitute the ideal model of what was defined by van Gennep ([1909] 1981) in *A Rite of Passage*, where the transition from one condition to the other is usually following a tripartite model: separation, transition, and transformation. These three phases could also be termed *preliminal*, *liminal*, and *postliminal*, and only upon reaching the third stage, and the related new status, the individual is again incorporated in the group (Turner 1967, 1969). The liminal phase is considered the most dangerous one, the individual being at this stage intrinsically unstable and essentially ambiguous (Turner 1969:95). For the very same reason, absent, incomplete, or incorrect performance of funeral rites can, in many cultures, give rise to a resentful spirit, or a ghost. The ghost constitutes the liminal, disturbing, and unsettling entity *par excellence*.

This tripartite correlation between the decomposition of the corpse, the dissolution of social ties, and the incorporation into a specific social group (the dead, the ancestors, etc.) constitutes also the model of the tamed, domesticated death described by Ariès (1977). A death less scary due to control mechanisms and ritual devices ensures the smooth transition in a critical time and the establishment of a sort of order in the relations between the living and the dead: after a long travel through the other world, which corresponds to the mourning time and the correct disposal of the body, the dead is finally "placed" in another dimension, finally pacified and kept under control. From that moment on, every relation is mediated through ritual or calendrical activities: the dead and the living can interact with each other only on certain occasion or at particular times of the year, and according to specific and particular dynamics. In the Indic context, this process is exemplified by the transformation of the dead from *pret* to *pitr*, from a restless ghost into a recognized ancestor[1]. The transformation of the individual into a member of the group of the ancestors is the direct outcome of the correct performance of the funeral practices. At the same time, the quiet belonging to that group is to be ensured through regular, and regulated, monthly offerings, i.e., the *śrāddha*.

While the exploration of mortuary rituals could give us additional materials to think about death and ghosts,[2] and acknowledging the obvious links between these two interrelated themes, when dealing with ghost stories we move partially away from the ritual and religious practices and we enter a different field, characterized by folkloric materials on one side, and narrative performance on the other. Several scholars of folkloric traditions identified in the oral heritage, and especially in stories about ghosts and the afterlife, the vehicle for the transmission and explanation of norms and social values.[3] It is certainly true that what may appear at first as an individual—a necrography *strictu senso*—tale about death and suffering, or about the supernatural, is not only an exceptional tale of the unexpected or the uncanny: each and every one seems to have a deeper meaning, a sort of subtext linking it to wider concepts and beliefs intrinsically tied with a system of thought. Ghost stories encompass and reflect, in fact, the individual stories of the ghost and the witness, intertwining them with conceptions or disbeliefs held by their narrators not only about the afterlife but also about established traditions and impending changes, moral issues or inheritance customs, social obligations or civic responsibilities, and so forth (Freed and Freed 1993: 85; Goldstein, Grider, and Thomas 2007: 13). The dead, through their stories, talk to the living about what happened and what will happen, but their voices, despite paradoxically coming from beyond, express always an insider perspective in relation to the parameters of the society. What is not always true is that, because of this, ghost stories are inherently conservative: often ghost stories are born around areas of individual or social conflicts, underlying the critical spots of a given culture, like a dark reflection of the inherent structural violence and injustice, whose victims, in forms of revenants, are forced to denounce again and again.

Mori (2012: 225) in his work on Japanese folklore describes the moment when, during the 1980s, ghost stories became an integral part of the mass culture and highlights their hybrid nature, in between folkloric materials and individual performance. This idea is very interesting, since, as it will also be evident in at least some of the following materials, it should be noted that ghost stories could constitute the conjunction points through which contents coming from various folkloric traditions can be transferred, through narration, into the society at large and even mainstream pop culture. Folklore and pop culture, after all, are to be considered intrinsically interrelated (Narváez and Laba 1986). Ghost stories, moreover, seem to be particularly tied to a juvenile context: the majority of "users" appear in fact to be constituted by teenagers and young adults. Through new forms of communication, like in the case of social media, elements of "traditional" culture are appropriated by the younger generations and flow into contemporary, urbanized settings. These appropriations equate to a form of commodification, making ideas and beliefs originally belonging to the religious sphere available as a form of entertainment. This phenomenon is not new, since ghost stories have been part of storytelling practices in almost every culture attested so far.

Phenomenology of the Indic Ghost

It has been said that the dead are scarier than death itself, because of their contextual presence and absence (Macho 2007: 961). Still here and yet no more, partaking of radically different dimensions at the same time, the dead person still has a residual force, or energy, or even better an agency on the living. This agency sometimes does not end with the dissolution of the physical body: belief in the survival of something belonging to the individual is not tied to the body or to physical space. The dead person is, in other words, *metà tà physiká*, metaphysics in the strictest sense. Beliefs related to this residual survival are shared by numerous cultures, and they are grounded on few similar ideas which could be summarized as follows: it exists in a dimension which is 1) objectively real and yet 2) separated and qualitatively different from the physical world, but 3) still enabling some kind of interaction between these two dimensions. These three conditions are followed by a more interesting one: that there are immaterial beings, which exist without a body. Among these, the ghost is the one without a proper place. The dead who have not been able to find the way to the otherworld, not pacified by the funerary rites, become restless and dangerous beings doomed to linger in-between worlds. Representation in ghost stories of these dead is tied to various, yet immediately recognizable, characteristics. Everyone is able to understand what a ghost is, yet its descriptions may entail radically different sets of appearances and behaviors. These differences are to be found not only between different cultures but also inside the same system of belief or worldview.

Pan-Indic beliefs about ghosts indicate that the concept could be applied to the

> disembodied spirit or shade of a dead person, who may haunt living persons and locations where the deceased lived or died. It may refer to the soul rather than the body of a deceased, to an apparition, specter, phantom, or wraith seen by a living person, or may be a haunting dream, memory, or image of the dead. (Freed and Freed 1993: 80)

Regarding this aspect, the ghost is usually described as resembling the living being he was. In many stories, in fact, witnesses do not immediately understand they are facing a ghost but deal with it like they would with the friend, relative, fellow human they used to know or they expect it to be. The interactions between them are "normal" until the realization that something is wrong: there are some criteria to identify beyond any reasonable doubt a ghostly being, which includes a lack of shadow, a nasal twang when speaking, feet pointing backward. In other stories a ghost occupies a corpse (a form of possession), reanimating it temporarily for its own purposes (like in the very famous set of stories titled, *vetālapañcaviṃśati*, the "twenty-five stories of the *vetāla*," see below). It could also appear as a glowing light, or an ethereal, pale, and luminescent body. Or, on the contrary, it could have the fierce aspect of an uncanny animal. Sometimes, and probably most of the time, a ghost is also not visible, but just "sensed,"[4] through noises, voices, whispers, or the movement of objects around the place.

Causes of death also play a pivotal role in defining ghosts. Several death typologies (collectively referred to as a "bad death") are recurrent in ghost tales: violent, extremely tragic, untimely or unjust deaths, suicides, and death during childbirth seem to produce, almost automatically, a restless, often vengeful, spirit.

> When a person dies, three main reasons are given for the soul of the dead becoming a ghost: (1) dying before the allotted time, (2) dying tortured, and (3) behavior contrary to village customs. The allotted time is set by Yama (for believers in ghosts) or Bhagwan (for disbelievers) based on their judgment of the sum of the soul's actions in past lives. Since no one knows the sum of a soul's actions, villagers interpret the allotted time in terms of the average natural length of a life, that is the average time villagers expect to live. When

people die before the end of the average life span, they are expected to become ghosts and haunt their families and village until their allotted time expires. (Freed and Freed 1993: 84)

A bad death in itself could be a legitimate reason for the dead to stay back, to come back, or to refuse to move on: sudden and tragic death in fact may give the dead a purpose or a duty to complete something, to punish a culprit, to avenge some injustice, to repay a debt or, simply, to reenact constantly a specific set of actions at recurrent times. The ghost's disposition toward the living could be, according to the circumstances, marked by hostility, benevolence, or indifference. During his research in the Himalayas, Berreman was repeatedly told that every dead is to be considered a ghost, and feared as such, for the first thirteen days after cremation (Berreman 1963: 110).

Times and places of ghostly apparitions are extremely variable. While the majority of them take place in deserted and lonely places (i.e., solitary country roads or paths, ruins, empty houses, graveyards, forests, locations where ancient battles were fought or heinous crimes committed) at nighttime, encounters in broad daylight in urban centers, in crowded streets, or while at work cannot be excluded. Other elements marking encounters with ghosts involve the displaying of what could be defined as supernatural skills like knowledge of past or future events, ability to move objects at a distance while being immaterial, the power of mind-reading, inflicting pain, shape-shifting, and so forth. In many stories, the possibility to stretch or elongate their limbs is also a recurrent features.

When talking about ghosts, then, people usually refer to a particular context of reference. That is to say, despite transcultural similarities, ghosts and ways to deal with them are also culturally determined. Specifically, in Nepal popular beliefs about ghosts are embedded in theories and worldviews about the afterlife variously influenced by Hinduism and Buddhism and several magmatic vernacular substrates influencing each other in turns, through multiple exchanges, local adaptations, reflections, appropriations, and translations from one set of ideas to the other.

In South Asian contexts influenced by Hinduism,

> A major belief among the villagers is that the soul of a person becomes a ghost at death and continues as a ghost for a time based on the sum of the soul's actions in past lives. Thus, ghosts are linked with the souls of the dead and are entwined with life and death. The fear of death and anxiety about becoming a ghost persist among villagers and are reinforced by a long history of many deaths, a relatively short life expectancy through centuries, and an ideological perspective about life and death deriving from Hindu beliefs about the soul (atman), the soul's actions (karma), and ghosts causing death. (Freed and Freed 1993: 15)

The term "ghost" in Nepal could be translated in various ways, the most popular being *bhūt* (Sanskrit *bhūta*[5]), usually used to refer to the spirit of a dead. Another word commonly used is *pret* (Sanskrit *preta*), used to indicate the hungry, wandering ghost, usually depicted as a being with a swollen belly and a minuscule mouth, devoured by a constant hunger. To these two categories or typologies, which refer specifically to human dead, we can add other classes of evil spirits (*piśāca*; *vetāla*; etc.) which are known to stalk and prey over human beings, in order to feed on blood and flesh, and thus are held responsible for illness and death. These beings are known to haunt crossroads, graveyards, and deserted places especially at night, lurking in the shadows and waiting for the solitary, incautious traveler to pass by. They can also possess the living, able to enter the human body through natural orifices,[6] especially during sleep or during the crossing of scary places as mentioned above, during the middle of the night. To cross the path of one of such spirit, or entering its domain is to be considered inviting troubles.

In Nepalese folklore the term *bhūta* denotes an entity, not necessarily malevolent, often the victim of an unfortunate and tragic event, as already mentioned when dealing with the topic of the bad death. As in many other cultures, the lack of funeral rites, their wrong performance, or negligence in performing the protracted practice of the *śrāddha* (Sanskrit), a ritual offering for the deceased (sskr. *pitṛa*) to be repeated over time on specific days in which the dead are given ritual food (sskr. *pinda*), could result in the creation of a vengeful spirit. The theme of the insatiable hunger of the *preta* is a common topic in ghost stories: if neglected, in fact, the ancestor spirits are able to unleash on their descendants misfortune and disgrace of different kinds. In many cases, when consulted through spirit-mediums they are known to ask for sweets and milk, while they refrain from salt and turmeric. Deceased persons whose life was undeniably marred by malevolence, greed, cruelty, and the like are considered prone to become *piśāca* and to keep tormenting the living. The usual outcome of an encounter with a ghost is a sudden fright and a precipitous flight, but other severe consequences are reported, too, such as: sudden death, slow consumption for an unknown disease, temporary or permanent madness, loss of speech and the like, among others. Narrations related to such encounters, often make use of the expression *bhūt-pret* to denote the *revenant*, thus conflating the two different classes of supernatural being into one.

Ghosts in Pan-Indic Classical Texts

References to ghosts appears in many classical religious texts, as, for example, in Vedic and Puranic literature. As already mentioned, a reference to the knowledge of the *bhūta* (*bhūtavidyā*) is mentioned in the *Chāndogya Upaniṣad* (CU 7.1, 2)[7] together with other sources of classical knowledge which include the four Vedas, the Mahabharata, grammar, astronomy, mathematics, ritual science, and other subjects. The *Atharva Veda*, which contains a long section on spells and charms to avoid hindrances and diseases sent by supernatural beings, is curiously devoid of direct references to disturbances provoked by the restless dead, focusing instead on other classes of evil spirits, like the demonic *rākṣasa* and the *piśāca*. These and other kinds of beings have usually been associated with the god Rudra, the "howler," associated with storms and wild hunts. As such, Rudra is considered the lord of terrifying hosts of warrior-spirits. Interestingly, in the most ancient texts the warrior-spirits were not conceived as monstrous beings, and the word *bhūta*, meaning literally "created," was used also for nature and gods (Chakravanti 1986: 53). The transformation into hideous beings apparently took place in the context of epic and Puranic literature, when the god Śiva[8] receives the appellation of *bhūteśvara*, "lord of the *bhūta*," and his retinues are openly linked with the cohorts of the denizens of the night and the graveyard. Several stories link the creation of *bhūta* entities with the infamous episode of Sati's death.[9] Ashamed that her husband, Śiva, was not invited to the great ritual held by her father Dakṣa, as referred to in several Puranic accounts, Sati committed suicide by jumping on the sacrificial fire. An enraged Śiva unleashed his fury over the ceremonial place, releasing an army of terrifying beings to avenge her death. The sacrifice was disrupted, with the participants killed or beaten.

According to the *Brahmāṇḍa Purāṇa* (henceforth *BP*)[10], Rudra, entrusted with the power of creation by Brahma, fathered a host of *bhūta* warriors (*BP* 1.2.6.70–80) of varied, wondrous, menacing appearance, described in great detail in a later section of the same text:

> stout, lean, tall, dwarfs, short ones, upright ones, those with hanging ears, those with suspended lips, those with long dangling tongues, those with small bellies, single-eyed, ugly ones, those with hanging hips, those with stout calves, black ones, white (fair) ones, blue ones, white-faced ones, red-faced ones, those of tawny colour, those of assorted colours, smoke-coloured ones, those who have reddish noses, those with hairs like Muñja grass, those with hairs standing on ends, those with serpents as their sacred thread, those with many heads, those with no feet, those with a single head, those with no heads,

fierce ones, hideous ones of disproportionate limbs, those with matted hairs, hump-backed ones, crooked ones, those of dwarfish stature, those who resort to excellent lakes, oceans, mountains, rivers and their banks, those with single ear, those with large ears, spike-eared ones, those with no car, those with curved fangs, those with claws, those without teeth, those without tongues, those with a single hand, those with two hands, those with three hands, those without hands, those with a single leg, those with two legs, those with three legs, those with many legs, those with great Yogic power, those with great inherent might, those with very good minds, those with great power, those who can go anywhere, those who have no obstacles, those having the knowledge of Brahman, those who can assume any form they wish, terrible ones, cruel ones, pure ones, those who consider liquor very pure, very virtuous ones, those with false teeth, those with big tongues, those without hair, those with deformed faces, those who eat with their hands, those who gulp down with their mouths, those who eat with heads (?) those with skulls, those having bows, those who wield hammers, those who hold swords and spears, those who have only the quarters for their clothes (i.e., naked ones), those with variegated dresses, those with garlands and unguents of diverse kinds, those who take in rice, those who habitually eat meat, those who drink liquor and those who drink Soma juice. (BP 2.3.7.359–370)

This long list of uncanny possibilities works as a blueprint, listing elements regarding the appearance, attitudes, and attributes of entities belonging to the *bhūta* class. The text gives also a time frame for their activities: "some of them are very terrible and they walk about during twilight hours; some of them are very gentle and they walk about during the midnight, the terrible ones among them stalk at night" *(BP* 2.3.7.371). The following section is devoted to the *piśāca* classes of beings, whose main characteristics seems to be their appetite for flesh, paired with a hideous aspect characterized by hairy bodies, protruding fangs, long claws or nails, and crooked limbs. Each *piśāca* group or family possesses specials abilities, habits, attitudes, and skills (see BV 2.3.7.374–400). Pitying their condition, the god Brahma granted them the power to become invisible and to shape-shift, to move at dawn and twilight, and the right to occupy and haunt empty houses or ruined mansions, roadways and riverbanks, trees, passages (entrance or exit places), as well as houses inhabited by people who do not behave properly or indulge in illegal and criminal activities, or where the rituals are neglected.

Ghosts appear also in the Buddhist Canon, where the afterlife stories of the hungry ghosts, the *preta* entities, constitute an important didactic and normative instrument at the hand of the Buddhist clergy. Ghosts, and their narratives of infinite sadness, suffering, and punishments, illustrate all the benefits of following religious precepts and behaving accordingly. In the Pāli canon, we find a collection of stories of the departed, the *Petavatthu*.[11] It contains fifty-one stories following a clear model. The stories are told by the Buddha himself, and relate an encounter between a monk and a ghost (*peta*[12]), in which the latter explains the reasons for his present condition. The narrative mechanism is to confirm the effectiveness of karmic retribution of sins, and as such it constitutes an *exemplum*, setting a model for behavior and constituting a warning against sinful conducts. Very often the appearance of the *peta* is directly linked to the sins committed in a previous life, as in the case of the ghost with a pig-mouth (*Petavatthu* 1, 2) or the one with the mouth full of worms (1, 3), both monks unable to restrain and control their speech in their previous existences. In another case (1, 6), a *peti*, a female ghost, described as smeared in blood and covered with flies, tells the reasons for her punishment: in her previous life, being jealous of the pregnant other wife of her husband, caused her an abortion and then denied having anything to do with it. Because of this, in this life she is doomed to give birth to five children every morning and five every evening, consuming their flesh as soon as they are born, due to her insatiable hunger. According to the Buddhist cosmology, being a hungry ghost is one of the six conditions of existence that an individual may attain at rebirth. Karmic retribution essentially determines the realm of existence of the next life, which may happen in the world of the gods, of the anti-gods, of the human beings, of the animals, of the ghosts, and finally among those damned to hell. The tormented dead, with their stories of sin and retribution, act as vivid warnings to the living. Their necrographies, the tales of their rebirth as hungry ghosts, are the dark reflection of their previous life, tainted by the retaliatory effects of their past actions.

Nepalese Ghost Stories and Local Folklore

According to popular opinion, ghosts are held responsible for several afflictions befalling the living. It is a well-known and pan-Nepalese belief that a ghost has the power to cause illnesses.[13] This belief is sustained by the activities of tantric exorcists, village-healers, shamans, and oracles. Nepalese shamans,[14] for example, usually intervene upon request from their sponsors to divine the origins of hindrances, misfortunes, or illnesses. During the divination ritual they try to identify the root cause of the problem, which may spring from natural causes, anger of the gods, witchcraft, soul loss, planetary obstructions, ghosts, misbehavior, sins, quarrelling, gossiping, and so forth. Among these the affliction, the one commonly indicated by the expression *bhūt lāgnu* seems to be quite common. That different groups possess different sets of terminologies for the malevolent spirits of the dead, seems to be inconsequential (Pigg 1989: 19), since the ways to deal with them usually follows a pattern that involves the identification of the spirits involved and a methodology for appeasement or banishment, normally through a range of rituals depending on the gravity of the situation, from the recitations of *mantra* formulas for the simpler cases, or the *jhar-phuk* (blowing mantras while sweeping the patient body), up to the practice of a full-scale ritual involving a sacrifice and an exorcism.[15]

As explained by shamans, other ritual specialists, and from narratives related to personal encounters with the dead, an encounter with these other-worldly entities is often a major cause for personal distress, opening inroads for an illness or even sudden death. It seems that ghost attacks can be differentiated into two kinds: intrafamilial dynamics (sickness, possession, etc.) involving family ancestors, which require addressing some family problems in order to solve them; and external, random attacks by casual encounters with the resentful dead. This difference leads also to a diverse modality of action: family ancestral dead have to be appeased, random ghosts have to be simply exorcised. These two kinds of ghost-encounters lead to a further differentiation, too, relevant to the topic of the present chapter. While the ghosts belonging to the first group, intrafamilial or ancestors, are highly individualized, identified and even given voices, through possession, to express their complaints, the random dead stalking the occasional passer-by are seldom identified beyond a vague idea of belonging to a specific class of malevolent dead (a suicide, a murdered person, etc.). There are of course exceptions to this, since in certain cases local ghosts haunting a specific crossroad, or a tree along a path, are well known by the locals, who are often able to enumerate a list of encounters happening in the same place and with the same connotations.

In her work on tantric healing traditions in the Kathmandu Valley, Angela Dietrich (1998) gives an overview of the many different ways religious specialists deal with the ghosts crowding the capital city of the Himalayan country. Special attention is devoted to the Newari beliefs, which enumerate a highly differentiated list of ghostly entities, among whom we find: the *sikha* (the ghost of a family member), the *ranke-bhūt* (a kind of *ignis fatuus* or will-o'-wisp), the *murkata* (headless ghost), the *lakhes* (originating from an evil human being whose sinful life transform him or her into a demonic being), the *khya*, further differentiated into the *sik khya* (vengeful revenant originating from incorrect funeral rites), the *barha khya* (ghost of a girl dead during the menstrual period of confinement), the *khya* haunting roads, passages, and fields, the *kichkandi* (a roadside female ghost luring passers-by and travelers by night), and so on

(Dietrich 1998: 45–48). One of the most interesting parts of her book is the appendix with the transcript of the questionnaire for the healers' patients, since it contains some interesting first-hand accounts of encounters with ghosts. Among these, a Newari retired maid who was at the service of the Rana[16] family reports having seen many women and children ghosts, including her own ghost babies, in a palace belonging to the autocratic family (ibid.: 250). According to many, the Rana aristocrats were often involved in the raping of their maids and the subsequent killing of the pregnant ones in order to prevent the birth of an illegitimate offspring. In another account, a Tamang thangka[17] painter reported his path was blocked by a weird tree rising up to reach the sky, an unknown force knocked him down, and released him only when he invoked the Buddha (ibid.: 253). A similar experience happened to a young Newari women, who on her way home, was grabbed by a hideous man who then disappeared upon her invocation of the goddess Kali (ibid.: 253). In another instance a middle-aged man stumbled upon a lady of great beauty one evening but got terribly scared when he saw that her feet were pointing backwards: "he tossed rice at her which had been given by the healer and she disappeared, so I knew she was a *kichkinni*" (ibid.: 254). A Nai (butcher caste) young woman reported having a *khya* haunting her house, "it is the spirit of a relative who died while a girl was in *gufa* (menarche confinement), since someone who dies during that time must get buried in the home" (ibid.: 257).

These are just a few cases, but sufficient to testify that the variety of ghosts populating Nepalese folklore is very rich, and every community adds its own peculiarity to it. Classical, vernacular, and indigenous traditions constitute the main sources from which healers and their sponsors draw. In this respect, ghosts are essentially transcultural beings, since they easily cross the boundaries between the different groups and cultures constituting the Nepalese society. Very often, in fact, when identifying the source of disturbances, a healer will point to a "foreign" ghost encountered when travelling outside the more or less safe boundaries of one's own community. So, for example, it is not uncommon to hear that a person's problems are derived by the casual contact with a restless dead encountered at a crossroad, along a path, or on a bridge, while visiting a relative in another town or village, or during a business trip abroad. The indefinite nature of the ghost is not a problem here, since the main problem is to get rid of its influence and to regain good health. The *bhūt-pret* affliction is a pan-Nepalese recognized syndrome, no matter if it was caused by a *saruwa*[18] (Pigg 1989), a *bai*[19] (Blustain 1976), a *theba*[20] (Michailovsky and Sagant 1992), a *shindi*[21] (Desjarlais 1992), or a ghost from the city of Varanasi or from London.

The discourse is radically different when the ghost affliction is derived from the intrafamilial spirit of a deceased person. One relevant example could be drawn from the cases documented by Michailovsky and Sagant among the Limbu people, a Nepalese indigenous minority inhabiting the eastern regions of the country. Ideally, according to the main tenets of Limbu indigenous religion, the ancestors (*theba*) are supposed to reside in the village of the dead (*khema pangphe*) after the correct performance of the funerary rituals (Michailovsky and Sagant 1992: 20). The ritual specialist, the *phedangma*, acting as a psychopomp, is in charge of leading the deceased to his new abode, located beyond the shores of a lake of tears (ibid.: 21). If, for some reason, the ritual is not performed correctly or adequately,[22] the soul of the deceased is not able to reach his destination, or gets lost along the way, it is bound to come back among the living. While the common assumption is that the malevolent ghost is prone to attack everyone, even the casual passer-by, Michailovsky and Sagant analyze ethnographic accounts and provide a counter argument: the vengeful ghost is more often than not coming back for a specific reason, to set right a wrongdoing and demanding compensation:

—a mother, swept away by a landslide, whose daughter sells her jewels for drink;
—an infant, dead because his mother has a new baby who drinks the milk destined for him;
—a father, a man of great reputation in the valley, whose son, out of avarice, does not hold a funeral equal to the dignity of his rank;
—a woman whose husband, widowed at a young age, finds and marries another woman, younger than the deceased;
—a man, killed in an avalanche, whose corpse is discovered by a group of yak herders who do not show the deceased the proper respect;
—a grandmother, drowned at the bottom of a well, whose newly married granddaughter carries away the grandmother's jewels to the husband's house;
—a man, also killed in an avalanche, whose house is used as a place of carousal without offering him something to drink, and whose belongings are stolen when his wife and son prudently decided to leave to live elsewhere.
All these cases have one thing in common: the deceased never complains of being forced to wander half-starved at the edge of the village. Nor does he or she refer to desires left unsatisfied by a premature death. The deceased complains instead of a wrong done to him or her. (Michailovsky and Sagant 1992: 28–29)

All these cases testify an extension of the individual agency beyond the natural limits of human life, extending their biography into the postmortem field. Their voices, the accounts of their lives (necrographies) in the afterlife, the exchanges and negotiations they still engage in with other members of their community constitute a clear example of their meaningful presence among the living.

The voices of the dead are not silenced. Through possession of their family members, spirit-mediums and shamans, they make sure everybody is listening. Among Tibetan-speaking Himalayan communities, there are memories of a specific class of religious specialists,[23] called *delog*, who are known to have travelled to the afterlife worlds, meeting the dead and the damned, in order to bring back messages for the living and, of course, to describe the torments of the suffering. In one case I have heard of in Helambu valley,[24] one family was destroyed by a fire that engulfed their house in a mountain village. The only surviving member of the family was a young woman living in Kathmandu. She knew that her relatives used to keep a cache of money and gold ornaments hidden somewhere on their property. She then went to visit a *delog*, asking her to reach her family in the underworld and ask them about the hidden valuable objects and money. During the ritual, the *delog* fell into a catatonic trance, lying still for hours. When she was revived, she claimed to have met the dead parents of the girl. They were in a boiling mud pool, forced to eat dirty things. "We were so rich during life—they complained—and here we suffer a lot because we were too greedy." That was the first message for the girl. Then there were instructions for the hidden cache: it is in a field, below such-and-such tree, you have to dig. She went digging for many days, but apparently the information was wrong, since she found nothing. Or was it a teaching on the uselessness of being greedy?

Nepalese Ghost Stories and Social Networks

Social networks have subsumed largely the function of receptacles of oral culture, and, despite their written, and more or less permanent content, are often employed to convey thoughts, impressions, and comments that were once mainly oral communications and exchanges. Even the writing form is different: it is a "spoken" way of writing. Writing on the internet, in dedicated blogs or through the social networks, enables the horizontal spread of cultural items beyond the usual limits imposed by other kinds of media. As such, social networks also provide a "space" where ghost stories can be traded and exchanged, told and compared between people on specifically dedicated web pages, blogs, or casual chats. These media have been defined *spreadable*, since items and contents can be easily shared by users over different networks, enabling a dispersion and diffusion that exponentially enhance their resonance (Jenkins, Ford, and Green 2013). The narrative experience of the ghost story is then enriched by visibility and access to a larger audience, who may also participate in the discussion by adding comments, asking questions, sharing similar experiences, and so forth. What is interesting is that these spaces are naturally not linked to a specific locale, giving rise to transcultural interpretations and comparative discussions. Transcendence of geographical, temporal, and cultural constraints is a peculiarity of these networks that constitute also alternative places for the appropriation and elaboration of cultural materials (Dawson 2000). As such, and especially in the field of religions, these networks could constitute poles of engagement that are not bounded by the "traditional" channels, and they may even directly challenge the authority of religious establishments (Campbell 2010: 251). While this is not the direct outcome of blogging about ghosts, it is nonetheless relevant to notice that some of the same mechanisms apply to this context as well. Materials from popular lore, including religious theories about the afterlife, are weaved into the narration of personal experience, as part of the background of the storyteller or to consolidate the narration itself by showing it as conforming to the general knowledge about the events and the actors involved. At the same time, the narration is enriched by individual details, which may derive from other sources, including popular memes, which have nothing to do with the original context of reference. Beyond the usual ghost story features, in fact, we find some interesting additions to the web version which seem to recur. Among these recurring traits, the first is a preamble of sort, where the narrators, despite being readers of such blogs for a long time and having an interest in ghost stories, justify themselves for not having shared their own one so far for fear of not being believed, reputed crazy, or simply considering themselves unfit for the task. To this, they often add that they are not credulous or superstitious, but skeptical and rational, and as evidence they often add their "credentials" of curricula of scientific-subject studies and the like. This preamble is also apt to create, consciously or unconsciously, the necessary suspense and add credibility to the story to be narrated. The second almost-constant feature is an explanation of local customs and practices related to the story, in order to clarify to external readers certain local customs which may appear extreme or shocking (e.g., reclusion of girls during the menstrual periods, arranged marriages, animal sacrifices, etc.) to a non-Nepalese reader, and that the narrator himself or herself seems also to implicitly criticize, as if to underline the belonging to a common "universal," cosmopolitan, educated middle class that is detached from, if not adverse to, what could be perceived as an excess of the local culture.

Many of the stories appearing on blogs and through the social networks, combine "traditional" ghost-lore of Nepal (with reference to

Hindu, Buddhist, and shamanic traditions), with more exotic details taken from, or inspired by other contexts. This is more evident with the most elaborate narrations that come closer to horror short stories, usually richer in details and with a profusion of elements to create suspense. This higher level of narrative skills adds also an aura of artificiality to some of the stories, highlighting their value more as entertainment or literary feats than an extremely disturbing encounter with a denizen of the realm of the dead. Linguistically less elaborate and brief, focusing more on the uncanny event without indulging in unnecessary embellishments, these stories appear more aimed at conveying the reality of the experience.

Conclusion

These stories, despite being just a minimum sample of the materials related to Nepalese ghost stories coming from various sources from classical to folklore texts, from web sources to local informants, highlight and touch upon several of the topics which could be usually linked to ghost stories locally and globally. As the ghosts of other cultures, the Nepalese revenant, too, appears preferably in isolated places (haunted houses, abandoned mills at the village periphery, cremation grounds, wells and fountains at night, etc.). In some of the stories, instead, the ghosts still haunt the places where they lived and died, sharing them with scared newcomers. Regarding the time of the apparitions, despite a marked preference for nocturnal encounters—it should be worth emphasizing, perhaps, the conceptions related to midnight, the witching hour, as the main temporal field for interaction with the uncontrolled spirit world, outside, distant and distinct from the daily routine of temple rituals where spirits appear to be tamed and domesticated by religious specialists—diurnal ones cannot be excluded. Very recently, in the Kathmandu center, in broad daylight several people claimed to have seen a ghost in a shop on New Road, causing a mass hysteria involving hundreds of persons poorly controlled by a small armed police force trying to cordon off the premises of the event, while local TV broadcasters were coming to document the phenomena. The rumors were started by the statements of the shop owner, who claimed to have been repeatedly slapped by the invisible hand of a ghost residing in the house where he has his shop on the ground floor (Adhikari and Gautam).[25]

In many stories there is an obvious link with food: ghosts request to the living to share food with them (food which invariably is contaminated by blood, pus, or feces—normal food for the damned spirits—or human flesh), or ask the living to cook for them in meals often disrupted when the salt element comes into play. Food as an element of exchange between the living and the dead constitutes the primary element of recognition between different realms of existence: nutrition modalities divide, once and for ever, the living and the dead, and to partake of the wrong (prohibited) food equates to sure damnation. It should be noted that food rules lay also at the base of the caste structure, where they constitute the practical boundary between different social groups. The same rules of commensality apply here: food-sharing is a highly regulated, almost obsessive, ideology related to the notions of purity and pollution.

Gender issues also play a pivotal role in ghostly matters as well: while the cause of being a ghost for male is usually tied to the lack of funeral rituals, a tragic death seems to constitute the norm for female ghosts. A tragic death is often caused by uncritical adhesion to models of submission and oppression of women: young girls who died while under reclusion during the menstrual period; murdered prostitutes (there is a partial overlapping of the prostitute with the spirit known as *kichkanya*, also in spatial terms: interestingly they seem to haunt and stalk the same premises of Kathmandu streets); or mistresses (a particular set of ghosts is considered to be the lovers or concubines tied to the aristocracy, murdered by killers to avoid scandals or to prevent them from claiming rights or blackmail their powerful lovers); and finally the huge numbers of those killed or who committed suicide after unhappy love stories, for forbidden inter-caste relationships, or in arranged marriages with violent men. As already mentioned, the ghost story acts upon a double sphere: supporting traditional customs and social conventions and norms, in one case, and angry critique and oblique (supernatural) attack to the structural violence of the establishment in the other. In this sense, the same ambiguity characterizing the ghost story is the very same ambiguity we find lingering nearby uncertain social boundaries and interactions which the ghost itself, with its presence, is challenging: different worlds, realms and dimensions exist side by side, separated yet intertwined; the food of the one and the food of the other, so radically different, and yet to be exchanged, and certainly due on prescribed occasions; sexual relations, parental and filial obligations, debts and credits. Among the causes of ghost presence we surely find in many ghost stories also envy for the living and greediness for the worldly things, and yet, not secondarily, also a just resentment for being a victim of injustice.

And finally, the ghost story, or its narration, is also essentially something to be shared. There is no ghost story without its sharing: the moment of the narration could be tied to several factors, from the urge to share a terrifying or inexplicable event experienced, or just heard and then transmitted from mouth to mouth, page to page, or blog to blog, to the opposite end to trick the credulous into believing, or to make a joke and entertain them. Whatever the truth behind them, ghost stories always reveal more than their surface value, conveying images and ideas not only of the story itself or the narrator, but also of the general context of reference. In all this, still at the crossroad, torn between different possibilities, the ghost still waits for a witness, as an opaque reflection of a living past retaining its agency.

Davide Torri is a postdoctoral researcher at the Heidelberg Centre for Transcultural Studies (HCTS), University of Heidelberg, Germany. He is active in the study of Himalayan indigenous religions and minority groups. His interests also include politics, religious violence, and Nepalese history. He has published several papers on shamanism and its interactions with Buddhist religions in the Himalayas; he is co-editor of *Shamanism and Violence. Power, Repression and Suffering in Indigenous Religious Conflicts* (Routledge, 2013) and author of the monograph *Il Lama e il Bombo: Sciamanismo e buddhismo tra gli Hyolmo del Nepal* (Edizioni Nuova Cultura, 2014).

Notes

1. On death and postmortem in the Hindu context see Filippi 1996. See also Parry 1994 for an examination of death and related topics in Varanasi.
2. See for example, Metcalf and Huntington 1979.
3. As in the case of the supernatural stories analyzed, for example, by Schmitt (1994) in *Les revenants. Les vivants et les morts dans la société médiévale*, such stories were diffusely employed by ecclesiastical apparatuses with didactic intentions, to highlight and flesh out contents supporting ideas about a Purgatory still to be systematized and fully integrated in the life of the people, functioning to establish a new branch of an economy of the sacred, managed by the Church and grounded on the much biased practice of selling of indulgences, while at the same time adapting to this purpose popular ideas, themes and beliefs about the bad death, ghosts, and tormented afterlives.
4. See also Sax 2015.
5. In the *Chāndogya-upaniṣad* 7.1.2 there are references to a so-called *bhūta-vidyā*, defined as the science of beings causing troubles and the ways to ward them off (Macdonell and Keith 1912: 107).
6. For example, ghosts are commonly supposed to enter the body through the nose or mouth when a person sneezes or yawns.
7. For a recent edition of the *Chāndogya Upaniṣad* see Muni (2007).
8. Śiva and Rudra are considered, in contemporary Hinduism, different aspects of the same deity.
9. One of the most detailed versions is contained in the *Vāyu Purāṇa*. References to it appear also in other Puranas like *Skanda Purāṇa*, *Linga Purāṇa*, and other classic texts.
10. For the *Brahmāṇḍa Purāṇa*, I have used the translation by Tagare (1983).

11. For the analysis of the *Petavatthu*, i am referring to the translations of Gehman (1974) and Hecker (2001).
12. The Pāli word *peta* corresponds to the Sanskrit *preta*.
13. See, for example, Oakley and Gairola (1977) and Lall (2014) anthologies of folk-tales, collected in various parts of Nepal.
14. I use the word shaman to denote a specific kind of religious specialist known in Nepali language as *jhānkri*. Despite the widespread use of this term among all the Nepalese groups, it must be said that different communities possess a specificity regarding the existence, abilities, and ritual knowledges of their shamanic religious specialists. This diversity is reflected also by a variegated and rich terminology. Without any pretension of being exhaustive, a short list of terms used to identify shamans among the different Nepalese groups will surely include the Tamang and Hyolmo *bombo*, the Limbu *yeba* and *phedangma*, the Gurung *pachyu* and *ghyabre*, the Sherpa *pormbo*, the Limbu *bijuwa*, and so on. The terminology referring to ghosts is equally varied and differentiated.
15. It must be said that the majority of healing rituals can be ideally considered exorcism, due to the belief in illness as the intrusion of a pathogen agent into the body of the patient, i.e., a form of possession.
16. The Rana family ruled over Nepal from 1846 until 1951, as hereditary Prime Ministers of the Shah Royal House of Nepal, which was deprived of almost all of the real power.
17. Thangka are traditional Buddhist paintings of religious contents.
18. The ghost of a deceased child, preying on pregnant women and newborn babies.
19. A ghost originating by the contaminating touch upon a corpse by a person belonging to another *jāti* or group.
20. The spirit of an ancestor, among the Limbu.
21. A restless dead, among the Hyolmo.
22. For example, because the *phedangma* is too weak, the offerings are not adequate, or the body is contaminated by the touch of an animal (Michailovsky and Sagant 1992: 21).
23. See also Pommaret-Imaeda 1989.
24. M. B., pers. comm., Timbu (Nepal), September 2014.
25. http://kathmandupost.ekantipur.com/printedition/news/2012-04-16/ghost-in-spooky-new-road-house-has-all-on-their-toes.html. Retrieved on 20 October 2017.

References

Adhikari, Ankit and Manish Gautam. 2012. "'Ghost' in Spooky New Road House Has All on Their Toes." *Kathmandu Post*, 16 April 2012. Retrieved 8 March 2019 from http://kathmandupost.ekantipur.com/printedition/news/2012-04-16/ghost-in-spooky-new-road-house-has-all-on-their-toes.html.

Ariès, Phillipe. 1977. *L'Homme devant la mort*. Paris: Seuil.

Berreman, Gerald D. 1963. *Hindus of the Himalayas*. Berkeley and Los Angeles: University of California Press.

Blustain, Harvey. 1976. "Levels of Medicine in a Central Nepali Village." *Contributions to Nepalese Studies* 3: 83–105.

Campbell, Heidi A. 2010. "Religious Authority and the Blogosphere." *Journal of Computer-Mediated Communication* 15(2): 251–76.

Chakravarti, Mahadev. 1986. *The Concept of Rudra-Śiva Through the Ages*. Delhi: Motilal Banarsidass.

Dawson, Lorne L. 2000. "Researching Religion in Cyberspace: Issues and Strategies." *Religion and the Social Order* 8: 25–54.
Desjarlais, Robert. 1992. *Body and Emotion: The Aesthetics of Illness and Healing in the Nepal Himalayas*. Philadelphia: University of Pennsylvania Press.
Dietrich, Angela. 1998. *Tantric Healing in the Kathmandu Valley: A Comparative Study of Hindu and Buddhist Spiritual Healing Traditions in Urban Nepalese Society*. Delhi: Book Faith India.
Filippi, Gian Giuseppe. 1996. *Mrtyu: Concept of Death in Indian Traditions*. New Delhi: DK Printworld.
Frazer, James George. 1913. *The Belief in Immortality and the Worship of the Dead*. London: Macmillan.
Freed, Ruth S., and Stanley A. Freed. 1993. *Ghosts: Life and Death in North India*. New York: American Museum of Natural History.
Gehman, Henry S. 1974. *Petavatthu: Stories of the Departed. Together with Excerpts from the Frame Stories from Dhammapāla's Commentary*. London: Routledge.
Goldstein, Diane E., Sylvia A. Grider, and Jeannie Banks Thomas. 2007. *Haunting Experiences: Ghosts in Contemporary Folklore*. Logan: Utah University Press.
Jenkins, Henry, Sam Ford, and Joshua Green. 2013. *Spreadable Media: Creating Value and Meaning in a Networked Culture*. New York and London: New York University Press.
Hecker, Hellmuth. 2001. *Peta-vatthu: das buddhistische Totenbuch; ein Text aus der Kürzeren Sammlung des Pālikanons*. Stammbach-Herrnschrot: Beyerlein und Steinschulte.
Lall, Kesar. 2014. *Folk Tales from Nepal: The Stolen Image and Other Stories*. Ratna Pustak Bhandar: Kathmandu.
Lévy-Bruhl, Lucien. 1927. *L'Âme primitive*. Paris: F. Alcan.
Macdonell, Arthur Anthony, and Arthur Berriedale Keith. 1912. *Vedic Index of Names and Subjects*. London: J. Murray.
Macho, T. 2007. "Morte," In *Le Idee dell'Antropologia*, ed. C. Wulf and A. Borsari, 960–978. Milano: Bruno Mondadori.
Metcalf, Peter, and Richard Huntington 1979. *Celebrations of Death: The Anthropology of Mortuary Ritual*. Cambridge: Cambridge University Press.
Michailovsky, Boyd, and Phillipe Sagant. 1992. "The Shaman and the Ghosts of Unnatural Death: On the Efficacy of a Ritual." *Diogenes* 40(158): 19–37.
Mori, A. 2012. "Japan," In *A Companion to Folklore*, ed. R. F. Bendix and G. Hasan-Rokem, 211–233. Malden, MA: Wiley-Blackwell.
Muni, N.P., ed. 2007. *Chandogya Upaniṣad: With the Original Text in Sanskrit and Roman Transliteration*. New Delhi: DK Printworld.
Narváez, Peter, and Martin Laba, eds. 1986. *Media Sense: The Folklore-Popular Culture Continuum*. Bowling Green: Bowling Green State University Popular Press.
Oakley, E.S., and Tara Dutt Gairola. 1977. *Himalayan Folklore: Kumaon and West Nepal*. Kathmandu: Ratna Pustak Bhandar.
Parry, Jonathan P. 1994. *Death in Banaras*. Cambridge: Cambridge University Press.

Pigg, Stacey Leigh. 1989. "Here, There, and Everywhere: Place and Person in Nepalese Explanations of Illness." *HIMALAYA, the Journal of the Association for Nepal and Himalayan Studies* 9(2): 16–24.

Pommaret-Imaeda, Francoise. 1989. *Les revenants de l'au-delà dans le monde Tibétaine: Sources littéraires et tradition vivante*. Paris: Centre Regional de la Recherche Scientifique.

Poo, Mu-chou, ed. 2009. *Rethinking Ghosts in World Religions*. Leiden: Brill.

Sax, William S. 2015. "Seeing Ghosts in India and Europe." In *Exploring the Senses: South Asian and European Perspectives on Rituals and Performativity*, ed. Axel Michaels and Christof Wulf, 110–19. Delhi: Routledge.

Schmitt, Jean-Claude. 1994. *Les revenants. Les vivants et les morts dans la société médiévale*. Paris: Gallimard.

Tagare, Ganesh Vasudeo, ed. 1983. *The Brahmanda Purana*. Delhi: Motilal Banarsidass.

Turner, Victor W. 1967. *The Forest of Symbols: Aspects of Ndembu Ritual*. Ithaca, NY: Cornell University Press.

———. 1969. *The Ritual Process: Structure and Anti-Structure*. Chicago: AldinePublishing.

Tylor, Edward B. 1871. *Primitive Culture: Researches into the Development of Mythology, Philosophy, Religion, Language, Art and Customs*. London: John Murray.

van Gennep, Arnold. (1909) 1981. *Les rites de passage*. Paris: Picard.

Chapter 11

Death Isn't What It Used to Be

Animist and Baptist Ontologies in Tribal India

Piers Vitebsky

You Are Not Fully Dead While Others Are Left Alive Who Remember You

Since I first studied them in 1975, the Sora people in India have shifted from animist to Christian Baptist. I shall use the ethnographic present, but the animist culture I describe, and in which I have been so immersed, is rapidly becoming extinct—or rather, transformed. The dead, who formerly spoke at such length, have now been silenced, and an anthropologist attending a Sora Baptist service today would have no way of reconstructing the previous, intense relationship between living and dead, or the vehement dialogues which used to pass between them through the mouths of shamans in trance. I have analyzed the old system of dialogues (Vitebsky 1993) and the current transition to Christianity (Vitebsky 2017a).

The Sora of Odisha (Orissa) in eastern India are a "Tribal" people who number some 300,000 (estimates vary). They speak a language of the South Munda branch of the Austroasiatic family, which is related to Cambodian and to the languages of the Orang Asli peoples of the Malaysian peninsula and of the hill tribes of Vietnam. The speakers of these languages generally lie at the jungly margins of the great empires and mainstream civilizations of Asian history (cf. Scott 2009). In India, they are generally considered more ancient and more aboriginal than the subcontinent's much larger Aryan and Dravidian populations. Although this picture is disputed for political as well as scholarly reasons, it is clear that their nonliterate cultures lie well outside the Hindu mainstream.

Since I started studying them in the 1970s, all young people in the core Sora area have become Baptist Christians (while young Sora in nearby areas are joining neo-Hindu cults). I shall call the remaining adherents of the old way of life "animist" to distinguish them from both Christians and mainstream Hindus. Among animists, there are numerous occasions when a shaman (usually female) goes into trance and a succession of dead people speak through her mouth, conducting casual conversations or impassioned arguments with groups of the living who squat around her. A dead Sora becomes a *sonum*, a term which partly corresponds to "spirit" but which we shall see can also be interpreted as a memory.

When an animist person dies, day or night, the men of the patrilineage gather to chop down trees and build a pyre. The next morning the dead person's ashes and soul are cooled with water and the ashes are buried. There is no remaining material residue of the body. Some time later, the men will plant a large upright stone as a memorial. To the accompaniment of drumming and dancing, this stone is dressed in cloth and fed with alcohol and the blood of numerous sacrificed buffalo, while women weep and embrace it. The stack of memorial stones for a populous patrilineage can number a thousand or more, perhaps going back centuries.

The stone is a representation of the deceased, but its personhood is limited: there is no writing in this animist culture, and people soon forget whose stone is whose. Previous stones receive no further attention and serve rather as a silent symbol of the lineage's unity. A more articulate memory of the deceased has migrated to another medium altogether. In what may well be the most elaborate form of communication between the living and the dead ever documented anywhere in the world, the dead speak with the living at great length. Animist Sora culture places an exceptional emphasis on verbal articulacy. Articulacy is the crucial indicator of consciousness, one could say of a phenomenon's existence. Even adverbial phrases of doing are constructed as phrases of saying. There is no indirect speech construction in the Sora language, so that in reporting a conversation one is obliged to imitate each speaker's words, and even intonation. This functions as a form of verbal perspectivism: in order to recount anything said by another person, one must performatively adopt their point of view.

Similarly, when conducting dialogues with the dead, the living perceive themselves not only from their own perspective but also from that of the dead, who are the agents of much of what happens to the living.

Dialogues with the dead serve as a portal to our knowledge of their condition, and their necrographies are elaborate and discursive.

There is a co-dependency between the dead and the living. The dead are underground and put their soul-force into the crops which the living eat, but they also cause the pain of illness and death. By talking with the living, the dead regulate kinship, control inheritance, and enforce morality. They do this in a way which is both embodied and highly verbal. It is through the pains of his body that a patient communes with the dead (for simplicity I use "he" for patients and "she" for shamans); it is the blood of the sacrificed animal which contains its soul and reaches the deceased; it is the shaman's body which absorbs the alcohol given to one ancestor after another during the séance, and which is drenched with tears by the mourners. A person's postmortem existence is thus of crucial importance to his living descendants—indeed, it is a major causative factor. And since each living person has known many people who are now dead, there is a dense web of causality bearing down on everyone.

It is through dialogue that the dead express their feelings, explain their motives, and make demands. All illnesses and deaths are caused by dead people who have themselves suffered from similar symptoms. Every time you fall ill, it is a reminder of your attachment to a dead person who has started to eat your soul, thereby repeating the same symptoms in you from which he himself died. The cure consists of offering him the soul of a sacrificial animal as a substitute for your own soul. If he accepts this substitute you recover; if not, you die from a repetition of his illness. Once you are dead, you will join him in a location on the landscape which corresponds to the symptoms you now both share. Thus, for example, people who die of smallpox reside in a place called Smallpox-House, those who are killed by a leopard, in Leopard-House, those who die from falls go up to the Sun, and so on. From there you will return as the most recent agent of that form of suffering to attack other living people who are close to you. A person's necrography is thus a direct continuation of their biography, and it starts from some aspect of their relationships which was salient at the time of their death.

The first time a dead person returns is on the morning after his death, when numerous ancestors will speak through a shaman to discuss the circumstances and causes. Most ancestors deny responsibility, but in the end at least one of them will admit to taking the deceased, through a mixture of love, anger, and other motives. At some point the dead person himself will appear to discuss his own situation, and feelings, in graphic detail. Between them, the living and the dead have started to construct a shared narrative about his death. This narrative will grow, be modified, and consolidated through a sequence of funeral rites over the next three years, plus numerous rituals of divination and healing for others even after this, as the dead person continues to turn up as an interested party.

For example, one young mother, who had married for love against the will of her patrilineal family, collapsed and died suddenly after returning from a village associated with her brothers. At the inquest the next morning she revealed that she had been taken by the ancestors of her own brothers' lineage, who resented her marriage. Their real target was her baby boy, since he reinforced her marriage as an heir in her husband's patrilineage. But she had bent down to protect her baby and the attacking sonums had eaten her instead. Months later, she was still repeating this story. I heard her when she turned up during a healing ritual for someone else, and insisted that her brothers' ancestors still would not allow her to join the ancestors of her husband:

> Dead woman: [faintly as she arrives from the Underworld] I got eaten up, I got drunk up, mothers!
> Mother-in-law: Ah my dear, it was so sudden, just like that, you ...
> Dead woman: After I came and married into your group, mothers—
> Mother-in-law: Yes, "this is my house, my home" you said ... have a drink of wine before you go.
> Dead woman: [same small, shaken voice] O dear, really I got eaten up, I got drunk up!
> Mother-in-law: ... didn't we do all your sacrifices, yet if only you'd been ill first [we could have done something] ... didn't we do all your sacrifices, yet—
> Dead woman: [becoming agitated] "Ah, really, help me, fathers, Ah, really, help me!" I cried, "Ah aunts Ah uncles, Ah mothers-in-law Ah fathers-in-law!"
> Mother-in-law: How could we see you?
> Dead woman: [tearful] "Where's my husband where's my husband, I want to be with him I want to speak to him, where's your nephew where's your son?" is all I cried. [quiet again] They ate me up fresh-and-alive.
> Mother-in-law: You can't say we didn't plant a memorial stone for you or didn't do your sacrifices, can you? [frantic torrent] Leave it, abandon it, that house, that home, that position, that location, that base, that hangout, leave it, abandon it!
> Dead woman: But they won't release me, they won't let me go! (Adapted from Vitebsky 2017a: 116–17)

During early appearances, the dead person emphasizes these feelings of pain, shock, and sadness. But a victim can also go on to become a perpetrator. Regardless of this young mother's personality, she will tend to seek further victims to pass on the form of her own illness or death. She will thus often be diagnosed as a cause, and even admit it in her own words while citing some grievance as justification. Over several years, at successive stages of the funeral, the mourners feed each deceased person with sacrificial animals (buffalo, goat, pig, or chicken according to circumstances) and seek to persuade him into a less distressed and aggressive state of mind. The shaman embodies, indeed envoices, the deceased and a range of his ancestors one by one; her assistants (one of which I became) impersonate his lineage ancestors collectively as they sing and dance to rescue him from the anti-society of his fellow illness-victims and lead him into the company of his patrilineal ancestors (who have died from a range of causes and have similarly each been rescued in their time).

Thus a dead person's necrography is progressive: through dialogue with the living, the person is induced to evolve. The stages of this can be seen in his trajectory through different categories of spirit and different cosmological locations. The emotional tone of dialogues shifts over time, as both the living and the dead come to terms with what has happened. As they gradually set each other at ease through a mutual persuasion and reassurance, the dead person becomes less dangerous and the mourners becomes less susceptible to a repetition of his illness (for a comparable talking cure in Freud's "Mourning and Melancholia" [1957], see Vitebsky 1993: 236–59).

In the early stages the dead person's transformation is unstable. Illnesses and deaths continue to occur because each rescue is not fully successful at first. The dead person frequently "reverts" from being an ancestor back to being immersed in his death-experience and continues to cause illness in others. These episodes can sometimes be seen to represent resurgences of grief among the living, or of the quarrels which were implicated in the interpretation of the death. Thus when the young mother above is diagnosed as the cause of an illness among her descendants, this is a reminder of the tension surrounding her marriage and the quarrel between the lineages of her husband and her brothers.

Gradually, the dead person's state becomes more stable, as all parties, living and dead, come to a compromise in their interpretation of the cause of the death and its social significance. An old ancestor who has been dead for many years no longer causes distress or illness. He continues to appear, but has less and less to say for himself (except to demand a drink which the shaman's body imbibes on his behalf) and rarely causes illness. Eventually he gives his name back to a new baby among his descendants, becoming the child's protector against attacks from others. We can perhaps say that it is only then that the mourning by the living is completed. Finally, a very old ancestor will die a second death in the Underworld, turn into a butterfly, and never appear again. When reconstructing genealogies, I came to realize that butterflies are people who have been dead for so long that there is nobody left alive to remember them.

Animist Sora practices of dialogue, based on evolution, construct a time which is shaped into constantly repeated cycles of repetition and resolution. A dead person dies of an illness, and then causes the same illness in others. He is gradually turned into an ancestor, but meanwhile his own victims have entered a similar trajectory. The first person's pain is resolved as he eventually gives his name to a descendant, and his victims will also come to a similar resolution in their time. In this way, each will contribute to the perpetuation of his own lineage. Whatever the circumstances of your death, a way will be found to connect it causally to someone who has died previously and to make it seem similar to that person's death. There is a contrast between good and bad forms of repetition, and Sora ritual is designed to adjust the balance between these and progress from one to the other. When the dead perpetuate their illnesses onto us soon after their death, this is bad repetition; as they evolve to the point of giving their names to our babies, this is good repetition. It is as if events have an impulse of their own, as they repeat themselves in the biographies—and necrographies—of new persons. The specific, individual circumstances of each event are reduced to patterns which are generic, and indeed I eventually worked out that all illnesses and deaths are ultimately reducible to around eight basic categories.

How are events classified together as similar, when circumstances may be so different? The key to this lies in the relationship between two complementary speech genres. Each of these entails a different kind of articulacy. Ritual verse is highly formulaic (Vitebsky 2017b), rather than discursive; it uses conventional imagery and specific signature tunes to characterize generic scenarios. These verse formats are thus a technique of conventionalizing and homogenizing the infinite variety of actual situations. The formal songs sung by the shaman's assistants sketch in the outlines of the situation. They sing their piece and then move off elsewhere for a drink; the shaman invokes her own helper sonums and then, as she enters trance, disappears herself to another life in the Underworld. Her main helper sonum promises through her mouth to lead on the dead, and then this persona too disappears from the shaman's vacant body. All the supporting formal structures of verse and music are withdrawn and you are finally left face to face with your own dead to speak with them on your own behalf, in a dialogue between your biography and their necrography. The formats of verse, the signature tunes, the styles of dancing, and the specialist roles of the shaman's assistants—all these were techniques of framing that led to this focal point of dialogues between the living and the dead, in ordinary language.

Often the stage for a dialogue is set through an exchange sung by the shaman's assistants in verse. The assistants form two teams. One team impersonates the deceased while the other impersonates a succession of living mourners. They sing their way through a series of exchanges between, say, a dead woman and her children, or else between a dead child and its mother, father, and siblings. Here is an extract from a song in the persona of a dead man's widow. The other team have just sung in the persona of the dead man asking to be let back into his old house (Vitebsky 2017a: 89–90). The team singing on the widow's behalf replies:

a'gadillen la a'gadillen la
a'gadillen la a'gadillen la
it can't be, *la,* it can't be, *la*
it can't be, *la,* it can't be, *la*

boten pımpımtai boten pımpımtai
boten pımpımtai boten pımpımtai
who's knocking who's knocking
who's knocking who's knocking

ayıngen la gamai ayıngen la gamai
ayıngen la gamai ayıngen la gamai
should I say, *la,* should I say, *la,*
should I say, *la,* should I say, *la*

iñaiten gamai iñaiten gamai
iñaiten gamai iñaiten gamai
should I say la should I say *la*
should I say la should I say *la*

bogad peng gamlai bogad peng gamlai
bogad peng gamlai bogad peng gamlai
I said perhaps I said perhaps

I said perhaps I said perhaps

ad-labon do sambarin
tıl-labon do sambarin
you're under the earth, *do*
you're deep in the earth, *do*

tungaren do la dinan u la
majaren do la dinan u la
halfway *do la* through the night, *u la?*
midpoint *do la* through the night, *u la?*

kukuren la juri ñen
dumıl do la juri ñen
it's my kukur-dove partner, *la?*
it's my turtle-dove partner, *do la?*

sibrung do la goden
pangrung do la goden
someone's come to pinch rice, *do la?*
someone's come to take rice, *do la?*

an-ubtar do la
jenumtar do la
someone's come to poke into my flower, *do la*
someone's come to eat my flower, *do la*

These formal exchanges lack the informality and flexibility of real dialogues. Rather, they are a conventional position statement made by each side in turn, set entirely in parallel phrasing. They sketch the outlines of what a husband or wife might say (or should say) in such a situation. By contrast, when this chant is over, the shaman goes into trance and the living widow finally gets to speak with her dead husband; their dialogue will be a naturalistic conversation between persons, reflecting the specificity of their situation. This is set in a language which is utterly ordinary. In talking with the dead, one speaks for oneself, in the language of one's own everyday life. It is though this genre, with its particular articulacy over repeated occasions, that the feelings of both living and dead will move towards resolution and "their soul will become cool."

In playing between the levels of the individual case and the generic scenario in which this is encapsulated, the series of funeral rites is in effect simplifying the personhood of the deceased. A dead person still speaks for himself but can be persuaded and manipulated in a way that goes beyond how one could manipulate a living person present in the flesh. As the dead person starts to undergo a progressive simplification, so his agency, his power to affect his descendant's life, shifts from resentful and dangerous to protective and nurturing. His individual necrography, however vivid and realistic, ultimately serves a larger purpose of sustaining the social structure.

The voices of the dead and their narratives are continually shifting and evolving. Another way of understanding this is in terms of memory. The dead have an effect on us because we remember them. This is what their necrography is. But how should we regulate this remembering? It is as if the sonums themselves are Memories (with a capital M, see Vitebsky 1993: 195–202; 2017a: 120–23), so that illness and death themselves are caused by Memories. It is these Memories that the shaman leads on stage in order to converse with their rememberers, like the young mother who expresses her own pain, her love for her husband and baby, and her rejection of her brothers. The more traumatic and upsetting these are, the harder it is to stop them from hurting us.

Sonums display one crucial difference from the usual understanding of "memories" in European languages: they are not contained inside an individual mind but exist and act outside the mind of any single rememberer. They have a collective existence, and each ancestor can address a roomful of living people. But this collective nature has multiple aspects, as the ancestor can also turn in conversation to address any one of the assembled rememberers with words that reflect their specific relationship of affection or jealousy, or inheritance of fields or personal jewelry. A dead person will remind each person in the room, not only of shared adventures, but even of each person's debts which are now inherited by his heirs.

Whatever else they may be, dialogues with the dead are an elaborate technique for structuring the processes of memory; they are equally a technique for regulating the pace of forgetting. Memories fade and are transformed as their rememberers too change with time, recovering from their grief but also aging and finally dying themselves. The old Sora culture had no access to photography, and when I collaborated with a Sora friend to circulate an album of photographs and texts I had collected in the 1970s (Vitebsky and Raika 2011), this revival of old dialogues and contexts stimulated conversations across Soraland of a sort which had never occurred before. Photographs are a static moment of memory, a freeze in time. So just as "remembering" is not so much a cognitive as a relational process, so too "forgetting" follows the evolution of social relationships, and the living gradually come to have less reason to talk with each dead person. Unlike photographs, unlike memorial books, this is the heart of Sora evolutionary necrography.

Baptist Christianity: A New Way of Being Dead

By the 1990s/2000s an entire generation across the Sora heartland came to embrace Christianity, generally in a Baptist form. Baptist Christianity radically reconfigures remembering, forgetting, and articulacy. A changed relationship with the living leads to a change in the nature of the dead. Having earlier been highly articulate, they have now become mute.

The effect of Christianization has run parallel to (and somewhat preceded) government development programs that finally managed to penetrate the Sora hills during the 1980s. A longstanding structure of isolation and feudal exploitation finally unraveled. The decisive advent of roads, schooling, literacy, and employment led to a seismic shift in consciousness, as generations of feudal extortion were transformed into a policy of government subsidy. Previously, animist Sora were living under a system of governance which put them under unremitting ethnic, economic, and political oppression. This power regime was starkly reflected in the shamans themselves. Even when operating their apparently un-Hindu tribal cosmology, Sora shamans gained their powers by marrying sonums in the Underworld. Unlike Sora ancestors, these sonums were not dead ordinary people but high-caste Hindu rajas, policemen, and government officers of the regionally dominant Odia (Oriya) ethnicity — that is, domesticated counterparts of the very people who exploited the Sora above ground. The nonliterate animist Sora saw writing as a magical technique of power and coercion wielded by police and government officers, and backed up with guns. This is the focus of the historical and ideological tension between generations: older Sora are afraid of being neglected after death, as dialogue with their descendants ceases; their children, now in quest of jobs as road laborers, church officers, or government schoolteachers, feel liberated from oppressive old attachments — whether with outside persecutors or demanding ancestors — as they read and write both their own language and the previously mysterious Odia language of the regional administration.

However, the possibility of Christianity had reached the Sora long before government largesse (Knight and Knight 2009), and among younger Sora these are now combined. Though the last of the Canadian

Baptist missionaries left in the late 1970s, they had already turned the Sora towards ideas which, though religiously conservative, were politically modernist. This new vision leaves no space for the agency of the dead. God, Jesus, and the missionaries' own hospital medicine directly undermine the principles of animist causality. The indigenous Baptist pastors, more militant than the foreign missionaries, suppress dialogues with the dead: these are the work of the Devil and distract people from a proper focus on God and Jesus. More specifically in the Sora context, they reinforce attachment between living and dead. But there is also less and less point to these dialogues, since what is there left to discuss? The dead are no longer thought to cause illness and death among the living, since these are now caused by germs (called "insects" in Sora). Tackling these insects is a specialist realm of knowledge known to doctors, nurses, and paramedics. Depriving the dead of voice, and thus of agency, releases the living from their claims. But it also leaves an explanatory gap. Now, illness and death come about through the "will of God." In a community which until now has put such an emphasis on narratives of causality, this is still a very opaque concept. Despite improved medical facilities, people keep falling ill and dying. However, God does not tell us anything about why he causes any of these events, and this leads to a new genre of speculation about people's ungodly behavior. Unlike the verdicts which emerge from dialogues with the dead, these speculations can never be "verified." Another consequence of the removal of the dead from the explanation of misfortune, is to strengthen another old genre: suspicion of sorcery by human enemies.

If the dead no longer cause events among the living, then by the logic of reciprocal dialogue the living have no role in managing the ongoing state of the dead. They can do nothing to feed or comfort them and must rely on God to look after them. They can pray for the dead, but do not receive any information in return. In the old Sora world death was a state of separation in which the dead craved acknowledgment and kept bringing themselves to the attention of the living. Among animists, their need to talk was matched by an equal need in their children. But now the parents of young Christians anticipate reaching out from the Underworld for dialogue but getting no response. The absence of long-term engagement with the dead is already clear at the moment of burial. Where animist cremation removes the body of the dead immediately and leaves nothing but the memorial stone, Baptists will need their bones again when Jesus returns, so they reject the animist pyre and bury the dead instead.

Christian tombs are elongated structures built up out of brick and cement. They are arranged singly or in groups of loosely defined kin (even including affines from other lineages). They are thus more individuated than the memorial stones of the patrilineage, and their clustering does not represent any demarcated social group. Yet this relative individuality does not give them an articulate necrography to match that of the animists. The tomb carries an inscription listing the person's name, date of death, and date of birth (known for literate young people, guessed for old-timers). But there is no story, and the dead person will never come back to talk about their life or afterlife. The (male) pastor reads from the Bible and leads prayers. There is no drumming or dancing, and little in the way of weeping or formalized laments. After this the tomb will never receive much attention ever again. A procedure which was at the heart of animist experience has dropped out of social life altogether.

Thus it is not only the logic of causality which is changed. So has the emotional universe of dialogue between the living and the dead. Animists say that both sides are comforted by such dialogues, and that they are simply an existential necessity. But Baptists deny both the comfort and the necessity. The old dialogues with the dead were a technique of remembering, in which a process of forgetting was carefully paced through a series of ritual encounters. In these encounters, the being of each dead person, and their pain, along with the grief of the mourner, was gradually attenuated. But the price of this was a form of relationality in which, as one young Baptist explained to me, "remembering makes you ill." This is not an existential necessity, but a leaning toward the side of the Devil. Animist cosmology presupposes an intimacy between generations which depends on continued communion, and a notion of time which is ultimately cyclical. But the Christian acquires none of the identity markers or the cumulative involvement of illness as constant reminders from ancestors which constitute so much of an animist's biography and personhood. This new kind of person starts as a *tabula rasa* and develops a cumulative persona through Christian relationships and events. Instead of ancestral names, Christian babies receive names from characters in the Bible. These take no cues from family history but instead serve as moral templates.

The dead Christian's silence leaves his current situation closed to enquiry. Unlike a dead animist, a dead Baptist does not evolve. The cosmic time of Baptism is utterly different from the time of the animists. Though exemplars from characters and scenarios in the Bible provide a template from the past, this is not the Sora past, which receives no validation ("our parents used to walk in darkness and worship devils"). Sora Baptism is ultimately future-oriented. All eyes are on the relationship between the present and the future, a relationship in which the past can be nothing more than a burden and an embarrassment. But what kind of future is this? The pace of the journey toward the future is unsure. In

Baptist ritual there is nothing—no structure, no phases, no acknowledged experience—between the moment of burial and the second coming of Jesus. Attention clusters around two focal points at opposite ends of the spectrum. At one end there is the moment of burial, with its prayers and construction of the tomb, at the other, Jesus' return, and who knows when that will be? Between these points, Baptist cosmology and practice skip over the middle ground of living memory. This is precisely the timespan of the animists' discursive procedures of dialogues with the dead. Those dialogues were the machinery of a cyclical vision of time and causality. But with a combination of Christian end-time and modern employment opportunities, who cares what the dead have to say, or how they are faring? The Baptists have abolished necrography.

Animists lived with an anxiety about sonum attack. Baptists live with a different fear, that they may backslide to old animist habits. Alcohol, tobacco, irregular sexual relations: every one of these old animist habits is perceived as a direct threat to the new regime. Alcohol in particular, so essential for animist ritual, is the key substance that attracts the dead and opens up communication. In this new polarization between ideas of good and evil, being good is hard work.

I also sense an anxiety about identity and doctrine. Sora Baptism seems like a religion still under construction, in which its demographic conquest of an entire generation has outstripped its ability to develop a fully formulated theory of existence, or the emotional forms to match. Perhaps this is an intrinsic problem in the early stages—or even throughout the history—of any totalizing ideology. Totalizing is exactly what the old religion was not. Peter Brown (2015), writing about early Christianity in Western Europe, provides a valuable long-term perspective. Around the second and third centuries AD, the trajectory of the individual soul after death was of limited interest since the entire universe was about to be transformed at any moment by the resurrection of the dead with the return of Jesus (Brown 2015: 9). By the seventh century, this moment had still not arrived, and the sense of cosmic time had stretched. "There was time for the trajectory of each soul to be charged with individual drama and interest. An entire history of the soul after death was spread out in all its richness" (ibid.: 14), since "each soul now had a story of its own.... Each was marked, for good or ill, by its own, irrevocable individuality, for which it had to give account in detail" (ibid.: 16).

The process I have witnessed among the Sora covers both of these possibilities, though in the reverse order. The early Christian view resembles that of Sora Baptists today, who give varied answers when I press them to explain when the dead finally reach God, or where they remain while waiting. The later view comes closer to Sora animism, but with one important difference. While the incompleteness of seventh-century European Christians lay in their sinfulness (a new Christian concept, Vitebsky 2017a: 221, 229–31), the incompleteness of the Sora animist dead lies in their unfinalized social and emotional relationships. This is why they have to be so articulate: their necrography is not just an extension of their biography, but it is also constitutive of the living (see the Introduction to this volume), and a powerful determinant of relationships among them. Just as relationships among the living are constantly shifting, so too are relationships among the dead, who may even marry and beget children in the Underworld as a reflection (or determinant) of living human relationships (Vitebsky 1993: 187–95).

In Soraland, the Baptist denial of a "history of the soul after death" enters subversively into an environment in which exactly this narrative history had a vivid and central function. For dead animists, dialogue makes each person's story emerge so as to become amenable to a specific resolution. Animist stories of individual death are assimilated to generic scenarios such as those associated with the Sun, the Earth, or the power of Leopard; and the resolution consists in reuniting the dead in the Underworld with their kin groups. But dead Baptists have no individual story. Only Jesus has a story, and this must stand for everyone's. While animist stories of individual death are assimilated to generic scenarios, Jesus' story is supergeneric. Jesus' necrography, as articulated in the Gospel, outweighs any interest in the inaccessible necrographies of his followers.

For today's Baptists old enough to have been formed under animism there are tensions which are hard to process. This generation contains the children of the Sora I have known best, those of my own generation who (because of the short Sora lifespan) have almost entirely moved on. To where? As one old friend told me with a laugh shortly before he died, "Maybe I'll go down to the Underworld instead of up into the sky with Jesus. But I don't care—at least the company's good down there!" These younger Baptists, children young enough to be my own children, are my "children," "nephews," and "nieces." I sometimes sense a longing in the ways they talk about their dead parents, and as a close friend of those parents, I am sometimes embraced in a way which suggests that I am being treated as a substitute for those parents. The last functioning shamans have been reduced to working for small circles of older animist clients. For Baptists, it is impossible to know how the dead are faring, because there is no channel for them to come and tell us. But sometimes these parents return in dreams, in effect reclaiming something of the voice that was silenced by the Christian funeral format. One young Baptist called Paranto, who is the son of one of my closest Sora friends, now deceased, was prevented from mourning his father in an animist way, but told me about a series of dreams:

> It was as if we were meeting in waking life:
> — "You've died, where have you come from?"
> — "I'm not dead," he said, "I remain, I exist."
> —I got up and looked around: it was the middle of the night—[amazed tone] there was nobody there! I cried, I was very sad: "I thought you were dead!" I met him under the tree on the way to his favorite drinking place: "Ai! where are you going?"
> — "I'm just wandering around." He looked just as he had when he was healthy.
> — "But how come your body was so sick, and now you're healthy again?"
> — "It's alright, I'm fine now."
> I looked around, there was nobody. (Adapted from Vitebsky 2017a: 208–10, cf. 191–92)

This is a particularly striking confirmation of the role and power of an articulate necrography. Paranto's church has repressed the format of dialogue between the living and the dead. His lineage's memorial stones—one of the main sites where such dialogues would have been staged—have been dismantled and re-used as building material, so that even their location is now hard to discern. Paranto's father calls out from the Underworld, but there is no format of articulation through which he can express himself, since his son will be sanctioned in church if he commissions an animist ritual or even attends one as a bystander. And yet the father has found a way through. Where an animist ritual would have staged a dialogue between son and father, both speaking out loud in a public event, here, privately and silently, the dream provides both sides of the conversation. The son receives a reassurance he craves, one which his new religion is unable to give. This reassurance comes through an imitation of an animist postmortem transformation. In further dreams the father went on to confirm that he had been healed of his terminal illness, that he was not going to pass it on, and that he now resided in a good place. This place is good in terms of the father's own cosmology, since he is not in the sky with Jesus (as Paranto is supposed to believe in waking life), but in the Underworld with his ancestors who led him there.

The format of Baptist services shows how much my view of what ritual is, or should be, has been conditioned by my association with shamans. As I started attending church, joining the congregation sitting on the floor under the platform (or sometimes being invited to come up on the platform and look down on the congregation), I found myself inside a new kind of performance in which dialogue is replaced by monologue and one participates not by speaking, but by being spoken to. Where an animist ritual persuades by negotiation, a Baptist service persuades by assertion, like a political speech. It is not so much a ritual as a rally, and the expected response is acquiescence and a feeling of belonging. The pastor's sermons and exhortations are perhaps no less performative than the trances of the shaman, but his performance is more emotionally restrained. Where mourners may sometimes embrace the entranced shaman and cling to her howling with grief, the pastor remains separated behind a table above them. He does not reproduce the voice of those they have loved but is a more distant mouthpiece for the words of God and Jesus, which are bound up with a written text: apart from the barely noticed grammatical necessity of quoting others verbatim, there is no format of impersonation in Sora Baptism.

The old religion had fetishized writing from a position of weakness by making it the key technique of spiritual power in which literate helper sonums enabled the articulacy of dialogue. Now, even while the universal literacy of young Christians makes the old-timers' awe at the mystique of writing seem pathetic, the inscription on the Baptist tomb takes the fetishization of writing in a new direction, that of bureaucratic annotation. Perhaps this was what the shamans' familiars used to do in their Underworld police stations: the animists did not really understand what was being written except that it gave the writers power over those who were being written about. But the Christians have captured this power more directly, by mastering it themselves rather than relying on shamans' familiars to do it for them.

Why do Sora Baptists no longer need a narrative about their dead? I believe the answer lies beyond Christianity itself. The Baptist church is not the only group identity available to young Sora today. Other Christian denominations are moving in, hoping to harvest souls from Baptist congregations. A prominent strand in the anthropology of Christian missionizing (e.g., Robbins 2007) looks for explanations within the logic or culture of Christianity itself. Certainly, evangelical Christian conversion has a strong rhetoric of rupture, but the Sora situation suggests that this cannot be the whole explanation: in some other villages, young Sora are converting instead to a range of forms of Hinduism which focus on the gods Rama and Krishna. I have argued (Vitebsky 2017a: 266–93) that all these new Sora religions represent ways for young Sora to emerge from their remote jungle and become more closely integrated, not only into the job market, but more broadly into the Indian nation-state. Young Sora are not so much converting *to* new religious forms, whether Christian or Hindu, but rather *away from* their previous isolation, poverty, and exploitation by outsiders.

This broadening of the field is accompanied by a change in the nature of the entities who serve as the focus of religious energy. For animists, the entire cosmos is ancestorized. The animist Sora had a cult of ancestors, but they did not worship them. Their dialogues were not devotional, because ancestors are not gods. They are our own people, just like us, who feel grudges and envy, but also love; we chat and argue with them, and when the conversation is particularly intense, we embrace them through the body of a shaman.

None of the new Sora religions, whether Christian or Hindu, holds dialogues with the dead. Instead they have a style of devotion which was unknown among animists. There is a shift of attention from ancestors to gods, from a more immanent to a more transcendent metaphysics. All use the same word *kittung* for their gods and bring this concept back from a remote figure in animist creation myths to the core of their faith. Jesus, Rama, and Krishna are objects of prayer, a format which was not part of animist religiosity. This is not dialogic in the same sense, since any response from the god is not made explicit or vocalized directly. Animist Sora had gods who made the world the way it is, but these gods then withdrew because there was nothing left for them to do, and their world now runs on sonum-power, in which causality lies in the hands of ordinary dead humans. But God and Jesus, Rama and Krishna, are still very active in the world.

If kittungs as creators contained a resonance of monotheism, this too was without the worship. The shift to currently active gods introduces a new level of respect for such beings, which is justified by a dignity that comes from a lack of neediness in their relationship with us. This dignity matches a reformist tendency throughout India, which I see as linked to a bourgeois aesthetic. Baptists replace messy sacrificial animals with the symbolic blood of Jesus, itself further sanitized by the Bible into wine, and thence by the temperance agenda of the Sora pastors into fruit juice; orthodox Hindus replace blood sacrifice with coconuts, fruit, and flowers. This is directly reflected in narratives about the dead. In contrast to all other Sora, my animist friends put an extraordinary emphasis on dialogical exchange, and their verbal articulacy allows them to act and feel as if they believe their performances literally.

All of this is set in history, and there is a close parallel between the spiritual and political dimensions of these dialogues. The culture that I witnessed in the 1970s combined an archaic metaphysics with an archaic system of domination. Sora dialogues with the dead were ultimately defensive in relation to everyone, from the most distant officials (who were domesticated in the Underworld by shamans through marriage) to one's own dead relatives. It was essential to know the necrographies of one's ancestors in order to modify their impact on one's biography, and the shaman's Underworld helpers provided the power to do all of this. Those dialogues were structured to deflect attack and to transform victimhood. Maybe those dialogues were themselves once a new religious form, a response to earlier violence from outside—an articulate necrography that emerged in its time and is now fading in a new time.

Piers Vitebsky is a social anthropologist specializing in the religions and languages of indigenous communities in Tribal India and the Russian Arctic. He was educated in Cambridge, Oxford, London, and Delhi, and recently retired as Head of Anthropology and Russian Northern Studies at the Scott Polar Research Institute at the University of Cambridge. He is Honorary Professor at the MK Ammosov North-Eastern Federal University in Yakutsk, Siberia. His books include: *Dialogues with the Dead: The Discussion of Mortality among the Sora of Eastern India* (1993); *Living without the Dead: Loss and Redemption in a Jungle Cosmos* (2017); and *Reindeer People: Living with Animals and Spirits in Siberia* (2005).

References

Brown, Peter. 2015. *The Ransom of the Soul: Afterlife and Wealth in Early Western Christianity*. Cambridge, MA: Harvard University Press.

Freud, Sigmund. 1957. "Mourning and Melancholia." In *The Standard Edition of the Complete Psychological Works of Sigmund Freud*, translated by James Strachey, vol. 14, 239–58. London: Hogarth Press. Originally published in German in 1917.

Knight, Kenneth, and Shirley Knight. 2009. *The Seed Holds the Tree: A Story of India and the Kingdom of God*. n.p.: Lulu.

Robbins, Joel. 2007. "Continuity Thinking and the Problem of Christian Culture: Belief, Time, and the Anthropology of Christianity." *Current Anthropology* 48(1): 5–38.

Scott, James. C. 2009. *The Art of Not Being Governed: An Anarchist History of Upland Southeast Asia*. New Haven: Yale University Press.

Vitebsky, Piers. 1993. *Dialogues with the Dead: The Discussion of Mortality among the Sora of Eastern India*. Cambridge: Cambridge University Press and Delhi: Foundation Press.

———. 2017a. *Living without the Dead: Loss and Redemption in a Jungle Cosmos*. Chicago: University of Chicago Press.

———. 2017b. "The Creation, and Abandonment, of Metaphor in Sora Parallel Ritual Verse." Paper presented at the 7th International Conference on Austroasiatic Linguistics, Kiel, Germany, September 2017. Available at https://www.academia.edu/35593854/The_creation_and_abandonment_of_metaphor_in_Sora_parallel_ritual_verse.

Vitebsky, Piers., and Monosi Raika. 2011. *Jujunji do yuyunji a banuddin: Sora jattin a sanskruti (Sora beran batte, aboi tanub)* [Indigenous Knowledge: a Handbook of Sora Culture (in Sora, Part I)], Visakhapatnam: privately printed. Available at https://www.academia.edu/5440444/Handbk_of_Sora_indig_kn_see_p.6_.

Afterword

The Necrographic Imagination

Magnus Course

The temptation one faces when asked to write an afterword such as this is to simply identify, usually somewhat arbitrarily, commonalities or overlaps between the essays presented and thus to condense them into a kind of singular direction, a simple take-home message. And it could be argued that, in a sense, anthropology in general, and the anthropology of death in particular, has taken a similar tack, frequently trying to consolidate into a kind of one-size-fits-all analytical framework. As Panagiotopoulos and Espírito Santo point out in their introduction to this volume, some of the most influential writers on death from Hertz to Heidegger fall into this kind of trap. Yet what struck me upon reading and reflecting upon these chapters was the deep-rooted and fundamental differences between many of the ethnographic cases described. These differences, however, do not seem random or arbitrary, but rather systematic and structured; they occur along particular lines. My goal in this afterword is therefore to sketch out some of these axes of differentiation, particular points or tensions from which practices diverge and take different paths. In some cases, these axes of differentiation occur between different ethnographic cases, but in others, the axis of differentiation can be observed within a particular case. I am going to focus on just two, but other axes of differentiation, perhaps to do with emotions, with senses, or with temporality could equally be identified. These axes occur within what I will call, the "necrographic imagination," a term through which I refer not to necrographies themselves, but to the conceptual space in which they are constructed, contested, maintained, and dismantled. Such an approach seeks to account for the fact that the ethnographic cases presented in this volume are as much concerned with the denial of necrography as to its revelation, a point to which I now turn.

Necrography as Biography, Necrography against Biography

We can loosely divide the chapters along a continuum, with those at one end seeking to engage with, to sustain, and to "progress" the dead, while at the other end of the continuum, the dead are to be dismissed, expelled, and forgotten. And we can approach these twin poles of continuity and discontinuity through the idiom of necrography, a concept laid out in both the Introduction and Panagiotopoulos's chapter to describe "the present situation, affects and effects of the deceased, whether these are present in the form of representation or exchange" (Panagiotopoulos, Chapter 3; Espírito Santo and Panagiotopoulos, Introduction; see also Panagiotopoulos 2017). Thinking through necrography helps us because, in a sense, the former pole—the emphasis on continuity with the dead, on their continued presence—is rooted in the desire to produce and sustain a necrography, a narrativized life-in-death, while the latter pole is specifically concerned with the very prevention of necrography, the absolute denial of any narrative (or even material) presence to the dead. Thus, as I explore below, some of the chapters are as much about the denial of necrography as its elaboration.

The chapters by Marouda on Vietnam, by Romberg on Puerto Rico, and by Robben on wartime Germany emphasize in one way or another a desire for the continued presence of the dead. Practices thus focus on the creation of spaces for the narrativization of the emergence and subsequent development of the dead, their "articulacy" to use a term used by Panagiotopoulos (2017). Here the dead really are gifted necrographies. And just as Bakhtin asserted that "biography is bestowed as a gift," so, too, is necrography (1990: 166). For it is the very narrativization of the dead which allows them to progress or to evolve. This gifting of necrography is perhaps nowhere clearer than in Marouda's description of the attempts of people in Vietnam to care for and propitiate not only their own ancestral dead, but also those "neglected" dead devoid of necrography and thus condemned to malignant wandering. Tellingly, it is biography—knowledge of the name, age, and date of death—that forms the first step in the construction of necrography, the narrative presence that will give the lost souls peace. A similar process seems to have occurred in the aftermath of World War II, when, as Robben describes, German survivors sought to retrieve their dead from the anonymity and obscurity of collective mass burials, and to rebury them as individuals.

This latter case clearly illustrates that the gifting of necrographies is far from democratic; for some necrography is allowed and sought, for others it is denied, a differentiation of the dead to which I shall return.

The chapters by Conklin on the Wari' and by Straight on the Samburu describe processes of forgetting and annihilating the dead, which head in the opposite direction. Any possibility of creating a necrography is forestalled, through the psychological, and indeed, physical destruction of the dead. The dead are not just dead, they are dead and gone. In Straight's term, the dead are "unanchored," unsupported by either a culturally-validated narrative or material presence. Yet the role of biography in the elaboration or foreclosing of necrography is not always clear-cut. While in the Vietnamese case described above, biography appears to be the prerequisite to necrography, in other cases biography eradicates its very possibility. My own work on Mapuche funerals has explored how in funeral oratory, biography is recited as a way of "completing" or "finishing" the dead, and thus denying them any further narrative presence through necrography (Course 2007). Perhaps the little bundles of a dead Samburu child's belongings reflect on a material register a similar process of condensation and annihilation. So, we can see how different cases occupy different positions on this axis of differentiation, some focused on the continued presence of the dead through sustaining necrographies, others focused on their dissolution through the removal of narrative possibility.

Yet many, if not most cases, are midway on this continuum. Walter makes clear that the relation between the dead and the living in Western Europe does not correspond simply to one of either "absence" or "presence" but to an ever-shifting configuration to the two. It is interesting to note that in the case of the *muertos* in Cuban Espiritismo described by Espírito Santo, a biography is assumed, but not elaborated; the premortem trajectories of the dead are of a generic, unspecified nature; "a gypsy," "a young man," and so on. Too much biography, it would seem, would erase the vitality of necrographic presence. This point can be extended to what one could call "auto-necrography," the self-awareness of the dead. Hence, the desire for Palo Monte practitioners to have "perros" who have been dead long enough to be aware of their deadness, but not long enough to have become enlightened, to have crafted for themselves a fully-fledged auto-necrography. Likewise, in the Jarê traditions of the interior of Bahia in Brazil, described by Banaggia, some dead are sought and cultivated, while others are dismissed and banished.

In other cases midway along this continuum between continuity or discontinuity of relations between the living and the dead, necrographies emerge as sites of tension and struggle. Thus in the Sora case described by

Vitebsky, widespread conversion to Baptist Christianity exiles the dead; the former shamanic dialogues with the dead aimed precisely at developing a necrography, a postmortem narrative of growth and appeasement, are banished. There is now no story for the dead to tell, other than the transcendent story of Christian salvation, a necrography so remote both socially and temporally to be of little immediate consequence.

Perhaps ultimately, the two opposed poles of this continuum are brought full circle, for it is striking that in many cases, the end goal of *both* those practices geared towards the enabling and reception of necrography, of giving the dead a life after death, *and* those practices which seek to annihilate the dead, is actually their ultimate transformation and subsequent control by the living. It is to this paradoxical process that Anne Christine Taylor refers in the title of her classic essay, "Remembering to Forget" (Taylor 1993). So it could be argued that two apparently very different ways of dealing with the dead ultimately end up doing the same thing; one just takes a short cut.

The Differentiated Dead

Death, we are sometimes told, is the great leveller; at death the inequalities of life disappear and all must face the same fate. The chapters in this volume demonstrate quite clearly that, for better or worse, this is rarely the case. A focus on necrography demonstrates that not only do the inequalities of the living carry over into death, but that such differentiation may also occur *after* death. We can see that one of the advantages of thinking through necrography is that it opens up a space for thinking about the dead's postmortem transformation and development. As Marouda makes clear in her critique, much thinking within the anthropology of the dead has assumed a teleological bias, thus death is presented as a static endpoint, a point also central to Robert Pogue Harrison's magisterial work on the dominion of the dead (2003). Yet as Conklin points out, even the gross materiality of a corpse is anything but static. Indeed, it is its very volatility and acceleration of change and transformation, which Wari' mourners find so shocking. In many of the cases described in this volume, the fate of the dead is not fixed or predetermined, but contingent on their relationships with the living. Thus in the Vietnamese case described by Marouda and the Nepalese case described by Torri, the division between benevolent ancestral spirits and malevolent ghosts is not fixed, but fluid and flexible, dependent upon the recognition and ritual care of the living. Likewise, in Cuba, the living provided the dead with the material bases for their rebirth, or what Espirito Santo fittingly calls, their "re-death." Whether or not death is seen as the absolute summation of human finitude à la Heidegger, or as one point in an ongoing trajectory of transformation, is, as Walter points out, itself subject to historical change and transformation.

Walter's point is that for Western society the presence or absence of the dead is linked to shifting economic and political transformations. This differentiation of the dead raises two points: first, that differential paths of the dead are frequently dependent on the living, through both modalities of "exchange" and "representation," to use Baudrillard's terms; and second, that in many instances, this differentiation is premised on our aforementioned axes of gifting or denying necrography; the creation of an undifferentiated dead is achieved, in part, through the negation of necrography (and in some cases, biography, too).

The Materiality and Immateriality of the Dead

The second axis of differentiation I want to highlight is that of materiality. Again, we can observe a continuum along which certain practices lean towards the increasing materialization of the dead, while at the other end, the materiality of the dead is eroded. In some cases, the material disintegration of the dead is—quite literally in the case of the Wari' described by Conklin—thrust into people's faces. Conklin describes how funerary cannibalism simultaneously gestured in two directions, on the one hand, towards the presence of the dead, but also towards their very deadness and the radical absence this implied for their surviving kin.

Some of the chapters describe an inverse movement, one towards greater materiality. This is the case of the dolls and cauldrons which Espírito Santo describes as providing material focal points for the Cuban immaterial dead. In the Cuban case, the materiality of the dead is not simply restricted to their materialization by the living, but also includes the literal incorporation of the dead's material remains as the powdered bones of the dead flow into incisions in the Palo Monte initiate's skin. The case of the Puerto Rican spirits described by Romberg illustrate that the materialization of spirits, primarily through the bodies of mediums in séances, is actually a medial point in their onward journey towards the disincarnate and immaterial conclusions of their necrographies as enlightened spirits.

The question of materiality is not just composed of the dead themselves, but on the practices surrounding them. This emerges clearly in the hurling of a deceased Samburu child's possessions into a fast-flowing river, in an attempt to annihilate all trace of him, to disperse, destroy, and dash downstream. It would seem perhaps that this materialization or dematerialization of the dead coincides with the construction or deconstruction of necrography. This point reinforces the idea that necrography (or its denial) is not limited to the linguistic or discursive, or indeed, the purely representational, but frequently takes a material register.

Necrography Within

What I have tried to do in this brief afterword is to highlight certain axes of difference; I want to think towards how, in different cultures, or even within the same culture, although the dead may be travelling along the same grooves, they might be moving in opposite directions. In some instances, from the material to the immaterial, in others from the immaterial to the material; at certain times, emerging towards us in the creation of necrography, at other times, away, removed from all processes of narrativization and recognition. Such an approach might constitute an initial step towards systematically working through both the striking commonalities and the striking differences presented by the dead.

I want to finish though by making a point which does not really fit at all into the schema outlined above, indeed, one which in some ways is tangential to it. I want to reiterate a simple, but fundamentally important point alluded to by Robben, but most powerfully elaborated by Bilinda Straight in her chapter on Samburu grief. In describing Samburu attempts to utterly and completely erase all trace of the deceased, Straight notes that although "it is better to throw these tiny things into a moving river, and to formally annihilate the meanings and implications of certain deaths by erasing the dead themselves. That this does not and cannot erase them from the memories of those who grieve." I take this point to reflect a broader truth, that the socially and culturally sanctioned approaches towards the dead—"collective representations" to use Hertz's term—whatever they may be, are never perfectly isomorphic with individual experience. No matter how extreme and how resolute any given society's mandate to distance or forget or eradicate the dead, we can never distance or forget or eradicate their part in our being, their existence within us. For the biographies of us, the living, are, to a certain extent, composed of the necrographies of the dead. Just as ninety percent of the physical self is a living other, so a large and ever-growing proportion of our social and emotional selves is too. Not living others of microbes and fungi, but dead others. All those who have loved us and hated us and been indifferent towards us, and whose voices now lend cadence to our own. For evidence of the dead, we need look no further than ourselves.

Magnus Course teaches anthropology at the University of Edinburgh. His research focuses on kinship, personhood, and death in both Europe and South America. He is the author of *Becoming Mapuche* (University of Illinois Press, 2011) and co-author of *Fluent Selves* (University of Nebraska Press, 2014).

References

Bakhtin, Mikhail. 1990. *Art and Answerability*. Austin: University of Texas Press.
Course, Magnus. 2007. "Death, Biography, and the Mapuche Person." *Ethnos* 72(1): 77–101.
Harrison, Robert Pogue. 2003. *The Dominion of the Dead*. Chicago: University of Chicago Press.
Panagiotopoulos, Anastasios. 2017. "When Biographies Cross Necrographies: The Exchange of Affinity in Cuba." *Ethnos* 82(5): 946–70.
Taylor, Anne Christine. 1993. "Remembering to Forget: Identity, Mourning and Memory Among the Jivaro." *Man* 28(4): 653–78.

Index

abolished necrography 238
abortion 53–5, 156, 215
Adorno, Theodor W. 20, 27
African-based religion 186
African-inspired culture 89
Afro-Cuban contexts 90
Afro-Cuban religion 84–6, 93, 100–1; approach to Palo Monte 86, 93; Bantu-Congo inspiration 86; Santería, *orishas* 89; religious cosmos 89; religious experts 103; religious sites 94
"Afro-Cuban" understanding of things 97
African religious practices 165
afterlife 135, 148, 152, 156, 165–6, 170–1, 205, 207–8, 211, 214, 218–20, 237
agency 18–9, 22, 24, 25, 30, 33–4, 55, 76, 105, 157, 166, 179, 206–7, 209, 218, 223, 234, 236
agency, nonhuman 168; moral agency of spirits 170, 173; agency in the corpse 115
agency of others 157, 165
agentive piece 90
agentive power 175
alcohol, key ritual substance 238

Alpizar, Ralph 89, 93
altar: ancestral/provisional 145–6, 150, 160–1; domestic 153; makeshift 154; spiritual 3
Amazonian eschatology 144
Amazonian systems 116
American-led forces 151
American Spiritualism 170
Amerindian Brazil 12
Amerindian Cultures 98
amulets: protective 178; ritually confectionate 90
anarchist socialists 170
ancestor-animals 117
ancestor: commemoration 142; newly-made 114; protective 206; religious ritual 94
ancestor-peccaries 119
ancestorized cosmos 241
ancestorhood 145–6
ancestral: figures 156; graves 150; spirits, benevolent 141, 146, 153, 155
Anderson, Benedict 29
animist casuality principles 236
annihilation 125, 135, 137, 186
"ancient money" 155
animacy 144

animal: flesh 121; magnetism, theory of 171; sacrifices 187
Animist: cosmology 237; cremation 236; culture 227–8 (no writing 228)
animist, Mongolian and Siberian 100
Antebellum North America 170
anti-colonial struggle 142
anti-hegemonic messages 170
apego (attachment) 91
aperterbis, Ifá dancing rite 86
aparelhos ("equipment/devices") 193
apparitions 157, 221
Arawete 144
Ariès, Philippe 18, 23, 63, 166, 207
Arendt, Hannah 57
artisanal miners 189
articulacy 5, 8, 228, 232–33, 235, 241–42, 245
articulation 8, 240
assemblages 90, 150
Atharva Veda 213
Auschwitz 29, 53
Austronesian kingdom of Champa 152

bad death 211
Bantu-Congo inspiration 87
"bank of the netherworld" (ngân hàng âm phủ) 155
Baptist Christianity 235
Baptist missionaries 236
basic components of the body 206
Battaglia, Debbora 144
"battle for Huế" 151
Battle of Stalingrad 40
Baudrillard, Jean 8, 10, 17, 64, 75–8
Becker, Ernest 66–8
becoming a ghost, three reasons 210
being, "enlightened" 91
"being toward the dead" 74
bereavement 43, 44
bereavement and rape 53, 54
Berreman, Gerald D. 211
"big clearance" (đại tường) 146
biographies 2, 3, 8–10, 12, 19, 21, 26, 63, 75, 79, 95, 106, 126, 128–9, 232, 249
biographical stories 95
biomaterial transformations 106–7

biomatter 121
biochemistry, spirit-ized bodily 96
biopolitics of death 100
births, abnormal 127
birth, cosmic 92
Bhils 127
"black magic" 88
Blauner, Robert 24
Bloch, Maurice 100
Blood 98–9, 107, 111–2, 114, 190, 192–3, 212, 215, 221, 228, 229, 242
blood: first vital fluid 192; menstrual 193; sacrificial animal 29, 89–92, 229
Bodhisattvas 157
body: "perspicient" body 96; "death-created" bodies 98; multiple "bodies" 102; embalmed body 107; prepare the body for roasting 108; intact body 109; living body/dead body 110; human body 116; cut body into pieces/dismembered bodies 118; ancestral body 145; body, decomposing 206; shaman's body 229
body-souls 102
body's postmortem trajectory 107
body's pregnant woman 128
body substance 111
Bolívar, Natalia 93
Bolivia 108
Bonelli, Cristóbal 99
Borchert, Wolfgang 40
born ready-made 200
Brazil 12, 98, 108, 112, 168, 174, 186–89
Brazilian Spiritists 170
Brazilian rainforest 108
Bride doll 129
"brief death" 196
Brown, Peter 238
brujo (Spiritist witch healer) 176
Buddha 174, 217
Buddhahood 129
Buddhism 120; Tibetan Buddhism 120
Buddhist: abbots 160; Canon 214; clergy 150, 214; cosmology 215; monasteries 157; monks 157, 159; settings 160

Burton, John 130
butterfly, very old ancestor turns into 231

caboclo Candomblé 187, 189, 191, 193
Calleja, Guillermo 89, 93
callendrical festivities 207
callendrical activities 208
Carbonell, Walterio 89
cannibalism 110–11, 118–21; Wari' funerary cannibalism 108
Caribbean Spiritism 170
Carroll, Bret 169
Casper, Monica 115
Castellanos, Isabel 94
Castellanos, Jorge 94
Catholic, alternative 165
Catholic religious elements 175
catatonic trance 219
categories of spirits, different 231
causas (bewitchments) 176–7
causation 33
Cementerio Colón, Havana's 91
Certeau, Michel de 176
Cham, the indigenous 142, 150, 152–3
chamalongos, oracles 88
change in the nature of the entities 241
Chapada Diamantina 187
Changó, *orisha*-god 89
Child's protector, old ancestor 231
childhood, anthropology of 127
children, nonhuman 127
child spirit 129, 135
Christian: Baptist 227; conversion, evangelical 241; funeral format 239; missionizing, anthropology of 241; tombs 236
Christianity, transition to 227
Christianization 235
Chukchi, siberian 101
City of Joined-Feet (*Cidade de Pé-Junto*), cemetery 200
Classical religious pan-Indic texts 213, 221; *bhūt* (Sanskrit *bhūta*), spirit of the dead 212; *bhūt-pret*, supernatural being into one; *revenant* 212
cleansing rituals 178

co-dependency between the dead and the living 229
Cohn, Clarice 98
Cold War 142, 149, 158
collective: existence of Sonums 234; forgetting 136; immorality 138; séances 175; representations 100; collective trauma 142
colonial state, Spanish Catholic 170
Conklin, Beth A. 98
commodificaction of the dead 21, 26
continued communion 237
consecration 92
contract between the living and the dead 32
cordón espiritual (group of spirit guides) 94
cordón muertos 96
Cordón spirits 95–6, 102
corpse 106–8, 110–11, 113–16, 119–22, 144–6, 207, 210, 218, 247; rotting corpses 116; meditation on corpses 120
cosmic time 237
cosmogony 97
cosmological: elaborations 189, landscape 142; locations, different 231; hierarchy of spirits of light 170
cosmology, distinct 143
cosmology of Self 95–6
Course, Magnus 4, 12
cremation 107, 109, 120, 211, 236; public cremation 50; cremation grounds 221
Creole independence activist groups 170
criado-prenda 89. See also Palero
Cuba 88–90, 95
Cuban Espiritismo 102
cult of ancestors 241
cult house 186
cuadro (spiritual power and protections) 173, 176–8
cyclical view of time 20

dancing barefoot (Jarê people) 190
Darhads, mongolian 101–2

Dayak society 72–3
dead: abscence or prescence of 18, 26; "dead agency on the living" 18, 33, 76; categories of the 141, 155; childless 143; children 129, 159; developed 96; hungry 153; ill-fated 150–1, 158; unanchored/dead, "sweet old" 138; unfortunate 142, 147, 149, 153, 156; unidentified, unknown 150; unpropitious 138; unquiet 30; Vietnamese 141, 145–6
"dead visionaries 3
deadness" 93
deads as legal agents 22
death-accepting/death-denying 100
death: anthropology of 11, 41–3, 45, 58, 244; domesticated 207; education 126; as an event 65, 68, 73; -experience 231;-as-change 75; -as-finitude 65–9, 71–78; as the end of existence 77; as the ending of all life 144; -as-an-instant 71; modern 167; as the most important source of all ghost stories 205; as "the object of a collective representation" 70, 72; -odor 115; of the Other 63, 64, 69, 70, 72; as a passage or threshold to another realm of existence 165; physical 144; as a relational phenomenon 73; as a renewal of cosmic cycles 119; rites 107, 113, 119–20; rituals 110; social implications of 143; sociological/ biological understandings of 143; songs 116; stages 231; as a starting point 145; tragic 135; as a transformative process 143, 145; as a transition 70–3, 77; untimely 207; the world of 92
Death Mills (Die Todesmühlen) 51
deaths, premature 137, 152, 158
Deceased children 132, 138; *nkiyo* 132
deceased: infants 158–9; meanings of the 134
deceased's transcendental transformation 146, 148

deities 3, 89
denial/acceptance model 63, 64, 69, 73, 75–8
denial "shut-upness" 68
Demske, James 2, 64–6
demography 19, 24, 31
Demossier, Marion 21
Denham, Aaron R. 127–8
destined for death 127
Devil 236
dialogues with the dead 229, 234; suppressed dialogues with the dead 236; not devotional, not worship 242
dialogue replaced by monologue 240
diamond-mining region 188
Dietrich, Angela 216
dignity, lack of neediness in relationship 242
"disappeared of Argentina" 30
disenchantment 167–8
dissonance, cognitive/sensory 116
divination 12, 79, 86–7, 95–6, 175–6, 178–9, 215, 230
divinity, incarnations of 137
Doka, Kenneth 126
doll spouse 129
Domanska, Ewa 30
Doyle, Arthur Conan 169
dreams 42, 239
Drumming Jarês 201
dualism 94, 96–7, 102–3; Aristotelian dualism 85; matter-spirit dualism 102
Durkheim, Émile 42–5, 49, 51

early Christianity 238
ecology 31
economy of death 78
ecoturism destination 188
eguns, Jarê spirits of the dead 199
Einarsdóttir, Jónína 127–8
elite, royal and mandarinal 157
embodiment of abjection 110
embodied sensation 111
Empson, Rebecca 26
"enchanted ones" (*encantados*) 199

encounters 206, 211–12; metaphysic encounter 190; encounters with ghosts 211, 217; personal encounters with (resentful) dead 216; ghost-encounters 216; nocturnal encounters 221
energy deficiency/excess energy 197
end of a specific cult house 194; deactivation of the cult house 200
enlightenment ideals 168
entidades 176
entities: ghostly 142–3, 147–52, 154–5, 157–8, 160–1; lowly 153; malevolent 206; other worldly 143, 216; unincorporated 192
entropic quality of the force 197
Espiritismo 90, 97
"Espiritismo científico" society 96
Espiritismo, Creole 86, 94–5; Espiritismo *cruzado* 94
Espiritismo, Cuban 94
espiritista 90; Espiritistas 100
espiritistas-brujos 168
espiritista-bruja 176
espiritistas, Cuban 96
espiritista-santera 176
Espírito Santo, Diana 90, 93–7
espíritus de existencia 176
espíritus protectores 94
ethereal fluids 171
"ethereal matter" 171
"ethnophysiological models of shared substance" 99
ethnocentrism 144
events 232, 236–7
evolution 232; of social relationships 235
evolutionism 165, 168, 170–1
excess of the local culture 220
Exchange 75–77; Exchange model 76; symbolic exchange (Baudrellardean sense) 75; living-dead exchange 25, 64, 143, 165–6, 168–9
exchange: dialogical 242; modern forms of 166; practices 130, 133

exchanges: human and spirits of the dead and light 175; of feeding and being fed 120; ritual 43, 207; with death, loss of 166
exchanging memories about the deceased 46
"existential anthropology" 109
existence: impermanence of 120; posthumous 150, 157, 161
ex-living-person 199
exorcism 216

Fabian, Johannes 78
fact of death, the; very fact 77; facts of death 107, 110
fates, changing 142, 161
fate, posthumous 160
father in sainthood (*pai–de–santo*) 195
"fear of death" 67; fear of the death of the Self 69
feasts, ritual 153, 159
feet pointing backward 217
fetuses 158, 161
Feutchang, Stephan 149
Figarola, Joel James 91
finitude, death as 65–8, 74–8
flows of intentionalities 199
"folklorization" 74
folklore and pop culture 209
folkloric traditions (Nepalese) 208–9
food as an element of exchange 222
forces: of Jarê, the 201; pernitious 193; sacred 129
food-sharing ideology 222
force-spirits 191
forebears, labor of 20, 21
"form of death" 147, 157
formal songs, Sora ritual 232
founders, ancestral 25
Fourier, Charles 172
fragmentation, bodily 120
Freed, Ruth S. 210, 211
Freed, Stanley A. 210, 211
Freemasons 170
French colonial project 153
Freud, Sigmund 43–5, 57, 66, 231
full-scale rituals 216

funeral rituals 108; precontact funeral 108–9, 113–4
funerary: cycle 146; process 145; treatment 146, 159

genealogy 28
genealogies, reconstructing 231
gender issues in ghostly matters 222
Gennep, Arnold van 207
Germany: post war 41, 54; West and East 56–7
ghost 2, 24, 30, 116, 141–3, 146–162, 174, 205–23, affliction 218; attacks 216; cô hồn 147; ghost's disposition toward the living 211; "dollarization" of the ghost economy 155; ghostly apparitions 141, 211; ghostly existence 143, 161; ghostly condition 149, 161; historic ghosts 150, 153; hungry 214; influence 217; malevolent ghosts 141; nonbecoming ghost 157; not visible, sensed ghost 210; stories 208, 219–20; story, sharing 222; -victims 142; victims of "fall of the capital" to the French 153
ghost-lore of Nepal 220
"ghost marriage" 129; African ghost marriage 130; Atuot ghost marriage 130
"ghosts of war" 142
give name to a descendant, to 232
God 236, 238, 241–42
godfather's *nganga* 92
godparents, religious 94
Gollancz, Victor 53
González Díaz de Villegas, Carmen 93
Gorodok Beckmann 40, 41
grief 42–3, 69, 72, 108, 117; collective grief 120; grief work 44; disenfranchised grief 126–8, 135; grief counseling 126; differentiating grief 134
"grieving rules" 126
groups, Kardecist espiritista 96
"guardian angel" 96
guardieros 70

Guinea-Bisau 128
Gustaffson, Mai Lan 147

Hallam, Elizabeth 130
Hare, Robert 171
Harrison, Robert Pogue 74
Havana 86, 88, 91, 94–5; Havana's Revolution square 3
Haunting dream 210
hazard 133–4
healer-medium 178
healing rituals 175, 230
Heidegger, Martin 64–8, 72, 244, 248
Heideggerian concept "being-unto-death" 65, 68, 72; "being toward death" 72
Heineman, Elizabeth D. 50, 55–6
heritage industry 28
heroic martyrs 29
Hertz, Robert 70, 72, 76–7, 100, 143
Himalayas 211
Himalayan communities, Tibetan-speaking 219
Himalayan country 216
Hinduism 241; ghosts causing death 211; neo-Hindu cults 228; mainstream Hindus 228; un-Hindu tribal cosmology 235; high-cast Hindu rajas 241; orthodox Hindus 242
high-caste Hindu rajas, sonums
Hockey, Jenny 130
Hollen, Cecilia Van 127
home-altars 176
Horkheimer, Max 20, 27
horror short stories 220
host, intimate 143
"house-centered morality of death" 147
human-animal relations 120
human body 94, 109–111, 116, 129, 212
human world of the dead 128
Huế 141–2, 145–7, 149–53, 155–59, 161
hüroroin, death and rebirth warriors ritual 117

Ifá, divination cult 86
illness: as constant reminders from ancestors 237; repetition of 229
"implotion" (of spirits within the body) 102
influences, malicious 158
incorporations 144, 187, 248
Indian ghost, phenomelogy 209–15; pan-Indic beliefs 210; specter transformation of the dead 208
Indian notion-sate 241
Indio, the (NativeAmerican spirit) 95
individual tale about death and suffering 208
Indochina conflict 150
infanticide 135
inheritance 21–2
initiation 94–5, 187
invisible beings 90
immortality 18, 30, 42, 44, 77, 114, 119; symbolic immortality 32, 42; reborn as an immortal being 115
immobility of feet 201
impersonate, to (Sora ritual) 232
inanimacy, lifeless 110
incorrect funeral rites 207
Indochina conflicts 157
instability 110
"internal entity" 93; *nsala* and *mwele* 93
interlocutors of the dead 143
"interrelated families" 151
intimacy 145, 159, 237; intimate exchanges across ontological divides 146; intimate interactions with the dead 168; intimate relations between people and their spirits 191
insatiable hunger, *preta* 212
invocation 217
iran, nonhuman child 127–8; 137
irrevocable individuality of the soul 238

jamixi' (Wari' principle) 110
Jarê 186–202, 246; older entities Nanã Borocô and Abaluaê 190; religious leaders 187, 194, 197, 199; temples 194

Japanese folklore 209
Jesus 171, 174, 236
Jesus, teachings of 172
Jesus' supergeneric story 239
Jesus necrography; Gospel 239
Jewish/non-Jewish women 47, 54–5
Jôbutsu, trascendent state of 129
joined feet, the 201
Judeo-Christian tradition 101
Juramiento, initiation 92

Kali (goddess) 217
Kardec, Allan 94, 165, 168, 173–5
Kardecean Spiritism 175
"karma" 92
karmic retribution 215
Kathmandu center 221
Kathmandu Valley 216
Kearl, Michael 18, 21, 26, 28–30
Kenya 125, 136
Kerestetzi, Katerina 92, 93
Kierkegaard, Søren 68
kin 98, 137; bereaved kin 116–18, 121; living kin 143, 146, 160
kinship 23, 28, 26, 31, 99, 116, 143, 149, 229; distinctive realization of 143; unilateral/bilateral 23
kinsperson 113
kittung, Sora gods 242
Klima, Alan 120
Kristeva, Julia 110, 136
Kwon, Heonik 142, 147, 155, 158

labor 20, 21
Lancy, David 127
Latin American Spiritism 170
Latin- and Luso-American Caribbean societies 165
Law, John 33
laws, Spiritists Spiritual 172
Law of Progress, the 172
Law of Love and Charity, the 173, 177–8
Law of Cause and Effect, the 173, 178
Law of Reincarnation 173, 177
Law to Aid Victims of War 56
Lestingrant, Frank 118

liberal revolutionaries 170
life-after-death 205
life and death as a continuum 4, 245–247
life-death/death-life 103
life-like existence 205
lifeworld 121, 156
Limbu people 218
liminal phases 207
liminality 41, 47, 58, 72; liminal period 71; liminal time 43, 59, 136
"living body" 93
living descendants 229
"living dispossessed" 149
living mourners 107
living, unborn 127
living worshippers 146, 151, 153
logic of ritual assemblages and fabrications, a 103
Lương Nghi, village 152
lunar calendar 141
Lunar New Year cycle 150

"maiden aunts" 142, 156
Malinowski, Bronislaw 43–5, 49, 167
market reforms 141–2
Marx, Karl 18, 27, 33
masses of dead 151
massive dead 42, 46, 53
massive losses 49, 58
materia 95
material beings 121
"material envelope" 93
material destruction 116
material substitute, human-like 129
materialism 170–1
materialize (to take on the form of sth) 90
meat-eaters 116
meat-eating 120
meat-sharing 116
Mebengokré-Xikrin 98
medium 96; mediumship 96, 99, 199; Espiritista medium 96–7; 175
mediums *cuadro* or *protecciones* 175
melody of death-keening 119
meritocracy, the ideology of 26

memorable dead 134
memorial stone, lineage's 240
memorial stones, stack of 228
memories: illness and death caused by 234; shared/private 22
memory: boom 28, collective/private 31, 34; memory, embodied 51
memory practices 135
Mesmer, Franz Anton 171
"metaphysical cuisine" of becoming 145
micro-lifeforms 106
"ministry of spirits", the 169
Michailovsky, Boyd 217–18
misa 94–95, 97; *misa espiritual* 94
missing dead 30
mistreatment of bodies 206
"modern disenchantments" 168
modern theories of death 168
Modern Western societies 17–9, 25–7, 32
modulate force 197
mollvün 99
Moore, Lisa Jean 115
moral charters 169
"moral specific gravity" 171
moral Spiritist way of life 169
moral templates 237
more-than-human-world 121
Morgan, Lynn M. 98
Mori, A. 209
Morris, Rosalind C. 142
mortal and divine relations 129
mortal spoils 206
mortician 107
mortuary: anthropology of 4; practices 128, 144; rites 130, 135, 143; rituals 208; shroud 133; treatment 143
movements: gothic and romantic 26; Spiritualist and Spiritist 169
mourning and recovery oscillation 54, 56, 58–9
mourning: communal 41, 43; cycle 160; experiences 138; memory-work 112; oscillation of humane 52–3; process 136; rituals 120; sociocultural/personal 46, 58; Wari' 109

Index 259

movement as a quality of life 196
mpakas 90
mpungo, Palo deity 89
mpungo Siete Rayos 89
muerteros 92
muerto(s) 87, 90, 94–8, 102, 176–7
muertos oscuros 90
"multinaturalism" 101
mystic procedures 192
mystic tellurism 189
"mystical birth" 93

Nai (butcher caste)
Nankani 127; "spirit children" 127
narrative: dimension 205; experience 219; shared 229
narratives of causality
narrators 208, 220, 223
national heroes (non-family dead) 26, 141
natural orifices 212
Nazi Germany's defeat 40
Nazi state, the 49, 50
necrographic frameworks 11, 15
necrographically emplaced 127–8, 130, 133, 135
necrography, necrographies 2–3, 8, 9, 79, 106, 126–9, 168–9, 208, 215, 218, 229, 232, 239, 242, 244–6, 248–9
necrography, sensory 107; pan-Nepalese belief 215
Nepalese: folklore 217, 221; ghost stories 205, 221; revenant 221; shamans 215; Nepalese society 217 (Limbu people 218); theories about the body and death 206 (Hindu knowledge and Buddhist 206, 221)
netherworld (Địa Tang) 157
newborns 158
new form of body 93
new forms of communication 209; social media 209
Newari beliefs 216–7
New Harmony Vision 172
Newton's gravity law 171
ndoqui, enlightened being 91
nfumbe 87, 90

nfumbi(s) (neophyte) 92
nganga (prenda) 87–93, 99
nganga spirit (protective spirit) 87
nightmares 135, 157
nineteenth century 165–6, 168–71, 175, 179
Nkai, Samburu divinity 134
nonliterate cultures 228
North America 17, 107, 126, 170
novenas 176
Nsambi, universal substance of spirit 90
Nsó Nganga 92–3

Ochoa, Todd R. 96, 102
Odé, the patron spirit of hunting 200
Odia (Oriya) ethnicity 235
offerings 32, 89, 132, 134–5, 138, 145, 189; monthly offerings, i.e., the *śrāddha* 208; votive offerings 155; substitute soul of a sacrificial animal 229
oral culture 219
oneiric, event 206
ontological divide 145, 149, 159
ontological others 161
ontology of spirits 168
oracle 96, 215
oral heritage 208
Orishas 89
Orula, Yoruba god of adivination
Owen, Robert 172

pagodô 190
Palero(s) 87–91, 93, 100
Palo 89–90, 98; Palo magic 90
Palo Monte 86, 91–4, 97, 99, 101–2, 246, 248
Palo cosmology of Self 93
Panagiotopoulos, Anastasios 3–4, 6, 8, 11, 18–9
Papel mothers 128
paradox of the body, the 121
parapsychology 170
"parochialization" 78
"partialization": "healthy stance" 68
Parry, Jonathan 100
pastors, indigenous Baptist 236

pastoralists, Samburu 125
patrilineage 228
pedagogy of the corpse 121
Pedersen, Morten 100–2
Pehueche communities 99
people's ungodly behavior 236
perpetuation of lineage 232
perro 88–91, 93; *perro de prenda* 87
persons 121
personal encounters with the dead 216
personhood 12, 73, 79, 98–100, 116, 125–7, 134, 228, 234, 237
performative adoption of their point of view 228
perspectivism 101
perspectivist ontology 101
philosophical premises of Spiritism (England, Spain and France) 168
"physio-logics" 98
plegaria 97
Poo, Mu-Chou 205
"positive cuadro", *protecciones* 177
positivism, social 165, 168–71
possession, embodied members 206, 210, 219
postburial practices 146
posterity, tangible 129
post-homicide ritual 114
postmortem existences 106, 229
postmortem phase 206
postmortem physical changes 109
postmortem rituals 207
"power of abscence, the" 30
power to mobilize 195
premonition 6
premortem/postmortem actions of the dead 33, 34
prenda(s) 87–89, 91
present, market-driven 161
Pret, haungry, wondering ghost 212
principles of Elightenment 169
prisoner-of-war camp 40
progressive necrography 231
Protestant Christianity 25, 34
Proyect, Humane Genome 106
pseudo bodies 90; agentive 86

Puerto Rican Spiritists 177
Puerto Rico 168

Rana 217
Rank, Otto 66, 68
rayado, initiated 91
rayamiento, Palo initiation 92
realm of the dead 221
reassurance 241
"rebirth" 92, 160
rebirth baptism 178
"re-dead" 102–3
"re-death" 94, 100–3
Red Army, The 53; Soviet troops, reformist tendency throughout India 242
reincarnation 26, 33, 170, 177
reincarnation, expiatory cycle of 172
religion 24
religiosos 90, 93
rememberers 234
"remembering" and "forgetting" relational process 235
"removing the hand of the dead person", funerary ritual procedure 195
repeated cycles of repetition and resolution 232
repetition: of illness 231; good or bad forms of 232
republican Romantic socialists 170
residual relatives 157
residual survival 209
resurrection 28, 30, 238
return of Jesus 238
Río, Natalia del 93
rite 94; initiation 92; Wari' funerary rites 109
ritual: animist 238; bathing 192; bell 196; communal 150, 152, 156; funerary 193; initiation 192; neighborhood 151, 154; waking 176
ritual economy of Jarê 196
ritual emancipation 142
rituals: market 154; periodic 150
Rondônia 108
rules of commensality 222

Index

saints 25
saints, Catholic 89
Saint Simonian socialist program 172
Sagant, Philippe 217–18
Samburu 125–6, 130–8
Sancti Spiritus, Cuban province 88
sangue real (royal/realblood) 192
Santería 89, 95, 97
"Santero" 95
Sarabanda, god of war 87
sea of the dead 103
"sense un-certainty" 96
Seremetakis, Nadia 111
scientific paranormal studies 170
"Scientific Spiritism" 175
shade of a dead person 210
"shadow" 199
Shamans 215, 219, 228–29, 231–32–35, 239–42, 247; Nepalese Shamans 215; shamans in trance 227
Shaman envoices the deceased 231
Shattshneider, Ellen 128–30
Sheper-Hughes, Nancy 127
Schieffelin, Edward 97
"shrine for the dead" 153
silence(s) 78, 227, 239; become mute 235
silence, dead Christian's 237
singing team (Sora ritual) 232
sirrum, Jarê funerary ritual 200
skin 98; Kayapó's "social skin" 98
"sky burial" 120
social erasure 138
social networks 220
"soft inheritance", theory of 171
sonic immersion 117
songs, identity-driven 97
sonum attack 238
sonum (a dead Sora) 228
sonums are Memories 234
songs in the persona of 233
sonumpower 242
Sora Baptism 237; future-oriented 237; cyclical vision of time and causality 238
Sora Baptist 227
Sora evolutionary necrography 235

Soraland 239
Sora people 227; nonliterate animist Sora 235
Sora ritual 232
soul 98, 100–1; angst-ridden souls 152; beleaguered souls 150, 161; disengaged restless souls 143; exembodied soul 101; ill-fated souls 143, 156; infant souls 157, 161; "neglected" souls 149, 156, 235; orphaned souls 149; soul-force 229; süns, *shadow* of the body 101–2
speculation, a new genre of 236
speech genres 232
spells and charms 213
specters 167, 210; historic specters 142, 152; of modernity 167
"spirit bodies" 86, 89, 90
spirit "fabrications" 90
spirit guide 90, 94, 96
spirit medium 95, 102, 156, 219
spirit-mediumship rites 3
spirit money 149, 155
spirit realms 142
spirit "voices" 102
"spirit world" 95, 114
"spirited modernities" 34
Spiritism 165–70, 172, 173–6
Spiritist centers 165, 168–70, 172–5
Spiritist medium 177
Spiritist séances 26, 167
spirits: of the dead 4, 165–6, 168–71, 175–6, 179, 186, 199–201, 216 disincarnate 94, 165; "enlightened" 165, 168, 170, 172–3, 175, 248; evil 213
free-floating malignant 146; of light 169–70, 173, 175, 177; propitiated 154; resentful 207; unfamiliar 153; vital 158; well-cared-for familial 143
spiritual: geographies 4; state 129; teachings 121
Spiritualism: Allan Kardec 94; Euro-American 96, 167; French and Anglo-American 94
stage for a dialogue 232
"stale revivals" 167

Standing, Guy 20, 21
stillborn child 127
storytelling practices 209
suicide 51, 53, 54, 213, 222
supernatural beings 213
suspicion of sorcery by human enemies 236
"sympathetic communion" 170
Swedenborg, Emanuel 171

taboo on mestruating women 193; *abajé* 193
Taita, godfather 93
Taitica, spirit of an invalid man 88, 91
Tamang thangka 217
"tangible prosperity" 129
tantric exorcist 215
tantric healing traditions 216
Taoist priest 156
Tata Nganga, the initiate's godfather 87
Taylor, Anne Christine 116
Taylor, Charles 99
Taylor, Janelle S. 99
"telluric metaphysics" 189, 191
temples, miniature 159
Tết offensive 151
terroir 21
Thai monastery 120
"theosophy" 167
Third Reich 49
ton ho', Wari' ritual 111
Tocqueville, Alexis de 27
Toradja of Sulawesi 127
Toraja 144
totalizing ideology 238
"tumbling over" (tombamento) 195
trajectories – paths 106; emotional 109
trajectory 97, 107, 111; body's social trajectory 118; death's social trajectory 118; symbolic trajectory 116
trance, bodily 94
transcultural: beings 217; transcultural interpretations 220; transcultural similarities 211
transformation of humanity into divinity 144–5

transition, Hertzian notion of 77
trascendental transformation 160
trauma: of dismemberment 119; of war 142
tripartite model 207
Trobriandes 44
Trobriand Islands 43; Trobrian islanders 167
trusts, philantropic 22
Tsintjilonis, Dimitris 143
Tsugaru, Japan region 128
Turner, Terence 98
Tylor, Edward B. 110, 167

unanchored deaths 125–6, 133, 13; "undeveloped" 158; unmarried persons deceased 126, 129, 158, 160
underworld 112, 114, 119, 242
Underworld 232, 236; marry and beget children in the Underworld 239; second death 231
unmade by death 200
unmarried man, *Imaasha* 136
United States 127, 155
unpropitious death 137
unpropitiousness 133, 136, 138

Vattimo, Gianni 167
Vedic and Puranic literature 212; classes of beings: *bhūta; piśāca* 214
veladas, nightly séances 175
vengeful ghost 218
verbal articulacy 228
verbal perspectivism 228
victims of civilian massacres 141
victimhood, transformed 242
Việt Nam 141–7, 152, 158–60; Buddhist 145; post-conflict and post-revolutionary 143
Vietnamese: cosmography 152; ghosts 161
Vilaça, Aparecida 98, 109
visceral: encounters 121; sensations 109; responses 110
visible/invisible deads 159
visible spirits 102
vital energy 186

Viveiros de Castro, Eduardo 98, 101, 144–5
voice(s) 78, 138, 236, 239; of the dead 208, 218–19, 234; ghostly voices 137

Walter, Tony 26, 44
Wari': 108–22, 246–7; cosmology 119; funeral 116–17, 119
waking life 206
Waterhouse, Helen 19, 26
web of causality, a dense 229
Weiner, Annette 44
well-care-for familial dead 149, 161
Western modern societies 167
widow(s) 43, 44, 56, 57; German war widows 47, 50
widowhood 52, 56
will 22, 33
"will of God" 236
"will power" 171
Willerslev, Rane 100–1
Winter, Jay 28
Wirtz, Kristina 96–7
witchcraft 89, 98–9, 215
witness 208, 210, 223
world: incarnated 165; spiritually enlightened 165
World War II 40–1, 47
work of curing 198
worship of the dead 206
writing as a magical technique of power and coercion 235

yaya, godmother 93
Yoryé, Ifá initiation ceremony 86
Yunke, Puerto Rican rainforest 176

Zambi, universal substance of spirit 90

www.ingramcontent.com/pod-product-compliance
Lightning Source LLC
Chambersburg PA
CBHW051533020426
42333CB00016B/1899